Central Bank Independence, Accountability, and Transparency

Central Bank Independence, Accountability, and Transparency

A Global Perspective

Bernard J. Laurens
Marco Arnone
Jean-François Segalotto

HG
1811
.L39
2009

First published 2009 by
PALGRAVE MACMILLAN

Palgrave Macmillan in the UK is an imprint of Macmillan Publishers Limited, registered in England, company number 785998, of Houndmills, Basingstoke, Hampshire RG21 6XS.

Palgrave Macmillan in the US is a division of St Martin's Press LLC, 175 Fifth Avenue, New York, NY 10010.

Palgrave Macmillan is the global academic imprint of the above companies and has companies and representatives throughout the world.

Palgrave®and Macmillan®are registered trademarks in the United States, the United Kingdom, Europe and other countries

ISBN: 978–0–230–20107–1   hardback

This book is printed on paper suitable for recycling and made from fully managed and sustained forest sources. Logging, pulping and manufacturing processes are expected to conform to the environmental regulations of the country of origin.

A catalogue record for this book is available from the British Library.

A catalog record for this book is available from the Library of Congress.

10   9   8   7   6   5   4   3   2   1
18   17   16   15   14   13   12   11   10   09

Printed and bound in Great Britain by
CPI Antony Rowe, Chippenham and Eastbourne

Contents

List of Figures

List of Tables

Notes on Contributors

Bernard J. Laurens is currently Deputy Chief, Monetary and Capital Markets Department, International Monetary Fund, USA. He began his career in the IMF in 1992. During his tenure, he has been extensively involved in domestic and external financial sector issues, and modernization and liberalization of countries' monetary frameworks and exchange and capital account issues. His recent publications include: *Coordination of Monetary and Fiscal Policies* (1998), *Managing Capital Flows: Lessons from the Experience of Chile* (1998), *Monetary Policy at Different Stages of Market Development* (2004), *Measures of Central Bank Autonomy: Empirical Evidence for OECD, Developing, and Emerging Market Economies* (2006), *China: Strengthening Monetary Policy Implementation* (2007), and *Central Bank Autonomy: Lessons from Global Trends* (2008). Prior to joining the Fund, Bernard Laurens worked for the Bank of France. He also holds a degree in economics from the Institut d'Études Politiques of Paris,

Marco Arnone is Director of the Centre for Macroeconomics & Finance Research (CeMaFiR), Italy, and Adjoint Professor of Economics and Finance of Emerging Markets (University of Eastern Piedmont), Italy. He has worked as an economist in the IMF's Monetary and Financial Systems and African Departments, and has taught at Milan's Catholic and State Universities. His recent publications include: *Primary Dealers in Government Securities* (IMF, 2005), *Venture Capital for Development* (2006), *Banking Supervision: Quality and Governance*, and *Financial Supervisors Architecture and Banking Supervision* (2007), *External Debt Sustainability and Domestic Debt in Heavily Indebted Poor Countries* (2007), *Central Bank Autonomy: Lessons from Global Trends* (2008), and *Anti-Money Laundering by International Institutions: a Preliminary Assessment* (2008).

Jean-François Segalotto is a Research Fellow at the Centre for Macroeconomics & Finance Research (CeMaFiR), Italy. His research work and interests focus on monetary economics and institutions. His publications include: *Central Bank Autonomy, Macroeconomic Performance, and Monetary Frameworks: a Global Comparison* (2005), *Measures of Central Bank Autonomy: Empirical Evidence for OECD, Developing, and Emerging Market Economies* (2006), and *Central Bank Autonomy: Lessons from Global Trends* (2008).

Alberto Brovida is a Research Fellow at the Centre for Macroeconomics & Finance Research (CeMaFiR), Italy.

Daniele Siena is a Research Fellow at the Centre for Macroeconomics & Finance Research (CeMaFiR), Italy.

Martin Sommer is a Senior Economist, Asia and Pacific Department, at the International Monetary Fund, Washington DC, USA.

Foreword

The International Monetary Fund (IMF) has always placed particular importance on the issue of central bank governance, since a robust central bank framework facilitates price and financial sector stability, which in turn is conducive to sustainable economic growth. Such a framework is important not only in conducting day-to-day central banking operations, but also for the evolving role of the central bank in the current global environment that is characterized by the extraordinary challenges facing policy-makers in the context of the global financial crisis.

The crisis, which started in August 2007 with the sub-prime market turmoil in the United States, has brought to the forefront important policy issues which are directly linked to the topics discussed in this book, in particular regarding the desirability and modalities of central banks' involvement in financial supervision. Furthermore, central banks around the world have responded to the financial crisis in ways which, at times, have departed from the conventional wisdom that prevailed before (i.e. widening the range of collateral and undertaking financial operations which used to be the prerogative of financial markets).

This book presents a comprehensive review of the literature on central bank independence, accountability, and transparency, as well as an analysis of the largest datasets ever published on these three pillars of central bank governance. The analysis reflects the importance given to the surveillance and technical cooperation work of the IMF's Monetary and Capital Markets Department in helping member countries to improve the structural, institutional, and operational aspects of central bank operations, and build strong monetary institutions.

I believe that this comprehensive review of the literature and careful consideration of central bank practice can provide useful guidance to policy-makers when they reflect on how to respond to the current challenges in ways which do not put at risk the advances achieved over the last 20 to 30 years. I also hope that this book, in particular the discussion on the sequencing of reforms to strengthen governance frameworks and their linkages with the stages of development of financial markets, will help policy-makers apply the general guidelines discussed in the book to the particular circumstances prevailing in their respective countries.

Dominique Strauss-Kahn
Managing Director
International Monetary Fund

Preface

"It is my desire for the Banque de France to be in the hands of the government, but not unduly so" (Napoléon).* We have certainly come a long way from the time of Napoleon, when the central bank (CB) was expected to be in the hands of the government, to the current consensus whereby CB independence has become a matter of pragmatic necessity, essential to ensure a firm commitment to price stability and financial stability. Indeed, the message that emerges clearly from the review of the literature presented in this book is that CB independence has increasingly been recognized as an essential aspect of their governance frameworks. With greater independence has come greater accountability, to both governments and the general public, requiring CBs to be increasingly transparent in conducting their operations. As a result, a sound CB governance framework is increasingly based upon three essential pillars: independence, accountability, and transparency.

This message is corroborated by a review of global trends in CB governance for a large group of CBs from advanced, emerging market, and developing countries. This book benefits from a wealth of information that is based in particular on the assessment of central bank independence for 163 CBs, representing 181 countries, and the assessment of CB accountability and transparency for 98 CBs representing 109 countries.

While it is valuable to review the literature and consider empirical evidence of CB practices in relation to governance, this book goes a step further by providing concrete guidance to policy-makers. A better understanding of the relationship between the three pillars of governance should assist policy-makers in determining the role of CBs in financial supervision and in sequencing reforms to strengthen the governance framework, taking into consideration the stage of development of the financial markets.

The book presents three main parts. In the first, it offers an overview of the literature on CB independence. It distinguishes base indicators of independence, which were first developed in the late 1970s, from the

---

*"Je veux que la Banque ... soit dans la main du Gouvernement mais qu'elle n'y soit pas trop." In Geneviève Iacono, *Le nouveau statut de la Banque de France, une étape vers l'union économique et monétaire*, Recueil Dalloz Siery 89 (March 1994).

subsequent literature. Also, it summarizes the literature on CB accountability and CB transparency from the time it started to appear in the late 1990s. On the basis of the literature, new indicators of CB independence, accountability, and transparency are presented in the second part. These are then applied to large samples of CBs from countries at different stages of market development (i.e. advanced economies, emerging market economies, and developing countries) with a view to drawing conclusions on global trends for each pillar of CB governance and on their interrelationships. The second part also offers new empirical evidence on the relationship between CB independence and inflation performance. Finally, the last part draws lessons for policy-makers regarding the relationships between the pillars of CB governance, the role of CBs in financial supervision, and how to sequence reforms to strengthen CB governance frameworks.

Given the current global financial crisis and the evolving role of CBs in attempting to minimize the turmoil, this book takes on even greater significance. This is therefore an opportune moment for the publication of this book, and I am most grateful to all the authors and contributors for their hard work.

Jaime Caruana
Counsellor and Director
Monetary and Capital Markets Department
International Monetary Fund

Acknowledgements

We are particularly grateful to Piero Ugolini, Chief of the Monetary Operations Division and Assistant Director, and to Stefan Ingves, Director of the IMF's Monetary and Capital Markets Department when this project began, for providing encouragement and support. At the time Bernard J. Laurens was Deputy Chief of the Monetary Operations Division, and Marco Arnone was an Economist in that Division.

We are grateful for comments and suggestions on draft sections of this book provided by Laszlo Balogh, King Banaian, Martin Čihák, Christopher Crowe, Alex Cukierman, Jakob de Haan, Andreas Freitag, Alessandro Gambini, Charles Goodhard, Arman Khachaturyan, Luis Jácome, Tonny Lybek, Donato Masciandaro, Fausto Panunzi, Marc Quintyn, Pierre Siklos, Andrea Sironi, Guido Tabellini, Michael Taylor, and participants at the conference: "Central Bank Independence: Legal and Economic Issues," sponsored by the International Monetary Fund and the Central Bank of Peru, September 19, 2007 (Lima) and at the following Bocconi University (Milan) conferences: "Central Banking Conference – Does Central Bank Independence Still Matter?," September 14–15, 2007; and "European Conference on Financial Regulation and Supervision – Designing Financial Supervision Institutions: Independence, Accountability and Governance," May 29–30, 2006. We are especially indebted to Donato Masciandaro for providing such a welcoming and stimulating environment, for his thought-provoking suggestions, and collaborative spirit.

We would also like to thank: Alberto Brovida, for his contribution to the definitions of our indicators of central bank accountability and transparency (in Chapter 4); Daniele Siena, for his contribution to building the database on central bank accountability and transparency, and analyzing their relationships with independence (in Chapter 5); and Martin Sommer, for his contribution to analyzing the relationship between central bank independence and inflation performance in emerging markets (in Chapter 6).

Our gratitude goes also to Luigi Campiglio, Carlo Bellavite Pellegrini, and Luigi Bonatti for their continuing support during this project.

This volume benefited greatly from the editorial assistance of Jo North throughout the production of this book.

We wish to dedicate this book to our families and friends.

Introduction

Starting in the 1970s and following a generalized trend towards enhancing the role of price signals in the general economy, central banks (CBs) around the world, starting with those in advanced economies, have moved away from administrative and rules-based instruments towards reliance on money market operations which they conduct as one participant in financial markets (i.e., open-market operations).[1] CBs in emerging market economies and developing countries have followed a similar path to a point where the practice of central banking has converged worldwide. In particular, in countries with developed capital markets, CBs have evolved from being governments' tools for achieving specific economic objectives into independent institutions devoted to maintaining a fundamental public good: price stability.

These evolutions have had far-reaching implications for CBs' governance frameworks. They have resulted in greater importance given to transparency in the monetary policy process. Indeed, nowadays only few central bankers would recognize themselves in a comment by Alan Greenspan the year after his appointment as Chairman of the Federal Reserve Board in 1988: "I guess I should warn you, if I turn out to be particularly clear, you have probably misunderstood what I said." In the current practice of central banking, transparency has become a pillar of CB governance. It is defined as follows in the 1999 IMF Code of Good Practices on Transparency in Monetary and Financial Policies: "... an environment in which the objectives of policy, its legal, institutional and economic framework, policy decisions and their rationale, data and

---

[1] See Laurens (2005) for a review of the implications of these changes for the conduct of monetary policy.

1

information related to monetary ... policies, and the terms of agencies accountabilities, are provided to the public on an understandable, accessible and timely basis ..."

By moving away from an institutional model whereby the CB's main objective is to be one tool in the hands of the government for achieving specific economic objectives, to one whereby its main objective is to preserve price stability, CBs have also become independent from the government. Such a move is based on the assumption, largely corroborated by empirical evidence, that CB independence has significant benefits for macroeconomic performance as it helps countries achieve lower average inflation, cushion the impact of political cycles on economic cycles, and boost fiscal discipline without any additional costs or sacrifices in terms of output volatility or reduced economic growth.

As the concept of CB independence gained strength, the associated concept of CB accountability emerged. Indeed, independence has made CBs far more "politically" accountable to public opinion directly and to parliament. Jean Claude Trichet, then Governor of Banque de France summarized that reality at a symposium on CB independence in these terms: "the independent central bank is accountable to French public opinion, the European central bank to the 293 million Europeans, and the Federal Reserve System to the 265 million Americans."[2] Accountability is a condition for the CB to build its credibility vis-à-vis capital markets and of its acceptance by the citizens in a democratic society.

Thanks to these evolutions, CB governance now includes the three concepts or pillars which *together* form the basis of the legal framework governing a CB and on which CB governance should rest, that is independence, democratic accountability, and transparency. Such a concept was eloquently summarized by France's Prime Minister, Lionel Jospin, at the above-mentioned symposium: "the independence of central banks was a matter of pragmatic necessity: it helps persuade economic players that price stability is essential." However "independence does not signify solitude," since controlling inflation concerns everyone. "Independence also means dialogue ... and it calls for accountability [which implies] transparency of decisions and the ability – and the necessity – to account for one's actions." At that symposium, Jean Claude Trichet also pointed out that price stability is "both a necessary condition and a normal consequence of a smooth-functioning democracy," and added

---

[2] Banque de France (2000).

that "it is one of our major responsibilities to communicate with public opinion as a whole as directly and precisely as possible."

This book brings together the three pillars of CB governance with a view to illustrate their linkages from both a theoretical and an empirical perspective. The book offers a review of the extensive literature on CB independence as well as the already large body of literature, though more limited, on CB accountability and transparency. It also proposes new indices of CB independence, accountability, and transparency which are afterwards applied to a sample of CBs in countries at different stages of economic development and from different geographic areas.

Our analysis allows us to identify six broad principles which represent the "consensus view" among policy-makers with regard to CBs' governance frameworks, irrespective of the level of economic development of the countries in which they operate, namely (i) setting price stability as the primary objective of monetary policy; (ii) curtailing CB lending to governments; (iii) ensuring full CB independence for setting its policy rate; (iv) ensuring no government involvement in monetary policy formulation; (v) ensuring that CB accountability corresponds to the level of CB independence; and (vi) ensuring that CB transparency corresponds to the level of CB accountability and financial market deepening.

Our analysis allows us also to link the various dimensions of CB business with the process of financial market deepening. It allows us to offer a possible sequencing of reforms to enhance CB governance frameworks, which associates the three components (independence, accountability, and transparency) with structural changes in the economy and financial system. Our analysis relies on the four-stage process for financial market development, from a post-conflict stage to the stage of financial market development, through a financial intermediation stage and an interbank market development stage. We identify three steps: (i) clarify CB's objectives with a view to establishing basic instrument independence; (ii) establish the building block of CB accountability; and (iii) further strengthening political independence, accountability, and transparency.

We also discuss the role of CBs in financial supervision and regulation, with a specific focus on banking supervision, and we present some empirical evidence on the architecture of supervisory and regulatory authority. In the last two decades many European and OECD countries have moved towards a more integrated financial supervisory structure. Such moves, which have reflected a trend towards reducing the scope of involvement of CBs in banking supervision, have led to establishing independent supervisory agencies covering a wide range of financial institutions on an integrated or unified basis, while at the same time the responsibility of CBs in financial stability was somewhat downgraded, although not altogether eliminated. The ongoing financial crisis that started in August 2007 with the sub-prime market turmoil in the United States and eventually became worldwide, has led a number of policy-makers and analysts to challenge that trend. It became evident that such a separation of functions did not facilitate crisis monitoring and resolution, and that barriers to communication between CBs and financial supervisors could potentially lead to delays in addressing mounting problems in the financial sector. Empirical evidence presented in this book also suggests that there are benefits from maintaining CBs' involvement in financial supervision. While it may not always be desirable for the CB to supervise financial institutions, there is a strong case for all CBs not to overlook financial stability issues. All CBs need to be involved, in ways consistent with countries' specific circumstances and history, in financial supervision so that they are in a position to identify systemic risks in the financial sector.

A defining feature of the book is to be empirical. Indeed, it includes the largest datasets for CB independence, accountability, and transparency ever published, including indices of CB independence as of end-2003 for 163 CBs representing 181 countries, and indices of CB accountability and transparency as of the end of the first quarter of 2006 for 98 CBs representing 109 countries. Regarding CB independence, a second defining feature of the book has to do with a methodology to calculate comparable measures of independence as of the late 1980s which allow us to present intertemporal comparisons with current levels of independence. The assessment of the individual levels of CB independence is based on a de jure index of independence which has required a detailed analysis of CB legislation. The assessment of the individual levels of CB accountability and transparency is based on the analysis of CB legislation and of official CBs' websites. The data were subsequently supplemented, when necessary, with information published by the International Monetary Fund and the World Bank in the context of the Financial Sector Assessment Program (FSAP).

It cannot be ruled out that in some cases the sources that were used did not provide all the information that may be needed to assess *actual* levels of CB independence, accountability, or transparency. In particular, there may be particular cases where de jure indicators may overestimate actual levels, especially in countries where the rule of law is limited. However, there may also be cases where de jure indicators may underestimate actual performance, for example in countries where monetary policy framework and operating procedures are specified in implementing regulations rather than in the law. While in a few cases the validity of individual assessments may therefore not be fully satisfactory, the lessons that can be drawn from a quantification of the levels of independence, accountability, and transparency should remain valid. Furthermore, adopting a de jure approach limits the scope for judgmental approaches; it also provides a salutary incentive for those countries in which legal frameworks have lagged behind actual practice to fill the gap by bringing their CB legislation in line with actual practice.

The rest of the book is structured as follows. Chapter 1 offers an overview of the literature on CB independence. It distinguishes base indicators of independence, which were first developed in the late 1970s, from the subsequent literature. Chapters 2 and 3 summarize respectively the literature on CB accountability and CB transparency from the time it started to appear in the late 1990s. On the basis of the literature, new indicators of CB independence, accountability, and transparency are presented in Chapter 4, which are afterwards applied to large samples of CBs from countries at different stages of market development (i.e., advanced economies, emerging market economies, and developing countries) with a view to drawing global trends on each pillar of CB governance and on their relationships (Chapter 5). Chapter 6 offers new empirical evidence on the relationship between CB independence and inflation performance. Finally, Chapter 7 draws lessons for policymakers regarding the relationships between the pillars of CB governance, the role of CBs in financial supervision, and how to sequence reforms to strengthen CB governance frameworks.

1
Survey of Models and Indicators of Independence

Introduction

In the 1990s a consensus emerged in the economic literature that price stability should be the primary objective of monetary policy, and the CB should have sufficient independence as a means to attain this goal.[1] These conclusions are based on a large body of literature that was developed starting in the late 1970s, and demonstrated that CB independence has undisputable benefits for macroeconomic performance. On average, countries with CBs enjoying significant independence were able to achieve lower average inflation, cushion the impact of political cycles on economic cycles, enhance financial stability, and boost fiscal discipline without any real additional costs or sacrifices in terms of output volatility or reduced economic growth.

Many of the empirical studies on the relationship between CB independence and inflation show that there is a robust negative correlation between the two variables. Initially, this result was based on research conducted on industrial countries, most of which showed a strong negative relationship linking average inflation or changes in inflation and CB independence. The indices used to proxy CB independence were mainly based on an analysis of CB laws therefore leading to de jure independence. Given that an indicator of de jure independence may overestimate the actual level of independence, especially in countries where the rule of law is limited, the scope of the research was expanded and led to the

---

[1] The literature (and this book) often uses "autonomy" and "independence" interchangeably, although the former entails operational freedom, while the latter points to the lack of institutional constraints.

definition of de facto indicators of independence.[2] These studies focus on the experience of developing countries; they show that the average and variance of inflation rates for these countries are negatively correlated to the de facto degree of independence, and they suggest that there is a positive correlation between economic growth and de facto independence indicators.

The most widely known and frequently used indices of CB independence are those discussed in Bade and Parkin (1977), Alesina (1988, 1989), Grilli, Masciandaro, and Tabellini (GMT) (1991), Cukierman (1992),[3] and Eijffinger and Schaling (1993). We refer to these measures as the "base indicators" of independence. More recent studies test the robustness of the statistical relationship between the distribution of inflation, growth, and CB independence. These studies have used different measures of independence, different time and cross-country samples, and additional determinants (such as political instability, trade openness, exchange regulations, per capita income, education levels, and proxies for the labor market structure) to explain geographic differences in inflation and growth levels. Most studies suggest that the relationship between independence and inflation is clear and robust, albeit with nuances. Regarding the correlation between CB independence and long-term growth, a number of studies have concluded that neither long-term output growth nor its variability is correlated to independence, at least for the more developed countries. Certain authors have argued, however, that disinflation costs grow as independence grows. The remainder of the chapter is organized as follows: the next section surveys base indicators of de jure and de facto independence; the following section surveys the subsequent literature and empirical studies on the base indicators; and the final section offers concluding remarks.

Base indicators of independence

The indicators of CB independence developed by Bade and Parkin (1977), Alesina (1988, 1989), GMT (1991), Cukierman (1992), Alesina and Summers (1993), Eijffinger and Schaling (1993), and Cukierman and Webb (1995) have been chosen as base indices because they constitute

---

[2] De jure independence may also underestimate de facto independence, for example in the case of several inflation-targeting CBs where the formal specification of the framework, which may not be included in the CB law, plays an important role in terms of CB independence (Roger, 2006).

[3] Cukierman (1992) states that, regarding chapters 19–21, he draws freely on Cukierman, Webb, and Neyapti (1991).

the body of research that forms the basis of, or the inspiration for, most recent empirical works. They represent the most diversified methodological source in this field; and offer nine indices in all; three of them serve as a de facto measure of independence, and the remaining indices serve as more or less detailed de jure indices.

First indicator of de jure independence: Bade and Parkin (1977)

Bade and Parkin (1977) is the first attempt to construct an indicator for CB independence, on the basis of an analysis of the relationships between monetary policy-making and the laws that define the powers of CBs. It contemplates the experience of twelve industrial countries (Australia, Belgium, Canada, France, Germany, Italy, Japan, the Netherlands, Sweden, Switzerland, the United Kingdom, and the United States) during the period 1951–75, based on the analysis of legal provisions regarding the CB's primary objective (does the law establish price stability as its sole and primary objective?), the CB board (is the CB the final monetary policy-making authority, and are government representatives sitting on the board?), and rules for the appointment of senior management (are less than half of them assigned to government officials?).[4] While combining the criteria leads to eight potential types of CBs, the authors show that four of them are not represented in the sample. The four remaining types of CBs are ranked from one (lower independence) to four (higher independence).

The authors find weak empirical evidence (Table 1.1) to suggest that pursuing price stability as the sole final policy objective is associated with achieving a lower level of average inflation, compared to cases in which this de jure objective does not exist or is not the sole objective.[5] They also find that CBs with some independence in terms of policy-making and board appointments may deliver a lower level of inflation, but not necessarily a low degree of variability in monetary policy[6] and monetary policy variability does not show a clear association with any of the CB groups. Finally, monetary policy-making does not seem to differ significantly among independent CBs and those dominated by governments when, in the first case, senior management is appointed by the executive branch.

---

[4] To minimize the arbitrary nature of combining the three attributes an equal weight is given to each of them.

[5] The result is probably due to the fact that only the Netherlands' CB shows the first criterion.

[6] This refers to the variability some of the most autonomous CBs showed in their monetary operations, in terms of higher coefficients of variation in monetary base growth and in the exchange rate (Table 1.1).

Table 1.1 Bade and Parkin ranking

Final authority/ appointment of senior management	Country	Percentage change in exchange rate	Annual growth in money supply		Annual growth in monetary base	
			Standard deviation	Variation coefficient	Standard deviation	Variation coefficient
Government/ government	Netherlands	33.44 (3)	4.62 (7)	55.1 (6)	3.99 (3)	61.67 (2)
	Australia	16.96 (7)	6.22 (11)	107.8 (12)	10.78 (11)	144.12 (12)
	Belgium	26.43 (4)	1.75 (1)	47.5 (5)	3.67 (2)	81.19 (6)
	Canada	3.39 (8)	5.49 (10)	89.4 (10)	5.26 (5)	76.23 (5)
	France	−22.47 (11)	4.02 (4)	36.7 (3)	8.69 (10)	115.10 (11)
	Japan	17.81 (6)	7.43 (12)	41.5 (4)	7.78 (9)	48.47 (1)
	Italy	−4.45 (10)	4.17 (5)	29.1 (1)	12.40 (12)	86.11 (7)
	United Kingdom	−26.05 (12)	4.82 (9)	103.4 (11)	7.60 (8)	109.67(10)
	Sweden	19.74 (5)	4.27 (6)	60.2 (8)	6.89 (7)	106.33 (9)
CB/government	United States	0.00 (9) (numéraire)	2.15 (2)	55.4 (7)	3.23 (1)	91.24 (8)
CB/government and others	Germany	41.35 (1)	3.20 (3)	33.6 (2)	6.79(6)	75.70 (4)
	Switzerland	40.97 (2)	4.65 (8)	65.5 (9)	4.80 (4)	69.46 (3)

Source: Bade and Parkin (1977).

Table 1.2 Results of Alesina, and Bade and Parkin

Country	Average inflation	Bade and Parkin (1977) independence index	Bade and Parkin (1985) independence index	Alesina (1988, 1989) independence index
Italy	13.7	1	2	1/2
Spain	13.6	–	–	1
New Zealand	12.0	–	–	1
United Kingdom	10.7	1	2	2
Finland	9.8	–	–	2
Australia	9.7	1	1	1
France	9.2	1	2	2
Denmark	8.8	–	–	2
Sweden	8.7	1	2	2
Norway	8.4	–	–	2
Canada	7.8	1	2	2
Belgium	6.9	1	2	2
United States	6.9	3	3	3
Japan	6.4	1	3	3
Netherlands	5.5	2	2	2
Switzerland	4.1	4	4	4
Germany	4.1	4	4	4

Source: Alesina (1989) and Bade and Parkin (1977, 1985).

Alesina's political response (1988, 1989)

Alesina (1988 and 1989) updates and extends Bade and Parkin's 1985 work, combining theories on political cycles and rational expectations. He finds that there is a negative relationship between the degree of independence and the average level of inflation. The author uses Bade and Parkin's index to link the level of a country's political instability to its macroeconomic results, and he extends the sample to five more countries: New Zealand, Spain, Denmark, Norway, and Finland. Table 1.2 summarizes Alesina's results for the seventeen countries over the time horizon of 1973–86, and the results of Bade and Parkin for their sample of twelve countries.[7,8]

---

[7] Alesina (1988) analyzes sixteen countries over the 1973–85 horizon; Alesina (1989) extends the sample by one country and one year: seventeen countries over the 1973–86 horizon.

[8] The difference between Alesina and Bade and Parkin concerns the Bank of Italy, which Alesina ranks higher with regard to economic independence following the "divorce" from the Treasury in 1981.

Table 1.3 Alesina: inflation, central bank independence, and government spending (1973–1985)

Country	Degree of central bank independence (1)	Average inflation rate (GNP deflator) (2)	Rate of government spending over GNP (percent) (3)
Italy	1/2	16.1	35.6
Spain	1	15.2	26.2
New Zealand	1	12.7	36.4
United Kingdom	2	12.3	37.3
Australia	1	10.5	28.4
France	2	10.2	39.1
Sweden	2	9.8	38.3
Denmark	2	9.1	39.7
Norway	2	8.8	38.3
Canada	2	8.1	23.1
United States	3	7.2	21.7
Belgium	2	6.8	36.0
Netherlands	2	5.8	35.4
Japan	3	5.0	16.2
Germany	4	4.1	29.3
Switzerland	4	4.0	9.0

Source: Alesina (1988).

Alesina (1988) examines how independence affects the magnitude of political influence on the economy and monetary policy. An independent CB is able to reduce fluctuations in monetary policy brought about by the election cycle, and, as indicated by Rogoff (1985), an inflation-averse CB can help to reduce the inflationary bias. Alesina argues that the creation of an autonomous CB is associated with lower levels of inflation, and reduces politically induced volatility in monetary policy and inflation. Countries that are shown to have the most autonomous CBs (Japan, United States, Germany, and Switzerland) have four of the six lowest rates of inflation, while the less autonomous CBs are associated with the highest inflation rates. Alesina points out that this apparent correlation does not necessarily constitute a causal relationship. In fact, the observed relationship may reflect the fact that a more pronounced aversion to inflation is more likely to result in a consensus in favor of establishing an autonomous CB.

Alesina also considers the size of the public sector, measured as the level of government spending as a percentage of GNP, and he points to a possible correlation between this variable and the rate of inflation. Such an assessment is based on the assumption that the highest levels of government spending should require higher levels of seignorage (Table 1.3). The

Table 1.4   Alesina: average inflation rates in selected periods (Germany, United Kingdom, United States) (GNP deflator, average in annual rate of growth, percent)

Country	(a)	(b)	Difference (a)–(b)	Bade and Parkin (1985) independence index
Germany	Social Democrats (1975–82) 4.3	Christian Democrats (1983–85) 2.5	1.8	4
United Kingdom	Labour Party (1975–79) 16.3	Conservative Party (1980–85) 9.0	7.3	2
United States	Carter (1977–80) 8.0	Reagan (1981–85) 5.4	2.6	3

Source: Alesina (1988).

author argues, however, that this correlation is not clear. Finally, Alesina asks whether an independent CB can reduce fluctuations in monetary policy caused by the political cycle (Table 1.4). To answer the question, the author uses the example of Germany, the United States, and the United Kingdom, since these countries experienced a change in the political alignment of their governments at the beginning of the 1980s. By comparing annual inflation under the various governments, Alesina provides convincing evidence. On the one hand, in the United Kingdom, where the CB's independence was somewhat low, monetary policy followed a rather "partisan" path during the transition period. On the other hand, in Germany, where the CB was more independent, the volatility of monetary policy, as expressed by the difference in the average inflation rate recorded under different governments, was lower. The intermediate case is that of the United States, where the effect of the change in government on inflation was in between the two extremes, in keeping with the level of independence of the Federal Reserve.

Grilli, Masciandaro, and Tabellini (1991)

Grilli, Masciandaro, and Tabellini (GMT) (1991) compare CB laws for eighteen OECD countries in the postwar years (1950–89), focusing on political independence – independence in setting objectives – and economic independence – independence in instruments. The authors confirm previous findings that countries with more independent CBs

Table 1.5   GMT: political independence index

Country	Appointment				Relationships with government		Charters		Political independence index
	(1)	(2)	(3)	(4)	(5)	(6)	(7)	(8)	(9)
Australia		1					1	1	3
Austria		1				1	1	1	3
Belgium				1					1
Canada	1	1					1	1	4
Denmark		1				1	1		3
France		1		1					2
Germany		1		1	1	1	1	1	6
Greece			1					1	2
Ireland		1				1	1		3
Italy	1	1	1		1				4
Japan							1		1
Netherlands		1		1	1	1	1	1	6
New Zealand									0
Portugal					1				1
Spain				1	1				2
Switzerland		1			1	1	1	1	5
United Kingdom					1				1
United States				1	1	1	1	1	5

Source: GMT (1991).

have a lower – or less variable – level of inflation. By defining *political independence* as the ability of the CB to select the final objectives of monetary policy, GMT examine three areas: (i) the procedures regarding the appointment of the CB board; (ii) the legal relationships that link the CB to the government in the formulation of monetary policy; and (iii) the CB's formal responsibilities (in the form of policy objectives) concerning monetary policy. The authors create a *political independence index* (Table 1.5).[9] Since the index rises with the increase in independence in the selection of objectives, it ultimately serves as an index of growing credibility in the CB's ability to autonomously pursue a low inflation objective. The index of *economic independence* is meant to measure the independence in the selection of instruments (Table 1.6). It encompasses the following items: (i) the government's influence in determining the availability of CB credit to the government; and (ii) the nature

---

[9] See Appendix III for a description of the indicator variables considered by GMT.

Table 1.6   GMT: economic independence index

Country	Monetary financing of public deficits					Monetary instruments		Economic independence index
	(1)	(2)	(3)	(4)	(5)	(6)	(7)	(8)
Australia	1	1	1	1	1	1		6
Austria			1	1	1	1	2	6
Belgium		1		1	1	1	2	6
Canada	1	1	1	1		1	2	7
Denmark		1			1	1	2	5
France				1	1	1	2	5
Germany	1	1	1	1	1	1	1	7
Greece				1		1		2
Ireland		1	1	1		1		4
Italy				1				1
Japan	1		1		1	1	1	5
Netherlands			1	1	1	1		4
New Zealand			1	1		1		3
Portugal				1		1		2
Spain			1	1			1	3
Switzerland		1	1	1	1	1	2	7
United Kingdom	1	1	1	1		1		5
United States	1	1	1	1	1	1	1	7

Source: GMT (1991).

of monetary instruments over which monetary authorities have full control. The rationale is that when the executive branch is able to influence the quantity and terms of credit available from the CB, it is also able (at least in the short term) to influence base money creation. The authors find that the correlation between the political and the economic independence index is not always positive; thus, a ranking that includes only one of the two dimensions of independence might be misleading. Therefore, the authors calculate a combined indicator as the sum of the two sub-indices.

The ranking of the CBs on the basis of their political and economic independence leads to classifying them into four groups (Figure 1.1): Group 1. The Netherlands, Germany, Switzerland, Canada, and the United States have CBs with the highest levels of independence with regard to political and economic independence; Group 2. The Bank of Italy enjoys a good degree of political independence, but a low level of economic independence; Group 3. Greece, Spain, Portugal, and New Zealand have less independent CBs from both points of view;

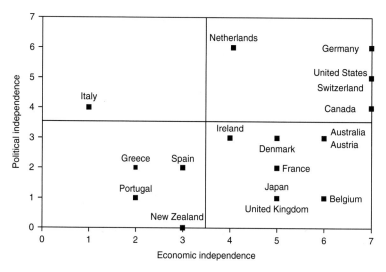

Figure 1.1   GMT: dispersion of independence
Source: GMT (1991).

and Group 4. Ireland, Denmark, Austria, Australia, France, the United Kingdom, Japan, and Belgium are shown to have CBs with a good degree of economic independence, albeit limited political independence. The authors note that three of the four countries that have less independent CBs (Greece, Portugal, and Spain) have also exhibited highly unstable political systems and risky public debt policies. They are also the countries that have made the greatest use of seignorage. Other countries may have had unstable political systems over the period under review (Austria, Belgium, Ireland, Italy, and the Netherlands). However, they still have relatively independent CBs (at least on one of the dimensions), and the use of seignorage since the end of World War Two seems limited (except for Ireland and Italy).

The authors argue that an independent CB could have provided benefits in terms of monetary stability and low inflation, even in the presence of political incentives towards less orthodox fiscal policies. By dividing the time horizon into four sub-periods (1950–59, 1960–69, 1970–79, and 1980–89) and regressing inflation data on the two independence indices, the authors show that the coefficients for both indicators always have the expected negative relationship. The economic independence index is statistically significant during periods of widespread inflation (as in the last two decades); while the independence index for objectives (political independence) is significant only for the 1970s. These results hold good for the average inflation rate for the entire period of 1950–89.

The authors also confirm previous findings by Bade and Parkin, and Alesina, that CB reforms brought positive results through their impact on policy credibility and the incentives they had on governments' behavior. In order to determine whether independence can influence the likelihood of treasuries adopting unsustainable debt policies, the authors regress primary deficits on the combined independence indicator and on three other variables that define countries' political environment (frequency of government changes, frequency of government changes from one political alignment to another, and the percentage of governments supported by a single party majority). They conclude that the independence index generally has a negative – and statistically insignificant – coefficient.

Finally, the authors find no systematic effect between independence and real growth. Similar results can be obtained by dividing the period under review into four sub-periods and adding the political instability variables indicated above as regressors. Replacing the growth rate with the unemployment rate, the authors find that an independent CB not only leads to a lower level of inflation but does not involve sacrifices in terms of macroeconomic performance. Such a conclusion constitutes what is commonly referred to as a "free lunch."

Two of the most widely used indicators: Cukierman (1992)

Cukierman is the first author to argue that there can be a wide gap between de jure independence and de facto independence. CB independence is certainly affected by the degree of de jure independence, but it is also determined by a host of other factors such as informal arrangements or actual practices, the quality of the research at the CB, and the personalities of key CB staff, the treasury or the ministry of finance. Cukierman points out the great difficulty in coding these elements so as to derive empirical measurements of independence. He argues that the degree of subjectivity in the selection of legal variables makes these (legal and practical) measurements highly arbitrary. The author argues that the use of de jure and de facto variables of independence, by partially offsetting the subjectivity of both approaches, helps in assessing actual independence.

Cukierman (1992) provides three indicators of independence, of which two (the LVAU-LVAW and TOR indices) have been widely cited and used in subsequent literature. The first of these (LVAU-LVAW),[10] which has

---

[10] LVAU is a simple legal index; LVAW is a weighted index (see Appendix I).

been calculated for some 70 countries, is characterized as a strictly legal index. It is made up of some sixteen variables that provide a detailed mapping of the legal structure under which CBs operate. Cukierman points out that, among the seven countries with the highest independence score, four are OECD countries, while of the seven lowest, six are developing countries. The average level of independence for the entire sample (0.33) is not far from that for developed countries alone (0.31), although there is a greater concentration of OECD countries in the top 10 percent of the distribution, while the bottom 10 percent is dominated by less-developed countries.

Cukierman also calculates for 58 countries a de facto independence index, defined as the turnover rate of CB governors – TOR – with a view to identifying actual deviations from the law. While easy to calculate, Cukierman cautions that a low TOR could be mistakenly perceived as a sign of independence in the case of a CB that is relatively subordinate to the executive branch and, consequently, tends to leave its position unchanged for a long period. However, the TOR is still a useful indicator based on the assumption that – at least above a certain threshold – a higher TOR does point to lower independence. In particular, in the event of a high TOR, the term in office of the governor may be shorter than the average term of a government, which dissuades the CB from taking a long-term view.

The author notes that it is unlikely that the TOR would have a practical meaning for more-developed countries. His ranking shows that TORs in developing countries cover a much broader range of values than in OECD countries (where values are all below 0.20 turnovers per annum), suggesting that this is not a reliable indicator for OECD countries. However, in developing countries, where practices that deviate from the law may be more common than in industrial countries, the TOR may be a good indicator of independence.[11] The last of the three indicators (QVAU and QVAW)[12] reported in Cukierman (1992) is based on responses to a questionnaire on CB practices by qualified staff at twenty-four CBs, therefore providing an assessment of de facto independence. In particular, the questions focus on the instruments that are under the control of the CB and the practices that are followed when they differ from the law. The two indices show a high correlation coefficient of 0.99.

---

[11] TOR values range from a minimum of 0.03 (which corresponds to an average term in office for the governor of some 33 years) to a maximum of 0.93 (which corresponds to an average term in office of just 13 months).

[12] QVAU is a simple de facto index; QVAW is a weighted index (see Appendix II).

Cukierman's main findings can be summarized as follows: (i) de jure independence (as proxied by the LVAU-LVAW) is more closely related to actual independence (as indicated by the QVAU-QVAW) in developed than in developing countries; (ii) the TOR and the de jure indicators seem to proxy different dimensions of CB independence, given the weak link between the TOR and the LVAU-LVAW; (iii) the overall contribution of individual groups of legal variables to inflation in the entire sample is not statistically significant. This is also true when TOR is added to the regression, although the improvement in results suggests that the TOR captures significant de facto independence factors; (iv) by regressing inflation against the TOR for the entire group of countries, the expected negative relationship is only significant above a certain turnover threshold; and (v) the TOR is a measure that best approximates the actual independence in less-developed countries. In particular, Cukierman finds that the index has a negative coefficient that is not significant for industrial countries, the opposite of what occurs for developing countries.

Regarding the impact of independence on inflation performance, Cukierman's main findings are as follows: (i) the regression of inflation on the LVAW and on a measure that captures compliance with the law with respect to the term of office of governors (i.e., the *comp* variable defined as the relationship between the average actual term of office and the legal term) shows that both have the anticipated negative sign, but only the *comp* is statistically significant for the entire sample. When only developed countries are considered, the opposite occurs: the effect of the *comp* variable is practically nil and the LVAW exhibits a significantly negative coefficient. This confirms the hypothesis that de facto measures would be better proxies for independence in less-developed countries; and (ii) the regression of inflation on the QVAU and QVAW indicators shows on the one hand that most of the questionnaire variables have the negative expected sign, and that the most significant are those referring to limits on the ability of the CB to extend credit to the government, while the overall contribution of the index to explaining inflation performance is low. Finally, adding the LVAW measure of independence does not provide much additional information, while adding the TOR measure does. This shows that, at least for the countries in the sample and limited to the 1980s, all the variables for explaining inflation are those contained in the answers to the questionnaire and in the TOR.

Aggregation of two legal measures: Alesina and Summers (1993)

Alesina and Summers (1993) construct an independence index covering both its political and economic dimensions on the basis of Bade and

Table 1.7 Alesina and Summers independence index

Country	Alesina index (1988)	GMT index (1991)	GMT index converted to Alesina scale (1988)	Average of Alesina (1988) and converted GMT index
Australia	1	9	3	2
Belgium	2	7	2	2
Canada	2	11	3	2.5
Denmark	2	8	3	2.5
France	2	7	2	2
Germany	4	13	4	4
Italy	1.5	5	2	1.75
Japan	3	6	2	2.5
Netherlands	2	10	3	2.5
New Zealand	1	3	1	1
Norway	2	–	–	2
Spain	1	5	2	1.5
Sweden	2	–	–	2
Switzerland	4	12	4	4
United Kingdom	2	6	2	2
United States	3	12	4	3.5

Source: Authors' elaborations based on Alesina and Summers (1993).

Parkin (1985), Alesina (1988, 1989), and GMT (1991). The index is the arithmetic mean of the combined GMT index (political and economic independence), and Alesina index (Table 1.7).[13] The index is then compared to macroeconomic measures, such as inflation, real GDP growth rates and per capita GDP, unemployment rates, and real interest rates, for the 1955–88 period.

The authors find a nearly perfect negative correlation between independence and both the average and variance of inflation. However, the relationship between independence and the average (and variance) of GDP growth is not clear. Similar results are found with regard to the relationship between unemployment and independence, as well as the relationship between independence and real interest rate movements. However, in line with expectations a negative relationship is observed between independence and interest rate variability.

---

[13] To review the conversion in detail, see the aggregation method section of the Alesina and Summers (1993) index in the Summary table of base indicators of de jure independence, in Appendix III.

Table 1.8   Eijffinger and Schaling policy types

CB final policy authority		No government official on CB board	Over one-half of CB board appointments made independent of the government	Potential CB type	Policy type	CB policy type does exist
g	0	0	1	(*a*)	–	–
g	0	1	1	(*b*)	–	–
b	2	0	1	(*c*)	–	–
b	2	0	0	(*d*)	–	–
b/g	1	0	0	(*e*)	–	–
b/g	1	1	1	(*f*)	–	–
b/g	1	0	1	(*g*)	–	–
g	0	0	0	(*h*)	1	(Australia, Canada)
g	0	1	0	(*i*)	2	(France, Italy, UK, Sweden)
b/g	1	1	0	(*j*)	3	(Belgium, Japan, US)
b	2	1	0	(*k*)	4	(Netherlands)
b	2	1	1	(*l*)	5	(Germany, Switzerland)

Source: Authors' elaboration based on Eijffinger and Schaling (1993).

A new legal indicator: Eijffinger and Schaling (1993)

In keeping with GMT (1991), Eijffinger and Schaling identify the degree of political independence with the ability for the CB to select its final objectives. Three areas are considered: the procedures for appointing CB boards; the relationship between the CB and the government in formulating monetary policy objectives; and the monetary policy objectives it is required to pursue. On that basis, the authors define twelve CB policy types and find that only five are represented in their sample (Table 1.8).

Political vulnerability of central banks: Cukierman and Webb (1995)

Cukierman and Webb develop an index of CB vulnerability to political instability with a view to explain inflationary trends among developing countries. It is motivated by the fact that de jure indices overlook deviations from the law, which presumably are more common in developing countries. The index, which draws on Cukierman's TOR, is measured as the CB governor's propensity to leave office in periods following a government transition or significant political change. The measure of

Table 1.9 Cukierman and Webb: frequency of changes in head of central bank

Economic group considered	Number of countries	Time interval (number of months from political transition)				
		0–1	*2–3*	*4–6*	*7–9*	*10 or more*
Total sample	67	0.063	0.026	0.025	0.013	0.015
All industrial economies	20	0.008	0.013	0.013	0.003	0.009
Only democratic economies	18	0.020	0.009	0.015	0.002	0.009
Mixed economies	2	0.060	0.000	0.000	0.024	0.013
All developing economies	47	0.096	0.041	0.034	0.022	0.018
Only authoritarian economies	9	0.046	0.016	0.065	0.011	0.025
Only democratic economies	16	0.089	0.017	0.006	0.025	0.015
Mixed economies	22	0.105	0.053	0.038	0.023	0.019

Source: Cukierman and Webb (1995).

vulnerability, which considers TOR close to a political change, allows distinguishing political TOR from other types of turnover.[14] Four political transitions are considered: *low instability* when a change in the head of government does not lead to change in government parties; *medium instability* with non-violent change in parties in government without a change in the form of government; *irregular transitions* whereby shifts from one authoritarian regime to another do not result in a change in the fundamental rules of government; and *high instability* when there are changes in the political regime detrimental to a democratic government or a return of democracy. The authors estimate the probability of a change of CB head, starting from the date of a political change (Table 1.9). They find that this probability decreases with the number of months from the political transition, and they define politically motivated changes in CB governor as those occurring within six months of a political transition. The authors also define the indicator of political vulnerability (VUL), and they find that close to a quarter of political transition events are followed by a turnover of the CB governor within six months, but the vulnerability is over three times higher in developing

---

[14] The data cover the period 1950–89, with two sub-periods: Bretton Woods period (1950–71); flexible exchange rates period (1972–89). Sixty-seven countries are analyzed: 20 OECD and 47 developing countries.

Table 1.10   Cukierman and Webb: central bank political vulnerability

Economic group considered	Vulnerability		Annual frequency of political changes
	Within six months	*Within one month*	
Total sample	0.24	0.12	0.27
Industrial countries	0.10	0.05	0.32
Developing countries	0.35	0.18	0.24
Industrial countries			
Only democratic economies	0.10	0.04	0.32
Mixed economies	0.12	0.12	0.33
Developing countries			
Only authoritarian economies	0.22	0.17	0.14
Only democratic economies	0.30	0.09	0.18
Mixed economies	0.39	0.20	0.30

Source: Cukierman and Webb (1995).

Table 1.11   Cukierman and Webb: correlation between various independence indicators

Indicator	Legal independence index	Total TOR	Vulnerability index	Frequency of political changes
Total TOR	−0.05			
Vulnerability index	−0.11	0.78		
Frequency of political transitions	−0.05	0.06	−0.11	
Non-political turnover at CB	−0.02	0.88	0.60	−0.21

Source: Cukierman and Webb (1995).

countries.[15] In addition, developing countries with high instability have more vulnerable CBs (Table 1.10).

The authors also investigate the relationships among different indicators, and between the political vulnerability index and type of political transitions. In a first set of regressions they compare four indicators (Cukierman, Webb, and Neyapti, 1992; de jure index; Cukierman's TOR; and their own vulnerability index) and show that most indicators exhibit no mutual correlation, even though the overall TOR is highly correlated to the two measures derived from it (Table 1.11). In a second set of

---

[15] $VUL(i) =$ Nb. of governors TOR within i months from political transition/Nb. political transitions ($i = 1$ to 6).

Table 1.12   Cukierman and Webb: political vulnerability within six months of transition

Economic group	Type of political transition			
	High-level	*Authoritarian*	*Medium-level*	*Low-level*
Total sample	0.58	0.46	0.15	0.19
Industrial countries	–	–	0.11	0.08
Developing countries	0.61	0.46	0.24	0.26
Industrial countries				
Only democratic economies	–	–	0.11	0.08
Mixed economies	0.00	–	0.12	0.17
Developing countries				
Only authoritarian economies	–	0.20	–	0.23
Only democratic economies	–	–	0.24	0.25
Mixed economies	0.61	0.55	0.24	0.28

Note: The values show political vulnerability within six months of the transition categorized by type of transition and applicable economic group. For instance, in the case of developing countries, 61 percent of high-level political transitions were followed by a replacement of CB leadership within six months.

Source: Cukierman and Webb (1995).

regressions they estimate the correlation between political vulnerability indices and the types of political transition, in addition to a dummy variable for authoritarian regimes and another one for developing countries. The latter dummy has a significantly positive impact on the vulnerability index calculated over a six-month time horizon. None of the political change indicators has a statistically significant effect. Low and medium-level political changes have no effect on vulnerability, while high-level changes exhibit a positive, but not statistically significant coefficient. However, CB vulnerability (over a period of six months) depends on the type of political change (Table 1.12). The highest vulnerability is associated with high-level political transitions, which occur only in developing countries. In these countries, irregular transitions from one authoritarian regime to another without changes in fundamental rules of government have an impact on CB vulnerability that is nearly twice as great as changes on a more modest scale. That second set of regressions shows that the political vulnerability is more pronounced in less developed countries and after major political transitions.

Finally, Cukierman and Webb (1995) expand on Cukierman (1992) with a view to assessing the relationship between inflation (and its variability), CB political vulnerability, the non-political turnover rate of the governor, and the various types of political instability. The results are comparable for vulnerability measures at one and six months, although vulnerability within the first month seems the most decisive. CB political vulnerability as well as non-political TOR has a significantly positive impact on the inflation rate and its variability. The authors also find that high-level political instability contributes to increased inflation variability, while low political instability contributes only marginally to an increase in average inflation. Results also show that medium-level instability (i.e., normal turnover of parties in a democratic context) has no effect on inflation. The low significance of the dummy variable, which incorporates countries with authoritarian regimes over the entire period considered, suggests that once CB and political instability variables are considered, the distinction of this type of regime does not help to explain the differences in inflation performance. Finally, once the TOR is broken down into its two components and the various types of political instability are considered, the distinction between developing and industrial countries no longer explains the differences in inflation performance. Hence, the differences in CB vulnerability to political instability, in the non-political TOR, and political instability fully account for higher inflation in developing countries.

Regarding growth performance, the authors show that greater CB political dependence tends to slow down growth. They assess whether independence has a significant impact on growth, once the contribution of other determining variables is defined (i.e., initial GDP, initial primary and secondary school enrolment rates, and ten-year rates of change in the terms of trade). Contrary to expectations, the non-political TOR has a marginally significant positive sign. However, after removing countries which have demonstrated solid growth rates despite high levels of political and non-political TOR (i.e., Brazil, Korea, and Botswana), a negative, statistically significant sign is obtained for the political vulnerability index within six months, suggesting that greater political dependence tends to slow down growth.

Finally, the authors find that the TOR increases the variability of real interest rates. Both the non-political TOR and the political vulnerability index increase the variability of real interest rates, while the legal index has little significance. However, with regard to the average level of real interest rates, the political vulnerability index exhibits a significantly negative sign, which probably reflects the higher implicit inflation tax in countries with politically dependent CBs.

Subsequent literature and empirical studies on base indicators

As discussed in the previous section, the base indicators literature found strong empirical evidence supporting the hypothesis that independence reduces the average rate and variability of inflation. Cukierman (1994) summarized these findings as follows: (i) among industrial countries, de jure independence is negatively correlated to inflation and its variability. On the other hand, de facto indices – in particular, the CB governor turnover rate – do not exhibit any correlation to inflation. In addition, de jure independence indicators are not significantly correlated with economic growth; (ii) among emerging economies and developing countries de jure indicators have no significant relationship with inflation, while de facto measures such as TOR do; and (iii) among developing countries and emerging markets, TOR is correlated with growth, but de jure indices are not. From 1994 to the present, a number of studies have challenged the theoretical foundations of independence and related empirical evidence from a variety of perspectives.

Theoretical and empirical clarifications on central bank independence

Much of the literature on independence makes little distinction between the concept of independence and the concept of conservatism. As already discussed, most legal indicators assign CBs a higher value when price stability is one of the CB's main objectives, even though this intuitively indicates less independence in terms of objectives. This is because in the theoretical setup, both independence and conservatism are important for inflation performance: if the CB has the same aversion to inflation as the government, its level of independence would not matter. Vice versa, if a CB was dependent on the executive branch, a higher degree of conservatism would have no effect. Following that line of thought, de Haan and Kooi (1997) assess whether the concept of conservatism (the governor's aversion to inflation) or independence (of the CB from the government's influence) is more important as a key factor of a good independence measure.

de Haan and Kooi (1997)

de Haan and Kooi (1997) relate CB independence to three areas in which the government's influence must be eliminated or at least restricted: (i) the independence of board members and the governor; (ii) financial independence; and (iii) the independence over monetary policy. The first criterion refers to de jure appointment independence, and thus includes criteria such as the government's representation on the board, appointment procedures, and terms of office and dismissal procedures. The second criterion concerns how easy it is for the government to obtain direct or indirect CB funding. The third criterion gives the CB room for manoeuvre in monetary policy conduct.

Following Debelle and Fischer (1994) and GMT (1991), the authors distinguish independence with respect to objectives and instruments. With regard to independence of objectives, it is necessary to evaluate the issues over which the CB has discretion, and whether price stability is the main objective of monetary policy.[16] It is no accident that the indices of GMT (1991) and Cukierman (1992) assign higher values the more stringent the price stability objective. Independence with respect to instruments proxies the freedom of the CB to use whatever means necessary to achieve its objectives.

The aim of the study is to find a measure capable of distinguishing the concepts of conservatism and independence, by breaking down two de jure independence indicators (GMT and Cukierman's LVAU). The process is based on the assumption that while the degree of an individual's conservatism cannot be objectively determined in practice, the degree of conservatism required by law can be measured in the form of the CB's commitment to price stability. Hence, the two indicators are broken down by isolating that degree of conservatism from other components that approximate respectively the independence of the personnel, financial independence, and the independence in policy.[17]

---

[16] The two components are (at least partially) negatively correlated since greater focus of monetary policy on the objective of nominal stability implies less independence in terms of objectives. This assumption reflects the fact that CBs whose sole objective is price stability are considered more independent since the level of priority given to this objective reflects the level of conservatism provided by law; see Cukierman (1992).

[17] With regard to Cukierman's LVAU all the (*CEO*) variables are retained for the personnel's independence measure; the (*PF*) ones, with the exception of the role of the CB in the formulation of the government budget, are retained for instruments independence; the (*OBJ*) is retained for the degree of conservatism required by law; the (*LL*) ones, with the exception of variables *ltype* and *lprm*, are retained to provide a measure of financial independence. The breakdown follows GMT's four criteria index: the first five points of the GMT political independence index contribute to determining the independence of CB staff; the

Consistent with Debelle and Fischer (1994), the regressions calculated by the authors generally show that instruments independence matters for inflation performance while conservatism and other aspects of independence are less important. Based on a sample of twenty-one OECD countries, and for the period 1972–89, the results of regressions of these new measures on the average level of inflation show that the coefficient on the independence index for monetary policy instruments is always significantly different from zero, which is not the case for the conservatism measure. The latter is never significantly different from zero for Cukierman's LVAU, and it loses its significance in the GMT index as soon as the indication of independence with respect to instruments is included. In addition, the calculations show that not even the independence of CB members is significant for explaining average inflation. Regressions of the same measures on the variability of inflation show similar results; the indicator showing the highest relationship with the dependent variable is instruments independence. Regarding variability in growth performance, no significant coefficient is found.[18]

Banaian, Burdekin, and Willett (1995 and 1998)

Banaian, Burdekin, and Willet look at the components of the Cukierman legal index to determine how strongly each of them is related to inflation performance. The authors observe that, despite the uniformity of the results, there is a considerable difference in the ways in which de jure independence is defined and categorized. According to the authors, the problem lies in the way in which the various indices are constructed, which does not rely on considerations based on economic theory. In a 1995 study, the authors had argued that economic theory suggested the need to give greater weight to attributes that describe the formal powers of the CB over monetary policy formulation rather than the provisions with regard to the limitation imposed on CB credit to the government. The authors highlight, for example, that Cukierman's (1992) index was constructed in such a way as to attribute to the restrictions on CB's participation in the primary market for public debt more

---

sixth and eighth points of the GMT political independence index proxy independence with respect to instruments; the degree of conservatism is isolated in the seventh point; and the level of financial independence is built on the first five points of the GMT economic index.

[18] Kilponen (1999) uses a similar procedure on Cukierman's index. While his results confirm the positive effect of instruments independence on inflation performance as in de Haan and Kooi (1997), the author finds that the degree of conservatism conferred to the CB by the law impacts on wage growth.

than three times the weight attached to the independence in monetary policy formulation. Along the same line of thought, the authors argue that GMT (1991) overlooked this fundamental aspect by giving the same weight to all the variables they consider.

The empirical results obtained by Banaian, Burdekin, and Willett led them to argue that among industrial countries inflation can be predicted more accurately using a simple policy independence index based on the CB's freedom from government interference in monetary policy formulation. In particular, using a sample of twenty-one OECD countries between 1971 and 1988, the authors find in their 1995 paper that the LVAU and TOR indices of Cukierman (1992) and the GMT (1991) index have no significance once a dummy variable on policy independence (i.e., the inability of the government to override monetary policy decisions) is included. In other words, in the absence of policy independence as defined above, the beneficial effects attributed to the other characteristics considered by Cukierman and GMT are seriously compromised.

In a 1998 article, the authors analyze the components of Cukierman's (1992) legal index in order to isolate the various attributes from the implicit weight assigned to them. Analyzing fifteen out of the sixteen variables, the authors conclude that most of the attributes have a non-significant or positive, rather than negative, relationship with the average level of inflation. This could mean either that there is no truly relevant attribute for explaining inflation within the Cukierman index or that certain attributes are relevant but were improperly coded by the author. Thus, the result suggests at least a certain caution in using Cukierman's (1992) legal index as a measure of independence. According to the authors, several of the problems discovered in Cukierman's index can be attributed to a faulty approach in categorizing the various degrees of de jure independence, in particular the attribute that pertains to independence in monetary policy formulation. The absence of significance for this attribute is the least reassuring sign for the authors. A further disturbing fact is that the CBs of Austria, Nicaragua, and Romania, the only ones to obtain the maximum ranking, are considered more independent than the Bundesbank for this attribute.

McCallum (1995)

There has been some criticism of the link between the theoretical foundations and the measurements of independence (Rogoff, 1985), as well as of the contractual solutions to the time inconsistency problem given by Walsh (1995) and Svensson (1997). One of the most cited criticisms is elaborated in McCallum (1995) who discusses two misleading interpretations of the literature on the foundations of the concept of independence. The first criticism concerns the assumption that if the monetary authority is not forced to behave otherwise, it will opt for suboptimal discretionary equilibrium. The author notes that there is no pre-commitment capable of ensuring the future behavior of the CB under all possible circumstances. However, there is no barrier either, that would prevent the CB from implementing optimal policies. The CB must recognize that benefits for the economy would be achieved sooner and more completely by abstaining from inconsistent policies. Another way of looking at this issue is to recognize that there is no required trade-off between commitment and flexibility (as argued by Lohmann 1992, and Debelle and Fischer 1994) when faced with the occurrence of unusually large shocks. In such cases, even a vigorous response does not necessarily imply inappropriate trends in the inflation rate.

McCallum (1995) also criticizes Persson and Tabellini (1993) and Walsh (1995) regarding the contractual solution to the problem of time inconsistency. McCallum argues that the incentive structure proposed by Walsh (1995) cannot solve the problem of the time inconsistency of discretionary monetary policy, but merely transfers it to the authority to which the CB is accountable. A government that must enforce the contract, and nevertheless suffers from the same (if not bigger) incentives to violate it, represents an evident inconsistency. McCallum argues that placing the contract at a higher legal level does not solve the problem. One example is the United States, where the constitution provides for a metal-based monetary structure, which has not formally existed since 1971, and ceased to exist de facto even earlier. McCallum does not deny the utility of such incentives but argues that they cannot influence the source of the inconsistent behavior.

Endogenizing the inflation bias

Inflationary bias has to do with the temptation for policy-makers to accept an inflation rate above its optimal level to boost growth. While there is broad agreement that monetary policy is not a first-best choice for correcting labor market inefficiencies, it is not clear how these inefficiencies interact with monetary policy. Several studies attempt to endogenize the inflationary bias by introducing the behavior of inflation-averse unions. Since those who bargain over wages are averse to inflation, they will moderate their demands. This modeling assumption undermines previous results, in particular Rogoff (1985), that an inflation-averse CB helps reduce the inflationary bias. According to this line of research, a not too conservative CB can achieve low inflation because such a behavior is more likely to reduce wage increases demands.

Cukierman and Lippi (1999)

Cukierman and Lippi (1999) offer an example of this second-best theory, by providing empirical evidence of the joint effect of independence and centralized wage bargaining on macroeconomic performance. The inclusion of a sufficient inflation aversion component in unions' behavior leads to a convex/hump-shaped relation between inflation and unemployment on one side, and the degree of centralization of wage bargaining on the other. This relationship is the consequence of two opposite effects of centralization: on the one hand, it reduces competition in the labor market; on the other hand, it increases the extent to which each union internalizes the inflationary consequences of its wage claims.

At low levels of concentration unions are too small to internalize the effects of increasing wage claims on inflation and a free-riding effect prevails. Therefore an increase in wage bargaining centralization, by reducing competition, results in higher real wages, inflation, and unemployment. However, as unions become large enough to value the consequences of their claims, this effect is offset because fewer unions lead to higher inflationary fears on the part of unions. This effect reduces wage demands; hence, inflation and unemployment decline.

Thereafter, the authors suggest a number of channels through which independence and its relationship with the level of labor market centralization affects the performance of labor markets. They argue that in a system with a limited number of unions, a study of the effects of various levels of centralization of wage negotiations should take into account the type of monetary regime. The convex relationship between unemployment (inflation) and wage bargaining centralization is stronger at a low level of independence and when unions are sufficiently averse to inflation. This convex relationship gradually weakens and eventually becomes monotonically increasing as the degree of independence increases. The main implication is that in countries in which there is a high level of independence, labor market decentralization (i.e., a high number of unions) is capable of reducing real wages, inflation, and unemployment.

The authors also assess the relationship between independence and unemployment. They identify two transmission channels. First, if unions are inflation averse, independence can affect the perception of unions regarding the consequences on inflation of their actions. Thus, at high levels of centralization, a more conservative CB leads to more aggressive wage negotiations and higher unemployment. Second, if there are several unions and some degree of substitutability between labor, there is a second effect that works regardless of the unions' aversion to inflation: a less inflation-averse CB leads unions to perceive any increase in individual real wage as more costly in terms of competitiveness; this effect moderates wage demands compared to a situation in which salaries are indexed, while this perceived reduced competitiveness decreases as CB conservatism increases. Both relationships disappear when wage negotiations are atomized at the firm level. Hence, in the presence of sufficiently concentrated unions that perceive the effects of wage claims, the Cukierman and Lippi model suggests that a higher degree of CB conservatism results in higher unemployment, as it leads to a relaxation of unions' fears with respect to inflation and competitiveness.

Empirical research on these issues is based on an analysis of data from nineteen OECD economies for the period 1980–94. The authors find a clear convex relationship between unemployment (inflation) and the bargaining centralization in the labor market for low levels of independence. Convexity disappears as the degree of independence grows. The authors show that previous studies, such as OECD (1997), did not find a convex relationship because they had omitted CB independence as a control variable in exploring the relationship between labor market structure and macroeconomic performance. The authors also show that the inflation-reducing impact that independence brings about is stronger at intermediate levels of union centralization, while there is a significantly positive effect of independence on unemployment for low levels of wage bargaining centralization.

Franzese (1999)

Franzese (1999) provides a politically oriented view that combines, amongst others, CB independence and union concentration models. He argues that the concentration and coordination of wage negotiations have an opposite influence on the anti-inflationary impact of independence. On the one hand, the power of labor unions, when the wage bargaining process is concentrated, lowers the natural rate of employment and therefore increases discretionary inflation. Coordinated bargaining, on the other hand, by internalizing the real costs of excessive wage claims, increases the natural rate of employment and reduces discretionary inflation. Hence, CB independence lowers inflation more in the former case (greater union power) than in the latter (greater coordination). Franzese also argues that independence is a matter of nuances: it can neither be absolute, nor completely absent. Hence, monetary policy and inflation are always partially controlled by both the CB and the government, and are affected by unions' behavior. As a consequence, he argues that the macroeconomic effects of independence and unions' behavior should be analyzed simultaneously. More generally, Franzese emphasizes that the inflationary impact of institutional and economic settings is not constant: any factor influencing unions, the government, or the CB's policy decisions, changes the impact of CB independence on inflation. Conversely, independence changes the inflationary impact of each of these factors. For instance, beyond the above-mentioned case of wage bargaining concentration and coordination, the author argues that independence reduces inflation more when the government is not conservative or there is higher inflation abroad than when the government is conservative or inflation abroad is lower. On the contrary, greater independence reduces inflationary differences between the polar cases.

Robustness of independence measures

We have already noted that it is difficult to construct a CB independence measure that is unbiased. In particular, even subtle differences in defining a variable, especially within de jure indicators, can generate large discrepancies in results. Furthermore, the possibility of comparing quantitative measures is made difficult given that the areas subject to the authors' discretion involve not only the selection of criteria of independence but also their interpretation or the method for aggregating the criteria. In that context, in the following paragraphs we review research having to do with the robustness of independence measures.

Mangano (1998)

Mangano explores interpretive and methodological discrepancies in measurements of independence and their impact on the robustness of resulting empirical evidence. Looking at the most widely used indicators (i.e., the GMT and Cukierman's LVAU indices), he finds a significant "interpretation spread"[19] equal to an average of 30 percent of the legislation reviewed. He also points to a "criteria spread"[20] that indicates that 40 percent of the variables contemplated by GMT are not present

---

[19] An interpretation spread indicates the subjective spread among researchers in reading laws and thus in interpreting the same criterion when it is included in an index of independence.

[20] The criteria spread is the way in which the personal preferences of the researcher influence the selection of criteria to be included in the index, and it is logically situated at a higher level than the first spread.

Table 1.13 Mangano: comparison of independence indices rankings

Country	GMT	LVAU	AL	ES	TOR	VUL
Belgium	7	11	5	5	6	4
Switzerland	2	1	1	1	6	8
Canada	4	4	5	12	3	1
Germany	1	2	1	1	3	11
Denmark	6	3	5	3	1	5
France	7	8	5	10	9	6
Japan	9	12	3	5	11	12
Netherlands	5	5	5	3	1	6
New Zealand	12	9	11	5	9	9
Spain	11	10	11	5	11	10
United Kingdom	9	6	5	10	3	1
United States	2	6	3	5	6	1

Note: AL: Alesina (1988, 1989); GMT (1991); ES: Eijffinger and Schaling (1993); TOR/LVAU are from Cukierman (1992). VUL is from Cukierman and Webb (1995).

Source: Authors' elaborations based on Mangano (1998).

in Cukierman's paper, while in the opposite case the proportion rises to 45 percent. Finally, he discovers a negligible "weighting spread."[21]

Mangano's work results in a ranking of existing indicators of CB independence. He notes that most of the recent empirical studies using more than one index or combinations of different indices, generally obtain results that agree with theory, but argues that it is not acceptable to merge indicators that suffer from subjective spreads. Accordingly, the author chooses to make a direct comparison of the rankings expressed by the measures rather than comparing absolute values. Looking at the twelve OECD economies that are common to the samples in the six indicators he compares, Mangano finds that there is little correlation among the rankings (Tables 1.13 and 1.14).

Mangano then uses the rankings as explanatory variables for several dependent variables for macroeconomic performance, including the average inflation rate, GDP growth rate, and their variability. With respect to inflation, the signs of the coefficients of the rankings are generally consistent with the anticipated negative relationship. However, it is disconcerting that the coefficient is significantly different from zero only for GMT and Alesina indices. Mangano reaches similar conclusions

---

[21] The weighting spread is defined as the way in which the selection of the weights related to each criterion included in the index influences its final value.

Table 1.14   Mangano: partial correlations between rankings

Indices	GMT	LVAU	AL	ES	TOR	VUL
GMT	1.00	0.75	0.82	0.31	0.55	0.23
LVAU		1.00	0.52	0.27	0.73	0.21
AL			1.00	0.26	0.39	0.09
ES				1.00	0.09	−0.57
TOR					1.00	0.51
VUL						1.00

Source: Authors' elaboration based on Mangano (1998).

regarding the variability of inflation, for which all coefficients have the anticipated sign, but only in one case is this coefficient significant. The results on growth are even more disconcerting: contrary to expectations, independence seems to have a negative effect on growth, although the results are not significant. Finally, Mangano does not find any significant relationship between the rankings assigned to the various CBs and the variability of GDP growth. Even if Mangano does not question the quality of the measures, he argues that the different measures of independence capture different aspects of the status of a CB, thus reducing the possibility of making meaningful comparisons of the empirical results.

Forder (1999)

Forder (1999) compares several independence indicators in order to identify a good proxy measure of independence. The author accepts that selecting an appropriate measure for independence inevitably involves arbitrary decisions, but also acknowledges that the results obtained indicate that CB independence lowers inflation and its variability. With those assumptions as background, Forder's goal is to challenge the view that measurement problems are minor, and to raise doubts regarding the concordance of results. Forder believes that measurement problems and the dichotomy between de jure and de facto independence are still too large to consider the results to be truly significant and persuasive.

Forder argues that independence indicators are nothing more than formal tests, since they identify a measure that is already actually negatively correlated to inflation, and that their authors are overly hasty in attributing to them the capacity to approximate independence. Indeed, none of the authors he reviews offers a test of the independence hypothesis, but only more or less plausible proxies of independence which are tied to inflation. Forder admits that all the studies provide reasonable measures, but there is no objective basis for making a selection among them. The fact that, except for the cases of Germany and Switzerland, the various studies do not succeed in reaching a reasonable consensus, confirms Forder's insights. Hence, Forder argues that although it is possible to talk about "degrees of independence" on a theoretical level, there is no correlation among different indices that indicates empirical agreement in this regard. Forder concludes that the assumption that there is a correlation between low levels of inflation and independence could indeed prove to be correct, but the literature has still not been able to offer an empirical concept of independence that would allow an effective test of this assumption.

Eijffinger, Van Rooij, and Schaling (1996)

Eijffinger, Van Rooij, and Schaling (1996) estimate a monetary policy reaction function for ten OECD countries, and analyze the response of money market interest rates to inflation, growth, and the current account surplus. The aim is to empirically identify a measure of independence by estimating reaction functions, so that the differences in independence can be seen as different structural pressures for an increase or decrease in money market rates. The reaction functions show a trend towards rising interest rates as a common reaction to inflation and economic growth. However, contrary to expectations the intensity of the response is higher in response to growth than it is to inflation. By ranking countries in decreasing order with respect to the new measure of independence (i.e., starting with the CB that has the strongest reaction as reflected in the increase in interest rates), the authors obtain a ranking where the CBs of Germany and the Netherlands are at the top, the Italian and British banks at the bottom, and the rest in between. After comparing the rankings obtained by their own and other indicators, the authors argue that most of the legal measures coincide rather well with their independence index (Table 1.15). This close relationship is confirmed by the correlations between the legal measures and their index of independence.

Causality of hypotheses on central bank independence
Posen (1993, 1995)

Posen (1993, 1995) argues that the strength of the financial sector's opposition to inflation could determine both the degree of independence and the level of inflation. The correlation between inflation and independence could run in either direction, or could alternatively be explained by a third factor such as the culture and tradition of monetary stability in a country. According to Posen, independence is not always a valid institutional recommendation, and instead may result as a "Pareto inefficient"

Table 1.15 Eijffinger, Van Rooij, and Schaling: empirical index and legal indicators

Country	Ranking based on empirical index	Eijffinger and Schaling index (1993) (Scale 1 to 5)	Bade and Parkin index (1988) (Scale 1 to 4)	Alesina index (1988, 1989) (Scale 1 to 4)	GMT (1991) political index (Scale 0 to 8)	GMT (1991) economic index (Scale 0 to 8)
Germany	1	5	4	4	6	7
Netherlands	2	4	2	2	6	4
Canada	3	1	2	2	4	7
Japan	4	3	3	3	1	5
Switzerland	5	5	4	4	5	7
United States	6	3	3	3	5	7
France	7	2	2	2	2	5
Australia	8	1	1	1	3	6
Italy	9	2	2	1/2	4	1
United Kingdom	10	2	2	2	1	5

Source: Authors' elaborations based on Eijffinger, Van Rooij, and Schaling (1996).

selection (even though it increases the relative level of welfare), since it was demonstrated (the author cites Debelle and Fischer 1994 and Walsh 1994) that the costs of deflation tend to rise with an independent CB. In addition, as argued by Cukierman (1992), in developing economies differences in the legal independence of CBs are not able to predict inflation rates. In practice, independence entails significant redistributive consequences, so there is no reason to believe that such an arrangement is always optimal. Posen argues that the preference for price stability, which the CB's conservatism should embody, needs significant political support. The only economic sector able to provide such support is the financial sector, since it sees independence as the only way to achieve nominal stability in the long run. Accordingly, it is very likely that changes in a country's financial or political systems will also have an effect on the CB's ability to maintain price stability.

Posen suggests that monetary policy decisions may embody the responses expected by those political entities that have the power to determine the CB's independence and powers. The financial sector is in a dominant position since it represents the greatest source of information, advisory services, and assessments for both the government and the CB regarding monetary policy. Posen quotes a sentence supporting his argument, taken from a 1993 parliamentary debate on the reform of the American federal monetary system: "If one's goal is to minimize inflation, Fed officials reason, then a sure way to achieve that goal is to have private bankers – who are among the world's fiercest inflation hawks – appoint the regional bank presidents."

Posen proposes an indicator of financial opposition to inflation (FOI). In order to elaborate the FOI, Posen asks two questions. First, which factors determine the financial sector's differing degree of unity in its opposition? Posen argues that the larger the number of financial institutions that share the same positions, the lower the cost of pursuing a joint objective. This implies that financial sectors with a "universal" banking system should have a more unambiguous feeling of aversion towards inflation, and the same should be true where the CB has no banking supervision responsibilities. Second, what is it that makes the financial sector stronger in one country compared to others? Posen assumes that for a less fragmented political system (as measured by the number of political parties), the financial sector's aversion to inflation should be stronger, and the same can be said for a decentralized administrative system where national issues (i.e., monetary policy) hold relatively greater importance.

Posen's FOI is made of four components. The first one has a positive value when banks are authorized to operate in at least two of the following markets: the financial intermediation market, insurance market, and commercial credit market. The second component has a full value when banking supervision is not under the control of the CB, and a partial value when this responsibility is shared between the CB and another agency. The third component approximates the existence of a federal administrative system. The fourth component (probability that two members of parliament selected randomly during the same legislative period belong to two different political parties) serves as an indicator of party system fragmentation. The first three components should increase FOI; the last should reduce it.

Posen's empirical work is based on a sample of 32 countries (of which 17 are OECD countries) with low and moderate inflation for the period 1960–89. It seeks to assess the ability of FOI to explain differences in the degrees of independence and inflation.[22] Analyzing OECD countries' differences over FOI and its components, the inflation rates, and the level of independence (as proxied by Cukierman's LVAU), Posen finds a positive relationship between independence and FOI and a negative relationship between average inflation and FOI. By regressing Cukierman's LVAU on FOI and its four components, he shows that the FOI, as well as its components with the exception of the one regarding the CB's supervisory power, exhibits a highly significant positive coefficient. Another set of regressions, in which inflation is the dependent variable, exhibits significant coefficients with the expected (negative) sign for FOI and for two of its four components (CB supervisory power and the existence of a federal administration). Furthermore, Cukierman's LVAU never exhibits statistically significant coefficients as long as the FOI variable is present. These results do not apply exclusively to OECD countries, even though they are stronger for them. In summary, Posen's work shows empirical evidence supporting a causal relationship between a high degree of FOI on the one hand, and a higher degree of independence and a lower inflation rate on the other hand.

Several authors, challenging Posen's results, have not found empirical evidence regarding the role of the FOI in explaining the various degrees of independence or inflation performance. de Haan and Van't Hag (1995) criticized Posen's results for OECD countries by arguing that they

---

[22] A higher level of FOI should lead to a greater degree of independence, and on average inflation should also be lower when financial opposition to inflation is widespread.

can be confirmed only if Cukierman's LVAU is used. Similarly, neither Campillo and Miron (1997), Temple (1998), de Haan and Kooi (2000) nor Sturm and de Haan (2001) find evidence supporting the hypothesis that the financial sector's opposition to inflation plays a decisive role in explaining the differences in inflation or the degrees of independence.

Crosby (1998)

Crosby (1998) suggests that countries that experience less variability in output should establish independence more quickly. According to Rogoff (1985), the highest cost of an independent CB is identifiable in the increase in output variability due to the governments' loss of control over discretionary and output-stabilizing monetary policy. Assuming an opposite causal relationship, Crosby suggests that countries experiencing low levels of output variability should establish an independent CB more quickly. He argues that the higher the inflationary bias, the less attractive the decision for discretionary monetary policy. Similarly, however, if real shocks to the economy are widespread, discretion is desirable since reducing output variability would be beneficial. Therefore, countries affected by real shocks of a lower magnitude or with a lower frequency may be more likely to opt for CB independence.

Using a sample of 44 industrial and developing countries for the period 1962–91, Crosby tests for the hypothesis that real shocks variability could explain levels of independence. He relies on Cukierman's LVAU indicator as a measure of independence, data on the variance of the terms of trade, plus a variable for measuring political stability (defined as the degree of polarization of the political system), which, according to Alesina and Gatti (1995), should increase the variability of output and inflation. Crosby finds that independence is a negative function of the magnitude of real shocks for the entire sample, but not for the subgroup of developing countries. On the other hand, there is no evidence that the degree of political stability determines the degree of independence. However, this does not reject the hypothesis of Alesina and Gatti (1995), which argued that the direction of causality moves from independence to the reduction in fluctuations brought about by political instability. Crosby cites Posen (1995) and his argument that independence could be regarded as endogenous and may depend on the support for such independence within the financial sector. Crosby argues that if the assumption of endogeneity is correct, the empirical correlation between inflation and output variability on the one hand, and independence, on the other hand, should not only imply causality moving from independence to inflation and output, but also in the opposite direction. Thus, the hypothesis proposed by Crosby, which is empirically confirmed at least for highly advanced economies, suggests that reforms in economic structures that can influence inflation and output variability should also change the degree of desirability for more or less independent CBs. Finally, contrary to Rogoff (1985), Crosby does not find evidence of the opposite effect. An explanation could be that delays in monetary policy transmission to the real economy make monetary policy unsuitable for reducing output variability. He brings us back to GMT's "free lunch" conclusion: independence can reduce inflation with no costs for growth or output variability.

Stella (1997 and 2003)

Stella is one of the few researchers who have analyzed the role of CB capital and financial independence on its performance. In the event of limited financial independence, the CB may face great difficulties in achieving its medium-term policy objectives. Moreover, the potential losses attached to the conduct of monetary policy, requiring continuous transfer of funds from the government, may undermine independence.

Several authors have argued that, despite losses, the CB always returns to posting profits in the long run, regardless of starting levels of operating costs and capital. The CB could operate with no capital as long as demand for base money is maintained. Stella (1997), however, shows that repeated losses may force the CB to abandon the goal of price stability, as well as lead to a decline in operational independence and the imposition of inefficient restrictions on the financial sector so as to achieve the objectives of monetary policy. If demand for base money does not rise, the CB may be forced to: (i) issue accelerating interest-bearing debt which would further reduce its capital; (ii) condition its ability to pursue its objectives to continuous infusions of capital by the government; (iii) impose high non-remunerated reserve requirements; (iv) lower interest rates to levels which would not be consistent with macroeconomic stability. Thus, financial strength and independence are preconditions for CB operational independence if financial repression is to be avoided. Stella (2003) also points to the positive relationship between CB financial weakness and high inflation rates. Bindseil et al. (2004) propose various explanations for this empirical finding, including possible large monetization of government's budget deficits at low interest rates.

Ize (2005)

Giving an empirical dimension to Stella's argument and building on the fact that inflation and interest rates control has proven costly for many

CBs, Ize (2005) is an attempt to assess the level of CB capital by following a net worth approach. The author builds a measure of CB "core capital," defined as the minimum amount of capital needed to maintain a credible inflation target,[23] and then uses this measure to show the amount of capital injection a number of loss-making and/or negative capital CBs needed from the government. Ize finds that in many low- and middle-income countries a substantially positive core capital is needed to make a low inflation target credible.

Furthermore, Ize argues that the financial strength of the CB may diminish due to the provision of cheap CB credit to the government or to failing banks. In such cases, there is a potential for a vicious cycle in which fiscal dominance results in a weakening of the CB's financial strength which feeds into the fiscal accounts only when a new capital injection becomes unavoidable, thus causing a large one-off fiscal effort.

Robustness and sensitivity of results, and search for new measures

A number of recent empirical works go beyond simple linear regressions to include additional control variables. They include Jenkins (1996), Campillo and Miron (1997), Fry (1998), Akhand (1998), Sikken and de Haan (1998), Oatley (1999), Lybek (1999), de Haan and Kooi (2000), Sturm and de Haan (2001), and Arnone, Laurens, and Segalotto (2006b).

Campillo and Miron (1997)

Campillo and Miron argue that previous analyses of differences in countries' inflation performances overlooked the effects of key determinants. In addition to the degree of CB independence, the level of trade openness, political instability, and the income level, the authors consider past inflation performance, and the level of taxation.[24] They show that the institutional characteristics of monetary policy, and especially independence and the foreign exchange regime, have no impact on inflation

---

[23] In this framework core capital is defined as a function of the (projections of) operating expenditures of a CB and the carrying cost of its international reserves, while core profits and core inflation are defined as the profits a CB would obtain, and the minimum rate of inflation it would need to target, in the absence of capital.

[24] Previous inflation performance is considered to account for the fact that countries with a history of high inflation were able to learn their lesson, and are less inclined to face a recurrence of similar episodes. The rationale for considering the level of taxation is that countries where government spending is high on average would be expected to show high levels of taxation, and the inflation tax is more substantial the less governments are able to maintain high levels of conventional taxation and the more inelastic the demand for money.

performance.[25] The variables that seem to play key roles are the degree of trade openness, debt as a percentage of GDP, the level of the inflation tax, political instability, and the level of income.

Brumm (2000, 2002) has challenged Campillo and Miron's view of an empirical uncoupling between independence and inflation, arguing that their estimation technique did not account for the measurement error that inevitably lies in a complex measure such as the LVAW. He argues that the use of legal proxies for independence as a substitute for actual independence is dubious, and that directly substituting a measured proxy for a latent theoretical construct in a regression equation may yield undesirable consequences. By using the analysis of covariance structures instead of OLS regressions, and adding Cukierman's TOR and Cukierman and Webb's vulnerability indicator, Brumm finds a strong negative correlation between CB independence and inflation. He also argues that the results in Posen (1993, 1995, and 1998) are questionable on the same grounds.

Fry (1998)

Fry explores the relationships between independence in developing countries and the level of fiscal dominance, based on a ranking of countries. He proposes two sets of potential discriminating variables: indicators of CB independence on the one hand, and fiscal and macro performance indicators on the other. He then estimates monetary policy reaction functions in which the change in domestic credit to the private sector is a function of current and lagged changes in net domestic credit to the government. Fry's independence index reflects the ability of the CB to neutralize (by reducing the amount of credit available to the private sector) the effects of lending to the government on money supply. He argues that the government can be financed in the following ways: borrowing from the CB at no cost (inflation tax); obtaining financing at below-market rates and forcing commercial banks to absorb the securities issued (financial repression); obtaining financing abroad in foreign currencies and/or at market rates in the private sector. Fry's "fiscal dominance hypothesis of independence" implies that greater reliance on the inflation tax and financial repression is associated with lower independence. Thus, the size of government deficits and the methods by which it

---

[25] The sample consists of 62 countries (the countries for which Cukierman, Webb, and Neyapti construct their LVAW measure) over a time horizon covering the period 1973–94.

is financed determine the degree of actual independence in a developing country.

Fry first estimates neutralization coefficients by selecting the country sample through three different measures of independence: a 1996 Bank of England (BoE) questionnaire, Cukierman's LVAU de jure index, and the TOR de facto index. The results of the BoE questionnaire turn out to be anomalous: CBs that consider themselves less autonomous neutralize 49 percent of any increase in credit to the government within two years, while more autonomous CBs do not neutralize them at all. With regard to Cukierman's de jure index, although less autonomous CBs show smaller delayed neutralization coefficients than more autonomous ones, neither seem to have a significant degree of actual independence based on the sum of current and delayed neutralization coefficients. Finally, with regard to the TOR, contrary to expectations, CBs with the lowest TOR exhibit high, positive neutralization coefficients. In view of these results, Fry argues that the CBs that are defined as autonomous have little or no independence in practice. This first set of results seems to suggest that coded measures of independence provide little information about how independently CBs actually behave in developing countries.

Thereafter, Fry tests his fiscal dominance hypothesis of independence by estimating neutralization coefficients when the country sample is selected on the basis of three fiscal attributes: average government deficit as a percentage of GDP; change in the amount of reserve money as a percentage of GDP; and the ratio of bank reserves to deposits, to capture the degree of financial repression. Fry's results indicate that: (i) CBs in countries with low government deficits have much higher neutralization coefficients; (ii) CBs in countries that rely less on seignorage have high neutralization coefficients, while in those countries where seignorage is high, no neutralization takes place; and (iii) countries whose banking system has a lower ratio of reserves to deposits show higher neutralization coefficients, whereas CBs in countries with high reserves to deposits ratios do not neutralize at all. These results are consistent with Fry's hypothesis that the degree of independence in developing countries is determined by the size of the government deficit and the way in which it is financed. By measuring independence as the degree to which the CB neutralizes the effects on money supply of an increase in credit to the government, Fry's research shows that larger deficits and greater government reliance on the domestic baking sector are associated with a lower degree of sterilization. The author stresses that this result may also reflect the fact that a CB that enjoys instruments independence is able to bring about some degree of fiscal discipline after neutralizing (in a painful manner for the private sector), for a certain number of periods, the increased financial requirements of governments. Finally, the author estimates neutralization coefficients by selecting the countries based on the level of inflation and economic growth. Fry finds that (i) as expected, countries with the lowest levels of inflation have more independent CBs in practice; and (ii) those with higher growth rates show the highest sterilization coefficients.

In summary, Fry brings three main contributions to the discussion about CB independence. First, Fry shows that the tendency to neutralize increases in credit demands by the government is a good proxy for actual independence in developing countries, since a higher level of independence can be associated with lower fiscal deficits, lower tendency to use seignorage, and financial repression on the part of the government, but is also associated with higher growth and lower inflation. This is not the case when independence is proxied using the conventional measures, in particular in developing countries. Second, Fry finds that large government deficits and greater reliance on the inflation tax and on financial repression are associated with a lower degree of neutralization of increased CB credit to the government. Therefore, he argues that empirical analysis confirms that the degree of independence in developing countries is determined by the size of the government deficit and the way in which this deficit is financed. Third, Fry finds that countries that have monetary institutions with the highest degree of independence have the highest growth rates. It may mean that fiscal policy or the executive branch end up influencing both growth and independence. But it could also mean that a competent and effective monetary policy fosters both growth and CB independence in a developing country.

Akhand (1998)

Akhand investigates the robustness of the empirical relationship linking growth to independence as proxied by several indicators. He argues that there is a lack of empirical studies supporting the hypothesis of a relationship between growth and independence. As we have seen, GMT (1991) and Alesina and Summers (1993) find no such relationship. Most likely, this is due to the fact that among OECD countries there is not sufficient variability in the dependent variable (the growth rate) or the explanatory variable being studied (the level of CB independence). Akhand specifically refers to Cukierman, Kalaitzidakis, Summers, and Webb (1993) as the article that inspired his study, arguing that the article is missing a systematic study of robustness for the relationship between growth and independence. To this end, the author uses the robustness test of Levine and Renelt (1992) on four measures of independence: the LVAW, the TOR of Cukierman (1992), the non-political turnover of CB governors (NOR), and the CB political vulnerability index (VUL) of Cukierman and Webb (1995).

Akhand confirms that the legal index and the indices that are more closely tied to actual practice cover different aspects of the characteristics of monetary institutions. His results indicate that there is a negative relationship between growth and de facto independence, but none of the independence indices he uses shows statistically significant coefficients in the base regressions. He concludes that he could not find a robust relationship with growth for any of the four independence indices, and that the result of Cukierman, Kalaitzidakis, Summers, and Webb (1993) of a negative relationship between growth and TOR may be due to the exclusion of the variable relating to the rate of investment as a percentage of GDP.

Sikken and de Haan (1998)

Sikken and de Haan investigate whether, in developing countries, there is a relationship between CB independence on the one hand, and the measure of fiscal deficits and degrees of monetization of deficits, on the other hand. The authors present several theoretical references and they indicate four possible channels through which government debt can lead to money creation and inflation: (i) government pressures to stabilize interest rates: if it is true that an increase in government debt leads to upward pressures on interest rates, the CB may be forced to absorb part of government debt to stabilize interest rates; (ii) time inconsistency in relation to monetary policy: this has to do with the ability to reduce government debt through capital gains that would result from a level of inflation exceeding the inflation-related premium in interest rates; (iii) optimum level of seignorage: this channel represents the amount of resources that the government may obtain through base money growth. In developing countries the tax base tends to be low. Therefore, seignorage plays a larger role, although beyond a certain limit inflationary expectations reduce the tax base at a faster pace than that of monetary expansion; and (iv) a fiscal dominance hypothesis: according to Sargent and Wallace (1981), in a situation of fiscal dominance, it is likely that money supply will become endogenous to the government's fiscal behavior. This occurs when the ability of the economy to absorb debt is saturated, and the CB has to purchase the remaining debt.

The authors explore the relationship between the government budget deficit and the level of independence. Following de Haan and Sturm

(1992), they regress the average budget surplus on different measures of independence.[26] The results indicate that none of these measures has a statistically significant coefficient. Thus, it does not seem possible to argue that in developing countries independence has a motivating effect on the government to reduce spending, or that none of the indices used is suitable for this purpose.

With regard to debt monetization, the authors regress money growth on current and past government surpluses. If it is true that a government deficit has a long-term effect on money growth, the coefficients corresponding to budget surpluses should be negative. The results indicate that eighteen of the thirty countries confirm the prediction, and six of these do so in a significant manner. However, in many countries government deficits have no major impact on money growth. The authors argue that this result is in line with previous studies regarding the monetization of debt in developing countries.

They also regress the growth rate of CB net credits to the government on its fiscal performance. Time series-regressions results indicate that in twenty-six out of thirty countries, a negative relationship exists, and in twelve cases the coefficient of the budget surplus is marginally significant. In order to compare these results with the level of independence, the authors perform second stage cross-section regressions using the coefficients estimated in these time series as dependent variables, and the various independence measures as explanatory variables. The results suggest, as expected, that an independent CB provides less monetary financing to the government through direct loans. However, significant coefficients are found only for the two de facto independence measures, confirming that legal indicators are poor proxies of independence in developing countries.

Oatley (1999)

Oatley investigates the robustness of the relationships found in previous research through the analysis of eight indicators of independence and how the results behave when a broader group of control variables is included.[27] The aim is to add control variables which, at least

---

[26] Countries are those in Cukierman and Webb (1995) reduced from 45 to 30 countries due to data availability. CB independence measures used are Cukierman's LVAW and TOR, Cukierman and Webb's VUL, and the LL heading in Cukierman's LVAU-LVAW index that approximates legal lending limitations on the CB.

[27] The sample is made up of ten OECD countries (Australia, Belgium, Canada, Denmark, France, Germany, Italy, Japan, the Netherlands, and the United Kingdom), and the period covered is 21 years from 1970 to 1990.

theoretically, have a relationship with inflation, including the degree of trade openness, fiscal policy, labor market characteristics, and other variables which had received little attention thus far (i.e., employment and macroeconomic preferences of various political groups). He argues that previous studies rely at most on four indicators of independence,[28] and he includes eight indicators: Cukierman's LVAW and TOR; GMT's three indices (political independence, economic independence, and the combination of these two); Alesina's (1988, 1989) index and two variants of the latter – one that presents a dummy variable for each level of independence identified by Alesina, and another consisting of a single dummy variable that distinguishes between high and low levels of CB independence. Three measures are used to approximate labor market structures: an index for union centralization (Cameron 1984), an indicator of union density (Visser 1991), and a multiplicative variable of these two. With regard to the measurement of policy preferences, Oatley opts for a measure on a five-point scale, which rises with the percentage of progressive representatives on the council of ministers. In addition, Oatley adds the government budget situation, the degree of openness of the economic system, and unemployment level as control variables.

Contrary to Campillo and Miron (1997), Oatley does not find a strong relationship between inflation and the government budget situation or the degree of openness of the economy. By contrast, the variable covering unemployment exhibits a high correlation to inflation. The coefficients are generally stable and statistically significant for all eight models, and the signs are negative as expected. The variables covering labor market organization and the political variables also exhibit a high correlation to inflation, and two out of the three variables proxying labor market structures (union density and the multiplicative variable) have significant and stable coefficients. However, even though the signs are in agreement with Calmfors and Driffill (1988), the magnitude of the interactive variable is too weak to attribute to it a conclusive negative effect on inflation. Finally, the coefficients of the variable reflecting the government's political orientation are generally stable and statistically significant. Oatley concludes that independence indices produced so far provide results that fall short of expectations. In fact, neither the more complex legal index (LVAW), nor the TOR, nor the three indices of GMT (1991) provides satisfactory results from the standpoint of the significance of the coefficients.

---

[28] See Cukierman (1992); Banaian, Burdekin, and Willett (1995); Eijffinger, Van Rooij, and Schaling (1996); Akhand (1998); Fry (1998).

Of the eight indices that are considered, it is the three simplest ones that exhibit statistically significant coefficients with the correct sign.

de Haan and Kooi (2000)

de Haan and Kooi use Cukierman's TOR to construct a new dataset of CB governor turnover.[29] They calculate simple regressions between the changes in the price level and the governor turnover rate and find a positive and statistically significant relationship. However, once high inflation countries are removed from the sample, no significant relationship is found. Thereafter, de Haan and Kooi attempt to verify the robustness of results by adding several control variables that Campillo and Miron (1997) found to be significant, including political instability (the total number of irregular government transitions in the decade); the degree of openness in the economy (the total of imports and exports as a percentage of GDP); the logarithm of per capita GDP in 1980; and public debt as a percentage of GDP in 1980.

In most of the regressions, the coefficient of the new indicator remains significantly positive in relation to inflation contrary to what was observed by Campillo and Miron. The discrepancy is likely due to the fact that these authors used Cukierman's legal indicator LVAW, which has limited value for developing countries. However, the result does not hold when high inflation countries are excluded.

With regard to the variability of inflation, the authors calculate several simple regressions between the standard deviation of changes in price levels and the TOR. The relationship between independence and the variability of inflation is negative and statistically significant although to a lesser degree than the relationship observed with average inflation. However, this conclusion is also shown to be valid only for high inflation countries. The authors stress that even when it is assumed that the order of causality does not move from independence to inflation or vice versa, but that both variables are affected by Posen's (1995) FOI, the results would not change. By following Sikken and de Haan (1998), the authors calculate the existence of any associations between government budget surpluses and the TOR, and do not find a significant relationship between these two variables.

By following the sensitivity analysis of Levine and Renelt (1992), the authors develop a growth equation. The independent variables are: a vector of explanatory variables that show some degree of robustness in explaining the differences in growth rates (the logarithm of the initial

---

[29] The study considers 82 developing countries between 1980 and 1989.

product, the average investment ratio over GDP, and primary and secondary enrollment ratios in 1980), the TOR, and an additional vector of explanatory variables which should affect growth (average population, ratio of government spending to GDP, and average rate of imports and exports as a percentage of GDP). The coefficients of the variables of the first vector are significantly different from zero, but by adding the TOR, sensitivity analysis indicates that there is not a robust relationship between growth and TOR, contrary to what was argued by Cukierman et al. (1993), but in accord with Akhand (1998).

Sturm and de Haan (2001)

Sturm and de Haan analyze the relationship between the TOR and inflation on the basis of a sample nearly twice the size of Cukierman's (1992), including some 97 developing countries and from the 1990s. Following Cukierman (1992) and de Haan and Kooi (2000), the authors use as a dependent variable the percentage rate of change in price level, and the TOR in a multivariate model by adding as control variables the degree of openness to trade within the economy, a political instability variable, the logarithm of per capita GDP, a dummy variable for the case of a fixed exchange rate, and the ratio of government debt to GDP. In order to compare results to those of Cukierman (1992), the time sample is divided into two sub-periods, from 1980 to 1989 and from 1990 to 1998.

The results are consistent with previous studies. With regard to bivariate regressions, the coefficient of the TOR is highly significant for both sub-periods, and has the anticipated positive sign (a higher TOR results in higher inflation). However, as already observed by de Haan and Kooi (2000), the result is significant only if high inflation countries are included. Moving then to a multivariate analysis, the coefficient of the TOR is not significantly different from zero. However, when using Cukierman's sample, the result improves slightly and, as in the case of bivariate regressions, the result remains significant only for high inflation countries.

Lybek (1999)

Lybek uses a new indicator to measure the degree of legal independence and accountability of fifteen CBs in the Baltic countries, Russia, and other countries of the former Soviet bloc at the end of 1997. The indicator assesses the following twenty-one legal attributes: (i) monetary policy targets (regarding price stability); and (ii) the supervision of the banking sector. In the policy independence area, the author considers

(iii) independence with respect to instruments and objectives; (iv) independence in exchange rate policy; (v) the coordination between fiscal and monetary policy; and (vi) the resolution of conflicts between the government and the CB. In the area of political independence, the index assesses regulations regarding: (vii) the appointment of the governor; (viii) the term of office; (ix) the regulations for the dismissal of the governor; (x) the representation of the government on the CB's board; (xi) the appointment of board members; (xii) the term of their office; and (xiii) dismissals. Regarding economic independence, the following items are considered: (xiv) limitations on loans made to the government; (xv) interest rates applied to such loans; (xvi) required collaterals; laws governing (xvii) the quasi fiscal activities of the CB; (xviii) monetary policy instruments; and (xix) cases of insolvency. Finally, in the area of CB transparency and accountability, the following items are analyzed: (xx) the publication of bulletins; and (xxi) CB auditing authorities.

Lybek looks for several empirical parallels between his index and changes in macroeconomic performance during the period 1995–97 that followed the introduction of these countries' own currency.[30] The author reaches three main conclusions: first, the degree of legal independence and accountability expressed by the index is strongly negatively correlated to average inflation, and this correlation remains valid when expanding and contracting the time horizon; second, a strong positive correlation is shown between this index and the average annual growth rate of real GDP, even though this correlation deteriorates by expanding and contracting the sample period, and disappears when taking into account per capita real GDP adjusted for purchasing power; and third, no relationship is found between macroeconomic performance (inflation and growth) in these countries and the degree of de facto independence as proxied by the TOR.

Lybek then asks whether causality moves from independence to inflation and growth performance or whether it was the strong political will to achieve reforms in those years that had a positive impact on all three variables. In partial confirmation of this viewpoint, Lybek argues that his new indicator is positively correlated with an index constructed by the

---

[30] These countries started a gradual reform process in the early 1990s: they enacted new CB laws between 1992 and 1995, and introduced their currency, for most of them, towards the end of 1993. Most prices were deregulated in the years that immediately followed. Excess liquidity inherited from the previous regime, the need to continue subsidizing inefficient sectors, and the problems of interregional trade led to inflationary pressures and output decline.

European Bank for Reconstruction and Development to measure progress in trade and financial reforms, and that strong political will and CB independence were complementary causes of inflation performance.

Arnone, Laurens, and Segalotto (2006b and 2008)

Arnone, Laurens, and Segalotto (2006b) present an update of the GMT index of CB independence based on CB legislation as of end-2003. The index is applied to a set of OECD and developing countries, and emerging market economies; this set is subsequently expanded in Arnone, Laurens, Segalotto, and Sommer (2008). For a smaller set of countries, the papers present a reconstruction of the GMT index based on Cukierman (1992) and assess changes in CB independence between 1992 and 2003.

Overall, the picture provided by the independence measures presented in these papers confirms a sharp move towards greater independence in OECD countries. A preliminary comparison of the data in GMT (1991) against the current data for the same group of OECD countries shows substantial changes in terms of both economic and political independence. In most cases, these changes are attributable to the implementation of the ESCB model to those CBs that had showed the lowest levels of independence in the earlier evaluation by GMT. Progress in OECD countries is not confined within the boundaries of the Euro area. The data also show significant progress – particularly in economic independence – for the other CBs belonging to the ESCB and for the extra-European banks that initially did not enjoy much independence. In sum, all the 2003 scores for the OECD countries have improved when compared to the results of GMT (1991).

Similar trends can be observed in emerging economies and developing countries. Some of these countries have reached levels of independence that compare well with those observed in OECD countries using the GMT methodology. Using data from Cukierman's (1992) legal measure, we could track the evolution of legislation in these countries as well. The results point to significant progress, since on average the measure for both political and economic independence doubled during the period under review.

Independence, credibility, and costs of deflation

Independence and conservatism are often considered the best way for enhancing CB credibility which, in turn, should help reduce the costs of deflation. This section reviews research work by Blinder (1999), Posen (1998), Cukierman (2002), and Fuhrer (1997) on the relationships between independence and credibility.

Table 1.16 Preliminary questions in Blinder questionnaire

(Q) Question	Answers and scores	Average (84 CBs)	Average (53 economists)
Q1: How important is credibility to a CB?	1 = unimportant 2 = of minor importance 3 = moderately important 4 = quite important 5 = of the utmost importance	4.83	4.23
Q2: How closely related are the concepts of credibility and dedication to price stability?	1 = unrelated 2 = slightly related 3 = moderately related 4 = quite closely related 5 = virtually the same	4.10	3.31

Source: Blinder (1999).

Blinder (1999)

Blinder asks why credibility is deemed important and how it can be established. The study relies on a questionnaire to 84 CBs from industrial and emerging countries and 53 scholars affiliated with the National Bureau of Economic Research (NBER). It seeks to assess which theoretical propositions have been most successful among central bankers, and what are the differences between academia and CBs. Responses to the first two questions (Table 1.16) show that CBs converge on the importance of credibility, a view not fully shared by economists. CB governors also showed greater confidence than scholars in identifying aversion to inflation as the main component of credibility.

The questionnaire investigates also some possible reasons why credibility should be considered an important element in policy-making, and the interviewees are asked to rank them (Table 1.17). CBs provided assessments which on average were higher than those of scholars. Central bankers and scholars agreed that the benefits of CB credibility were most evident with regard to inflation performance and to improve the short-term trade-off between inflation and unemployment. However, central bankers and scholars did not agree on the ranking of other reasons why credibility should be considered important.

The final part of the questionnaire aims at comparing viewpoints about how to best create and maintain CB credibility. Interestingly, both groups rank equally the seven proposed considerations (Table 1.18). In particular, the best way to achieve credibility is to establish a tradition of honesty. CB independence, as a way to create and maintain credibility

Table 1.17 Blinder: reasons why credibility is deemed important

(Q) Question: Why is credibility deemed important?	84 CBs			53 economists		
	Average	Standard deviation	Ranking	Average	Standard deviation	Ranking
Q3: Less costly disinflation	4.13	0.78	2	3.83	1.12	2
Q4: To keep inflation low	4.39	0.60	1	4.17	0.83	1
Q5: To change tactics (provides strategic flexibility)	4.38	0.54	5	3.97	1.03	3
Q6: To serve as a lender of last resort (during a financial crisis)	4.12	0.77	6	3.74	1.07	4
Q7: To defend the currency and exchange rate	4.29	0.70	3	3.47	1.04	5
Q8: Public servants should be truthful	4.00	0.84	7	3.30	1.07	6
Q9: For support for independence (to justify public support for CB independence)	4.34	0.75	4	3.19	1.00	7

Source: Blinder (1999).

is ranked second; the consensus view seems to be that an independent CB can be less credible than a more dependent institution that has managed to establish a solid reputation. A history of fight against inflation is ranked third, confirming the view that a tradition of honesty does more to increase credibility than one of inflation aversion. Blinder expresses some surprise at the fact that transparency, as a way to create and maintain credibility, is ranked fourth, as this would go against a view that some secrecy may help ensure that credibility is not affected by a change in strategy. Surprisingly, government's fiscal discipline is only ranked fifth. This result may well reflect progress made in enhancing fiscal discipline in the most recent period. Finally, the last two ways to create and maintain credibility refer to the CB's pre-commitment to a fixed rule and the personal incentives included in the optimal contracts proposed by Walsh (1995) and Svensson (1997). As could be expected, central bankers express a low score with regard to the pre-commitment to a fixed rule, given that they probably rank highly their own ability to conduct monetary policy. However, it is surprising that the scholars attribute an even lower score. With regard to personal incentives, Blinder refers to an answer stating that the loss of reputation is already an effective

Table 1.18   Blinder: how to create and maintain credibility

(Q) Question: Method	84 central banks			53 economists		
	Average	Standard deviation	Ranking	Average	Standard deviation	Ranking
Q11: CB independence	4.51	0.63	2	3.99	0.86	2
Q12: Transparency	4.13	0.71	4	3.44	1.18	4
Q13: History of honesty	4.58	0.52	1	4.30	0.80	1
Q14: History of fighting inflation	4.15	0.67	3	3.83	0.86	3
Q15: Constrained by a rule	2.89	1.01	6	2.32	1.06	6
Q16: Incentives (personal loss)	2.15	1.10	7	1.95	0.96	7
Q17: Small fiscal deficit/debt	3.92	0.93	5	3.27	1.14	5

Source: Blinder (1999).

mechanism for creating credibility, even in the absence of a personal incentive. Here also, the even lower assessment expressed by the scholars may be considered somewhat at odds with the widely cited theory.

Posen (1998)

Posen looks for empirical evidence of the "credibility bonus" that a commitment to price stability should theoretically entail if a CB is conservative and independent. In particular, he investigates the public and private sectors' behavior in a sample of seventeen OECD countries for the period 1950–89 by looking for changes in credibility, which is proxied by the deflationary capability of the CB. Posen provides several theoretical predictions regarding the impact of greater CB independence on deflationary processes and wage negotiations. First, the announcement of a credible deflationary policy should lead to good inflation performance with limited output or employment costs. Thus, the risk of a recession should be limited to the case in which money growth is lower than what was predicted by the public. By reducing the gap between expectations and actual outcomes, a more credible monetary policy should therefore imply lower costs of deflation, all other conditions being equal. Second, if we assume that the public (in an environment with little inflation and limited uncertainty over future inflation) prefers to enter into contracts for a longer period, a monetary regime that offers greater credibility in terms of price stability should encourage greater rigidity in nominal wages. As a result, Posen argues that higher inflation (hence lower independence at the beginning of a deflation episode), should ensure lower costs during that process. Finally, it is likely that in an environment of perfect credibility, the period required for the deflation process is significantly shorter since credibility should reduce the degree of stickiness in the reduction of nominal compensation.

Posen shows clear empirical answers for a possible relationship between his theoretical predictions and Cukierman's LVAU indicator of independence. The first of the four empirical predictions (more credibility lowers the cost of deflation) is analyzed by regressing the costs of deflation[31] on the LVAU index, the duration of the episode, the total change in inflation, and a measure of nominal wage rigidity. The results do not support the prediction, which is therefore rejected.[32] Regarding the second prediction (credibility leads to rigidity in nominal wages), Posen regresses two measures of nominal wage rigidity[33] on the LVAU index. The results are inconsistent with expectations. However, neither of the two measures of nominal wage rigidity has a statistically significant relationship with CB independence. Thus, negotiating behavior seems to be partially invariant with respect to the monetary environment, and therefore the positive relationship between CB independence and the costs of deflation does not seem to depend on that particular channel. The third prediction (low independence at the beginning of the deflation episode leads to lower costs during deflation) is addressed using a set of regressions of the sacrifice ratio, and by replacing CB independence with the level of inflation at the beginning of each episode of deflation. This variable does not exhibit significant coefficients. The author concludes that there is no evidence confirming that a less inflationary environment leads to greater nominal rigidity, and therefore that the negative relationship between CB independence and inflation does not seem to have the desired effect when the increase in credibility is the source of price stability. Finally, as for the fourth prediction (perfect credibility reduces the duration of a deflation process), two measures

---

[31] The cost of deflation is proxied by the total annual increase in the unemployment rate from the beginning of the deflationary maneuver divided by the corresponding reduction in inflation (so-called sacrifice ratio).

[32] As further proof, Posen cites Ball and others (1988) who regress the estimated trade-off between output and inflation on independence and two wage rigidity measures. They find that the coefficient of the variable regarding independence has a negative sign.

[33] Rigidity index of Grubb, Jackman, and Layard (1983) and Bruno and Sachs (1985) complementary measure.

are regressed that approximate the speed of the deflationary episode: the number of quarters the episode lasts and the number of percentage points of inflation eliminated during the episode in relation to the length of the episode. Posen finds that the coefficient of independence has a small negative sign and is significant in only one of the regressions.

Posen also assesses what should be the effects of an increase in independence on the government's behavior. The laws that ensure independence should increase the CB's ability to resist debt monetization, protect the governor's position once appointed, and ensure the priority of price stability as the objective of monetary policy. Two additional predictions are proposed to reflect these considerations: all other conditions being equal, where independence is greater, government's recourse to seignorage should be lower; and there should be less economic policy manipulation for electoral purposes. Posen does not find empirical evidence supporting these last two predictions.

In summary, Posen does not find empirical evidence supporting the hypothesis that the channel through which independence leads to a situation of low inflation is brought about by an increase in credibility. In other words, deflation is more costly and lasts longer in countries with relatively independent CBs. Similarly, countries with independent CBs do not exhibit either nominal wage and price rigidities or less government debt monetization and less manipulation of macroeconomic policies for election purposes. According to Posen, two questions arise from these considerations. First, why does independence not increase the credibility of a deflationary policy? He argues that it is unlikely that the legal indicators used could capture the entire spectrum of a CB's actual discretion; other factors may influence its actual independence. Second, why is there a negative correlation between inflation and independence? He argues that if there are no fiscal restrictions on the government, it will be impossible to make a tight money policy credible in the long run, and independence does not seem to prevent recourse to seignorage or monetary expansion in pre-electoral periods. However, if a CB is autonomous from the executive branch, neither of the two will be interested in implementing expansionary policies, and thus the commitment should be credible. Therefore, the lack of a private sector reaction to independence can be seen as a reaction to unchanged behavior in the public sector.

Cukierman (2002)

Cukierman (2002) seeks to provide a conceptual review of the relationship between the level of CB independence and the greater sacrifice in employment during deflationary periods. Posen (1998) showed that the sacrifice ratio is higher in OECD countries that exhibit greater independence. Gartner (1995) and A. M. Fischer (1996) reach a similar conclusion, while Debelle and Fischer (1994) note that during the deflationary period that followed the oil shocks, the employment sacrifice was greater in Germany than in the United States. Cukierman argues that there is not necessarily a negative relationship between the sacrifice ratio and social welfare.[34] On the contrary, there is a credibility bonus: the higher the level of CB independence (and thus, the better its reputation), the higher the expected value of social welfare. In other words, social welfare is a growing and monotonic function of independence and reputation (which is assumed to be positive in relation to independence). This result is obtained regardless of the size of the sacrifice ratio and the sign of its relationship with CB independence. Thus, although it is empirically true that countries with greater independence incur a higher increase in unemployment during deflationary periods, one cannot infer that it is not desirable to increase independence since it increases expected social welfare monotonically. That conclusion explains why the sacrifice ratio is a rather poor measure for analyzing the long-term desirability of independence.

Fuhrer (1997)

Fuhrer's objective is to reassess previous assertions about independence and inflation. Fuhrer (1997) states that, in keeping with S. Fisher (1996), "effective central banks must be independent from undue political interference, and they would do well to target the rate of inflation directly." Fuhrer examines the empirical evidence to support these assertions. After reporting several previous theoretical solutions to the problem of inflationary bias (Rogoff 1985; McCallum 1995; and Walsh 1995), Fuhrer suggests that the CB's independence and credibility are inescapable ingredients in any resolution of this issue. However, he also notes that there is an alternative solution, which consists in pegging the exchange rate to a currency whose CB is independent.

---

[34] Cukierman argues that the relationship between sacrifice ratios and welfare is not monotonic for at least two reasons. First, if we focus only on deflationary periods, we lose sight of the fact that a higher sacrifice ratio also implies greater output performance during expansionary periods. Second, for the same reason, temporary employment-related costs tend to obscure the long-term benefits derived from price stability.

The author stresses that the major macroeconomic developments at the beginning of the 1980s occurred without any formal obligation for monetary authorities. Several countries between the 1980s and the 1990s began reviewing their legislation in response to the concept of inflationary bias and time inconsistency, with a view to ensuring that price stability would be the primary and often only objective of monetary policy. However, the author stresses that the deflation of the early 1980s was brought about by monetary authorities in the United States, United Kingdom, Germany, and France without any formal obligation to do so, and it occurred without either changes in their degree of independence, or the formalization of strict rules, or the announcement of an explicit inflationary target. In essence, the authorities' will, which was probably accompanied by public support, was sufficient to bring about those changes. Thus, credibility (defined as the behavior which is sufficiently systematic and permanent to generate a public perception that it is the norm) seems to be the determining factor for successful deflation. If a CB earns this credibility bonus through its actions, it is unlikely that the announcement of new monetary policy rules or changed inflation objectives would serve as an effective substitute (Blinder 1999). However, Fuhrer (as in the case of Debelle and Fischer 1994) acknowledges that the empirical evidence contradicts the existence of a credibility bonus in case of deflation (see Posen 1998; Cukierman 2002; and Debelle 1996).

Fuhrer also moves to earlier empirical studies in an attempt to reconfirm that independence is a key ingredient for successful monetary policy. He initially shows the results obtained by Alesina and Summers (1993), indicating a strong negative correlation between the degree of independence and inflationary levels. Then, he regresses the data on inflation used by these authors on Cukierman's LVAU. Fuhrer finds that the strong negative correlation weakens and becomes statistically less significant. Then, by using a broader sample of countries divided by geographic areas, and measuring CB independence using Cukierman's LVAU, Fuhrer concludes that for the sub-group of OECD countries, the relationship is weaker and less significant than the relationship observed by Alesina and Summers (1993). For Latin American, Asian, and sub-Saharan African countries this correlation is not statistically significant, and it is positive, rather than negative, in the two former cases.

Fuhrer then attempts to infer conclusions on the possible existence of a credibility bonus by measuring the degree of correlation among Cukierman's LVAU and Ball's (1994) sacrifice ratio for the Alesina and Summers (1993) sample of sixteen OECD countries. The results indicate that the correlation between CB independence and the sacrifice ratio is significantly positive primarily due to the values scored by Germany and the United States. According to Fuhrer, it is these two CBs that contradict the hypothesis of a credibility bonus. To check the robustness of this result, Fuhrer expands the number of countries and scope of his analysis, including data on inflation, unemployment, real growth, the ten-year average LVAU, short-term interest rates, public deficits as a percentage of GDP, and a variable that measures exchange rates in various European countries against the Deutschmark. As a result of these additional variables, Fuhrer finds that with regard to inflation, none of the regressions on the entire sample of 70 countries exhibits any significant correlation with the degree of independence. The only negative relationship is confirmed to be the one observed for the sample of Alesina and Summers (1993), in simple bivariate regressions. He also finds that the coefficient of independence with respect to inflation also loses significance for OECD countries, although the explanatory power of the regressions is good. Regarding the variability of inflation, the only specification for which Fuhrer finds a significant correlation between this and the degree of CB independence is in the simple bivariate regressions on the sample of Alesina and Summers (1993), and the correlation vanishes as supplementary variables are added. Finally, when the dependent variable is the real growth rate or unemployment rate, Fuhrer's calculations contradict the "free lunch" hypothesis. The only statistically significant correlations suggest a negative relationship between independence and real growth and a positive relationship with unemployment. In summary, Fuhrer's work generates considerable doubts over the robustness of the correlation between independence, inflation level and variability, real growth or unemployment. In general, the inflation-related benefits attributed to CB independence are found only in bivariate regressions. Once other supplementary variables related to international differences are included, the correlation disappears. These conclusions are still distorted by the fact that the author uses a legal indicator of independence such as Cukierman's LVAU for a sample which included a number of developing countries.

Conclusions

The empirical results in the base literature were brilliantly summarized by Cukierman (1994) with three considerations. First, among industrial countries there is a strong negative relationship between de jure independence and inflation, while the same measures of independence exhibit no correlation to real macroeconomic performance, most likely because the underlying causes of growth are too complex for a regression on simple independence to provide significant results. Second, de facto independence is useful for analyzing inflation performance in emerging and developing countries. Third, de facto measures of independence are good proxies to explain growth performance in less developed countries.

Among the studies on de jure independence, Bade and Parkin argue that setting price stability as the primary objective of monetary policy is associated with lower inflation, although not necessarily lower variability. Alesina argues that there is an inverse relationship between independence and average inflation, and he notes that where a CB is not independent, monetary policy tends to follow the course of political cycles more closely. The analysis of CB independence by GMT finds similar results: independence brings about lower inflation, and it does not seem to have costs in terms of growth or output variability. Cukierman's LVAU and LVAW indicators show that the contribution of de jure independence to inflation is negative and statistically significant for developed countries, but not for developing countries. Finally, Alesina and Summers find a strong negative correlation between independence and inflation and no clear relationship between independence and growth. The analysis of the behavior of the unemployment rate shows similar results, while negative long-term effects are observed with regard to the relationship between CB independence and the variability of real interest rates.

In view of the limited reliability of de jure measures of independence for developing countries, the literature has relied on measures that approximate de facto independence. Cukierman proposes an indicator based on the average frequency of CB governor turnover (TOR). He finds that, at least above a certain threshold, the TOR is positively related to average inflation and its coefficient is statistically significant for developing countries. Cukierman develops two other de facto independence indices (QVAU and QVAW) and finds that most of their variables have the expected negative sign, with the most significant measures being those concerning the presence of intermediate monetary policy objectives and those concerning limitations to CB credit to the government. These indices' overall contribution to explaining inflation performance is not very significant, however, and this leads the author to favor the use of the simpler TOR measure. Cukierman and Webb propose a substitute for the TOR during periods of political transitions which has a significantly positive impact on inflation.

As a follow-up to base indicators, a number of authors have analyzed specific issues, therefore contributing to an already large body of literature. McCallum has branded as too simplistic Rogoff's proposal of reducing inflationary bias by delegating monetary policy to an independent CB. The author also criticized the solution proposed of making use of incentive-compatible contracts for CBs, since such mechanisms would simply redistribute the time-inconsistency problem but not solve it. Banaian, Burdekin, and Willett have searched for the single criterion that would have the best performance in explaining inflation dynamics. They show that a dummy variable based on the government's inability to override the CB's policy decisions is statistically more significant than more complex measures. Finally, Cukierman and Lippi have attempted to endogenize the structural imperfections of economies in order to better assess the determinants of inflationary biases, in particular by studying the interaction between CB conservatism and various degrees of centralization in wage bargaining. The authors confirm that there is a convex relationship between the unemployment rate or inflation and the centralization of wage bargaining. This relationship is valid only at low levels of CB independence, however. In addition, the inflation-reducing impact of CB independence is greater at intermediate levels of union centralization, while there is a significantly positive effect of independence on unemployment for low levels of centralization in wage bargaining.

There is also a group of authors who analyze the direction of causality in empirical relationships, and others who investigate the robustness and sensitivity of previous empirical results. Posen argues that CB independence does not affect inflation if the calculations include his measure of the financial sector's opposition to inflation (FOI) as an additional variable. He argues that the FOI is theoretically able to increase independence and, at the same time, significantly reduce inflationary bias without the need to assume any direct causal relationship between these two variables. With regard to the robustness of previous empirical findings, Campillo and Miron show that CB independence cannot explain inflation when several additional control variables are added, such as the degree of openness of the economy, the ratio of debt to GDP, political instability, the level of income, or previous inflation experience. Oatley shows that the assumed negative relationship between CB independence and inflation is not modified by the inclusion of a set of economic and political-institutional control variables. Contrary to what was observed by Campillo and Miron, neither the government's budget situation nor the degree of openness of the economy exhibits a strong relationship with inflation; whereas unemployment, the structure of the labor market, and the government's political preferences provide good results. He also argues that five out of the eight most complex indices of CB independence that he has analyzed fail to capture the assumed relationship with inflation, while the three simplest indices perform better. Sturm and de Haan calculate the TORs for a new sample of 97 developing countries, in order to substantiate Cukierman's conclusions on de facto independence. They show that once some control variables are included, the TOR coefficient is not very significant. The authors also observe that the TOR coefficient is significant only when high-inflation countries are included. Finally, Stella and Ize analyze the role of CB capital and financial independence on its performance, a promising area in which more empirical research is warranted.

In exploring the relationship between independence, credibility, and the costs of disinflation, we again cited Posen. Looking for the actual existence of a credibility bonus, which (if the monetary authority is independent and conservative) makes deflationary policies less costly, he investigates the behavior of the public and private sectors in a sample of OECD countries by looking for changes in credibility consistent with common measures of independence. He could not find evidence, however, that greater CB independence and conservatism lead to significantly lower costs of deflation. Finally, Mangano offers an analysis of the reliability and comparability of different independence measures. He uncovers different interpretations of central bank legislation among researchers as well as preferences in the selection of the variables to be included in the independence index which are not neutral on the final result, resulting in low correlation between the CB rankings obtained with these measures. Mangano's results caution against the potential abuse of independence indicators if they are deemed to be interchangeable, and suggests that analysis of independence should rely on a set rather than a single index.

Appendices

Appendix 1 Variables in Cukierman's LVAU-LVAW indices

GROUP/ Variable name	Definition of variable	Levels of independence and their meanings	Numerical coding
CEO			
Too	Term of office of CEO in years	1. *too* ≥ 8	1
		2. 8 > *too* ≥ 6	0.75
		3. *too* = 5	0.50
		4. *too* = 4	0.25
		5. *too* < 4	0
App	Who appoints the CEO?	1. CEO appointed by CB board	1
		2. CEO appointed by council composed of members from executive and legislative branches as well as from CB board	0.75
		3. CEO appointed by legislative branch (Congress, king)	0.50
		4. CEO appointed by executive branch (council of ministers)	0.25
		5. CEO appointed through decision of one or two members of executive branch (e.g., prime minister or minister of finance)	0
Diss	Provisions for dismissal of CEO	1. No provision for dismissal	1
		2. Dismissal possible only for non-policy reasons (e.g., incapability or violation of law)	0.83
		3. Dismissal possible and at discretion of CB board	0.67
		4. Dismissal for policy reasons at legislative branch's discretion	0.50
		5. Unconditional dismissal possible at legislative branch's discretion	0.33
		6. Dismissal for policy reasons at executive branch's discretion	0.17
		7. Unconditional dismissal at executive branch's discretion	0
Off	Is CEO allowed to hold another office?	1. CEO prohibited by law from holding any other office in government	1
		2. CEO not allowed to hold any other office in government unless authorized by executive branch	0.50
		3. Law does not prohibit CEO from holding another office	0

(Continued)

Appendix I Continued

GROUP/ Variable name	Definition of variable	Levels of independence and their meanings	Numerical coding
POLICY FORMULATION			
Monpol	Who formulates monetary policy?	1. CB alone has authority to formulate monetary policy	1
		2. CB participates in formulation of monetary policy together with government	0.66
		3. CB participates in formulation of monetary policy in an advisory capacity	0.33
		4. Government alone formulates monetary policy	0
Conf	Government directives and resolution of conflict	1. CB given final authority over issues clearly defined in the law as CB objectives	1
		2. Government has final authority only over policy issues that have not been clearly defined as CB goals or in case of conflict within CB	0.8
		3. In case of conflict final decision up to a council whose members are from CB, legislative branch, and executive branch	0.6
		4. Legislative branch has final authority on policy issues	0.4
		5. Executive branch has final authority on policy issues, but subject to due process and possible protest by CB	0.2
		6. Executive branch has unconditional authority over policy	0
Adv	Is CB given an active role in the formulation of government's budget?	1. Yes	1
		2. No	0
CB OBJECTIVES			
Obj	Objectives of CB	1. Price stability mentioned as the only or major goal, and in case of conflict with government CB has final authority to pursue policies aimed at achieving this goal	1

	2. Price stability mentioned as the only goal	0.8
	3. Price stability mentioned along with other objectives that do not seem to conflict with price stability (e.g., stable banking)	0.6
	4. Price stability mentioned with a number of potentially conflicting goals (e.g., full employment)	0.4
	5. CB charter does not contain any objectives for CB	0.2
	6. Some goals appear in the charter, but price stability not one of them	0
LIMITATION ON LENDING		
Lla	Limitations on advances	
	1. Advances to government prohibited	1
	2. Advances permitted but subject to limits in terms of absolute cash amounts or to other types of relatively strict limits (e.g., up to 15% of government revenues)	0.66
	3. Advances subject to relatively accommodative limits (e.g., advances can exceed 15% of government revenues or are specified as fractions of government expenditures)	0.33
	4. No legal limits on advances; their quantity subject to periodic negotiations between government and CB	0
Lls	Limitation on securitized lending	Specification of levels identical to those for advances
$Ldec$	Who decides control of terms of lending?	
	1. CB controls terms and conditions of government borrowing from it	1
	2. Terms of CB lending specified in the law, or CB given legal authority to set these terms	0.66
	3. Law leaves the decision about the terms of CB lending to government to negotiations between CB and executive branch	0.33
	4. Executive branch alone decides the terms of CB lending to government and imposes them on CB	0
$Lwidth$	How wide is the circle of potential borrowers from CB?	
	1. Only central government can borrow from CB	1

(Continued)

Appendix I Continued

GROUP/ Variable name	Definition of variable	Levels of independence and their meanings	Numerical coding
		2. Central and state governments as well as all political sub-divisions can borrow from CB	0.66
		3. In addition to the institutions mentioned under 2 public enterprises can borrow from CB	0.33
		4. CB can lend to all of the above as well as to the private sector	0
Ltype	Type of limit when such limit exists	1. Limit specified as absolute cash amount	1
		2. Limit specified as a percentage of CB capital or other liabilities	0.66
		3. Limit specified as a percentage of government revenues	0.33
		4. Limit specified as a percentage of government expenditure	0
Lmat	Maturity of loans	1. Maturity of CB loans limited to a maximum of 6 months	1
		2. Maturity of CB loans limited to a maximum of one year	0.66
		3. Maturity of CB loans limited to a maximum of more than one year	0.33
		4. No legal upper bounds on the maturity of CB loans	0
Lint	Restrictions on interest rates	1. Interest rate on CB loans must be at market rate	1
		2. Interest rate on CB loans to government cannot be lower than a certain floor	0.75
		3. Interest rate on CB loans cannot exceed a certain ceiling	0.50
		4. No explicit legal provisions regarding the interest rate on CB loans	0.25
		5. Law stipulates no interest rate charge on government's borrowing from the CB	0
Lprm	Prohibition on lending in primary market	1. CB prohibited from buying government securities in primary market	1
		2. CB not prohibited from buying government securities in primary market	0

Source: Cukierman (1992).

Appendix II Variables in Cukierman's QVAU-QVAW

Variable name	Definition of variable	Definition of criteria	Numerical coding
Qto	Tenure overlap with political authority	Little overlap	1
		Some overlap	0.5
		Substantial overlap	0
Qll	Limitations on lending in practice	This scale measures the tightness of limitations on lending and how they have been adhered to in practice as evaluated by the respondent to the questionnaire. The scale has four points where the maximum stands for the most binding limitations	1
			0.66
			0.33
			0
Qrc	Resolution of conflicts	In some cases clear evidence of resolution in favor of CB	1
		Everything except what is covered under the first and last items	0.5
		Clear evidence of resolution in favor of government in all cases	0
Qbcb	Who determines the budget of CB?	Mostly CB	1
		Mixture of CB and executive or legislative branches	0.5
		Mostly executive or legislative branches	0
Qsp	Who determines the salaries of high CB officials and the allocation of CB profits?	Mostly CB or law	1
		Mixture of CB and executive or legislative branches	0.5
		Mostly executive or legislative branches	0
		Whenever the decision about salaries and the allocation of profits is not done by the same institution, the answer is coded according to the identity of the institution determining salaries	
Qst	Are there quantitative money stock targets?	Such targets exist and are well adhered to	1
		Such targets exist and there is mixed adherence	0.66
		Such targets exist and are poorly adhered to	0.33
		There are no stock targets	0

(Continued)

Appendix II Continued

Variable name	Definition of variable	Definition of criteria	Numerical coding
Qirt	Are there formal or informal interest rates targets?	No	1
		Yes	0
Qpps	What is the actual priority assigned to price stability?	First priority assigned to price stability	1
		First priority assigned to a fixed exchange rate	0.66
		Price or exchange rate stability are among the objectives of monetary policy, but neither has first priority	0.33
		No mention of price or exchange rate stability as objectives at any priority level	0
Qsc	Does CB function as a development bank that grants credits at subsidy rates?	No	1
		To some extent	0.66
		Yes	0.33
		CB is heavily involved in granting subsidized credits to the private and public sectors	0

Source: Cukierman (1992).

AUTHORS	Robin Bade, Michael Parkin (1977).
TYPE	Legal indicator of political independence.
SAMPLE	Period: 1951–1975. Countries: 12 OECD countries (Australia, Belgium, Canada, France, Germany, Italy, Japan, Netherlands, Sweden, Switzerland, the United Kingdom, and the United States).
CHARACTERISTICS ANALYZED	(i) Legal policy objectives of CB; (ii) relationship between CB and government in the formulation of monetary policy; and (iii) procedures followed for appointing members of the board.
INDICATOR VARIABLES	(A) Legal policy objectives: (p) the price stability objective is clearly codified as the sole CB objective [Netherlands]; (p-u) the price stability objective is accompanied by other macroeconomic objectives [Australia, Canada] or there are no explicit legal objectives (-) [Belgium, France, Germany, Italy, Japan, Sweden, Switzerland, the United Kingdom, and the United States].
	(B) Ultimate monetary policy authority: (g) CB authority is dominated by the government; (b) the CB is the sole ultimate authority [only in the case of the United States, Germany and Switzerland. Also Canada before 1967].
	(C) Members of government or its representatives on the board: number of ministers (or their representatives) on the board. [(1) for Australia and Canada; (2) for France and Japan; (0) for the other eight countries.]
	(D) Percentage of senior managers appointed by the government: the cutoff point is set where such percentage is greater than half the members; in most cases, senior managers are all appointed by the government (value of 1). [The only exceptions are France (14/15 appointed by government), Germany (10/21), and Switzerland (5/8).]
AGGREGATION METHOD	The authors categorize the 12 CBs into four groups from marginally independent CBs (group 1) to CBs with the greatest independence (group 4). The four variables considered would produce 24 possible combinations, and the 12 countries considered would end up having 12 different formulations. In order to group part of these under similar categories, the authors reduce the first variable (A) and group the second and third variables (B and C). Legal policy objectives fall from three to two: countries where there is no unambiguous price stability objective (p-u) are combined with countries where there are no specific objectives (-). A CB is considered the ultimate authority of monetary policy only if it satisfies requirement (B) (i.e., the CB is the only ultimate authority; case b), and there are no members of government or their representatives on the board (i.e., variable (C) = 0). At the end of this process, the potential categories drop to eight, four of which remain empty in the sample considered. The four remaining categories are as follows: those belonging to

(Continued)

Appendix III Continued

group 2 [the Netherlands] are CBs that have the specific legal objective of price stability (i.e., variable (A) = p), are not the sole ultimate authority of monetary policy (i.e., variable (B) = g), and over half of senior managers are appointed by the government. Group 1 (the least independent CBs) [Australia, Belgium, Canada, France, Italy, Japan, Sweden, and the United Kingdom] includes CBs that do not have a specific legal objective of price stability, or this objective is ambiguous (i.e., variable (A) = p-u or -), that are not the sole ultimate authority of monetary policy (i.e., variable (B) = g, or (B) = b, but (C) does not equal 0), and more than half of senior managers are appointed by the government. The CBs in group 3 [the United States] do not have a specific legal objective of price stability (as in the case of group 1), but have ultimate monetary policy authority (i.e., variable (B) = b and variable (C) = 0), and more than half the senior managers are appointed by the government. Finally, we have the last category (group 4) [Germany and Switzerland], where the law does not assign the CB the sole legal objective of price stability, but it is still seen as the undisputed ultimate authority of monetary policy, and less than half of senior managers are appointed by the government.

AUTHORS	Alberto Alesina (1988–1989).
TYPE	De jure index of political and economic independence.
SAMPLE	Same sample as in Bade and Parkin (1977) plus Denmark, Norway, New Zealand and Spain in Alesina (1988), and Finland in Alesina (1989). Period: 1973–1986. Countries: 17 OECD countries (Australia, Belgium, Canada, Denmark, Finland, France, Germany, Italy, Japan, New Zealand, the Netherlands, Norway, Spain, Sweden, Switzerland, the United Kingdom, and the United States).
CHARACTERISTICS ANALYZED	(i) Institutional and formal relationships between the CB and the executive branch; (ii) the extent of informal contacts between the CB and the executive branch; (iii) the existence of rules forcing the CB to automatically accommodate fiscal policy.
INDICATOR VARIABLES	The author states that he is directly referring to the extension of Bade and Parkin (1977) found in Bade and Parkin (1985) and illustrates only the variables analyzed with respect to characteristic (i): (A) who appoints the CB governor and his/her term of office; (B) the existence of government representatives on the CB board; (C) any requirements for the approval of monetary policy by the government.
AGGREGATION METHOD	Consistency of the results with Bade and Parkin (1985) for the same period and sample (with the exception of Italy) suggests the same methodology for aggregating variables, i.e., the sum of values obtained by the CB

for each variable. However, it is important to stress what Eijffinger and Schaling (1993) indicated regarding this indicator. First and foremost, the author (Alesina 1988: 41) clearly acknowledges that the strictly political attributes appear more relevant for the purposes of his own research. Secondly, the score of 1/2 (1.5) assigned to the Bank of Italy (and the criticism made against Bade and Parkin (1985) for not having duly considered the 1981 "divorce" of the Bank of Italy from the Treasury) indicates a different structure of weights used in the total, or perhaps even an internal inconsistency in the indicator given the movement of the Bank of Italy from 2 to 1/2 rather than to 3. Only Italy has a score of 1/2. At the same time Australia, New Zealand, and Spain are classified with a score of 1. The CB category with a score of 2 is made up of: Belgium, Canada, Denmark, Finland, France, the Netherlands, Norway, Sweden, and the United Kingdom. Japan and the United States have a score of 3, while Germany and Switzerland were assigned a score of 4 (maximum independence).

AUTHORS	Vittorio Grilli, Donato Masciandaro, Guido Tabellini (1991).
TYPE	De jure index of political independence; CB independence with respect to objectives.
SAMPLE	Period: 1960–1989. Countries: 18 OECD countries (Australia, Austria, Belgium, Canada, Denmark, France, Germany, Greece, Ireland, Italy, Japan, New Zealand, Netherlands, Portugal, Spain, Switzerland, the United Kingdom and the United States).
CHARACTERISTICS ANALYZED INDICATOR VARIABLES	(i) Procedures for the appointment of board members; (ii) relationships between CB boards and governments in the formulation of monetary policy; (iii) formal monetary policy responsibilities of CB. Appointments: (1) governor not appointed by government; (2) governor appointed for more than five years; (3) board not appointed by government; (4) board appointed for more than five years. Relationships with government: (5) no government representatives participate in board; (6) government's approval not required for formulation of monetary policy. Charters: (7) there is a charter (or legal, or even constitutional) provision requiring the CB to pursue monetary stability as one of its primary objectives; (8) there are legal provisions strengthening CB's position in the event of conflict with government. [There is an asterisk for items (1) to (8) if variable applies.]
AGGREGATION METHOD	The authors believe they can reduce arbitrariness of the indicator by using a simple sum of values (asterisks) obtained (min = 0, max = 8). Overall "political independence" index grows as level of independence rises. Australia, score of 3 (variables 2, 7, and 8 apply); Austria, score of 3 (variables 6, 7 and 8); Belgium, score of 1 (the only applicable variable is 4); Canada, score of 4 (variables applicable are 1, 2, 7, and 8); Denmark,

(Continued)

Appendix III Continued

	score of 3 (variables 2, 6, and 7); France, score of 2 (variables 2 and 4); Germany, score of 6 (variables 2, 4, 5, 6, 7, and 8); Japan, score of 1 (variable 7); Greece, score of 2 (variables 3 and 8); Ireland, score of 3 (variables applicable are 2, 6, and 7); Italy, score of 4 (variables applicable are 1, 2, 3, and 5); New Zealand, score of 0; the Netherlands, score of 6 (variables 2, 4, 5, 6, 7, and 8); Portugal, score of 1 (variable 5); the United Kingdom, score of 1 (variable 5); Spain, score of 2 (variables 4 and 5); the United States, score of 5 (variables applicable are 4, 5, 6, 7, and 8); Switzerland, score of 5 (variables present are 2, 5, 6, 7, and 8).
AUTHORS	Vittorio Grilli, Donato Masciandaro, Guido Tabellini (1991).
TYPE	De jure index of economic independence; CB independence with respect to instruments.
SAMPLE	Period and countries: same as political index.
CHARACTERISTICS ANALYZED	(i) Availability, terms and conditions of CB direct credit to the government and monetary financing of public deficits; (ii) nature of monetary instruments under the control of the CB.
INDICATOR VARIABLES	Monetary financing of public deficits: (1) direct credit not automatically extended; (2) direct credit provided at market rates; (3) direct credit is explicitly temporary; (4) direct credit subject to limitations on amount; (5) CB does not participate in primary market for public debt. Monetary policy instruments: (6) discount rate set autonomously by the CB; (7) banking supervision not assigned to the CB (*); banking supervision not assigned only to the CB (**). [There is an asterisk for items (1) to (6) if the variable is applicable; one or two asterisks for item (7).]
AGGREGATION METHOD	Simple sum of values (asterisks) obtained (min = 0, max = 8). Overall "economic independence" index grows as the level of independence rises. Australia, score of 6 (variables 1, 2, 3, 4, 5, and 6); Austria, score of 6 (variables 3, 4, 5, and 6, and double asterisk for 7); Belgium, score of 6 (variables 2, 4, 5, and 6, and a double asterisk for 7); Canada, score of 7 (variables 1, 2, 3, 4, and 6, and double asterisks for 7); Denmark, score of 5 (variables 2, 5, and 6, and two asterisks for 7); France, score of 5 (variables 4, 5, and 6, and double asterisks for 7); Germany, score of 7 (variables 1, 2, 3, 4, 5, and 6, and a single asterisk for 7); Japan, score of 5 (variables 1, 3, 5, and 6, and a single asterisk for 7); Greece, score of 2 (variables 4 and 6); Ireland, score of 4 (variables 2, 3, 4, and 6); Italy, score of 1 (variable 4); New Zealand, score of 3 (variables 3, 4, and 6); the Netherlands, score of 4 (variables 3, 4, 5, and 6); Portugal, score of 2 (variables 4 and 6); the United Kingdom, score of 5 (variables 1, 2, 3, 4, and 6); Spain, score of 3 (variables 3 and 4, and a single asterisk for 7); the United States, score of 7 (variables 1, 2, 3, 4, 5, and 6, and a single asterisk for 7); Switzerland, score of 7 (variables 2, 3, 4, 5, and 6, and a double asterisk for 7).

AUTHORS	Alex Cukierman (1992).
TYPE	De jure index of political and economic independence.
	Name of index: LVAU (simple index) and LVAW (weighted index).
SAMPLE	The sample is one of the largest, both in the number of countries analyzed and the periods covered. It covers the period 1950–1989, divided into four sub-periods: 1950–1959, 1960–1971, 1972–1979, and 1980–1989, corresponding to the dollar standard period, the period of dollar convertibility, the period of the two oil shocks and the deflation and debt crisis period. The sample of countries covered is among the largest including 21 OECD countries and 49 developing countries.
CHARACTERISTICS ANALYZED	(i) Variables concerning the appointment, dismissal, and term in office of the CB governor or president; (ii) provisions concerning the resolution of conflicts between the executive branch and CB, and the degree of CB participation in the formulation of monetary policy and the formulation of the government's budget; (iii) the final objectives of the CB as provided for in the charter; and (iv) laws that restrict the government's ability to obtain loans from the CB. The characteristics considered in this section are grouped under the following headings: CEO (*chief executive officer*), PF (*policy formulation*), OBJ (*final objectives*), LL (*limitation on lending*).
INDICATOR VARIABLES	The strength of the Cukierman indices lies in their unquestioned depth. Each of the four headings described above can be further broken down resulting in a total of 16 variables as follows:

• CEO, composed of: (1) *too* (*term of office*), the governor's term in office in years; (2) *app* (*appointment*), the entity delegated to appoint the governor; (3) *diss* (*dismissal*), legal provisions for the dismissal of the governor; (4) *off* (*other offices*), the ability of the governor to hold other offices.

• PF, composed of three variables: (1) *monpol* (*monetary policy*), the entity in charge of formulating monetary policy; (2) *conf* (*conflicts*), for government directives and conflict resolution; (3) *adv* (*advisory*), analyzes whether the CB has an advisory role in formulation of the budget.

• OBJ: (1) *obj* (*objectives*), CB objectives.

• LL is the deepest category, with eight variables: (1) *lla* (*limitations on advances*), limitations on advances to the government; (2) *lls* (*limitations on securitized lending*), limitations on securitized loans to the government; (3) *ldec* (*limitations on lending – who decides*), i.e., who has the authority to control loan terms; (4) *lwidth* (*width of potential borrowers*), i.e., the entities that have access to loans provided by the CB; (5) *ltype* (*type of limit*), the type of credit limit, if any; (6) *lmat* (*maturity of loans*), the maximum maturity of

(Continued)

Appendix III Continued

possible loans; (7) *lint (interest on loans)*, restrictions on rates applicable to CB loans; (8) *lprm (primary market lending)*, provisions on CB participation to the primary market for public debt.

Each of the 16 variables is coded using a standard scale that measures the degree of independence from 0 (minimum independence) to 1 (maximum independence). The number of levels presented for each variable depends on the specific nature of data for each individual legal characteristic. If n_j is the number of levels of legal variable j that can vary from a minimum of two to a maximum of seven, the scale [0, 1] is divided into $n_j - 1$ equal intervals providing n_j numerical values, or one for each level of independence.

Due to problems of availability of the large number of the postulated variables (due to the fact that laws do not provide sufficient information for coding all 16 variables in each country), Cukierman initially regroups them in order to form eight more comprehensive legal variables. The procedure followed consists in combining the four CEO sub-divisions into a single variable called *ceo*, which is calculated by computing their arithmetic mean. The three sub-divisions of the PF heading are combined under the notation of *pf* using a weighted average in which the weights are respectively 0.5 for *conf*, and 0.25 for *monpol* and *adv*. Finally, the last four variables of the heading LL (*ltype, lmat, lint, lprm*) are combined into the variable *lm* also using an arithmetic mean. The proposed combination produces a single variable for each of the first three headings (CEO, PF, and OBJ) and some five legal variables for LL. Cukierman then proceeds to a second and final level of aggregation in order to obtain a single legal independence index by country and sub-period. Two different indicators are calculated: a simple and weighted index.

The simple index is constructed through the simple arithmetic mean of values obtained in each of the eight variables obtained at the first level of aggregation.

In order to arrive at an index in weighted form, the weights, which the author insists are entirely subjective (Cukierman 1992: 379), are organized as follows:

AGGREGATION METHODS

Aggregated legal variable	Weight assigned
Ceo *(chief executive officer)*	0.20
Pf *(policy formulation)*	0.15

75

Obj (objectives)	0.15
Lla (limitations on lending – advances)	0.15
Lls (limitations on lending – securitized)	0.10
Ldec (limitations on lending – who decides)	0.10
Lwidth (limitations on lending – width)	0.05
Lm (limitations on lending – miscellaneous)	0.10
	1

AUTHORS	Alberto Alesina, Lawrence H. Summers (1993).
TYPE	De jure index of political and economic independence.
SAMPLE	The period covered by the sample is 1955 to 1988. The countries in the sample are the same 16 OECD countries used by Alesina (1988) [Australia, Belgium, Canada, Denmark, France, Germany, Italy, Japan, the Netherlands, Norway, New Zealand, Spain, Sweden, Switzerland, United Kingdom, United States].
CHARACTERISTICS ANALYZED INDICATOR VARIABLES	The analysis is based on the joint characteristics of the indices of Alesina (1988, 1989) and Grilli, Masciandaro, and Tabellini (1991). (1) The sum of values provided by the general index of Grilli, Masciandaro, and Tabellini (1991) (i.e., the sum of the two political and economic independence indices), and (2) the values obtained through the Alesina (1988, 1989) indicator.
AGGREGATION METHOD	The index of Grilli, Masciandaro, and Tabellini is converted into a scale of 1 to 4, like that of Alesina (1988), using the following procedure: for aggregate index values greater than 11 the score assigned is 4; for values between 7 and 11 the score is 3; if the value of the aggregate index of Grilli, Masciandaro, and Tabellini is between 4 and 7 the new value is 2; and finally, for values less than 4 a score of 1 is assigned. The Alesina and Summers index is obtained using the arithmetic mean of the index of Grilli, Masciandaro, and Tabellini, converted as noted above, and the Alesina (1988, 1989) index.
AUTHORS	Sylvester Eijffinger, Eric Schaling (1993).
TYPE	De jure index of policy independence.
SAMPLE	The period covered is for flexible exchange rates between 1972 and 1986.

(Continued)

Appendix III Continued

	The sample of countries is the same as used by Bade and Parkin (1977): 12 OECD countries [Australia, Belgium, Canada, France, Germany, Italy, Japan, the Netherlands, Sweden, Switzerland, United Kingdom, and the United States].
CHARACTERISTICS ANALYZED	The authors refer directly to Grilli, Masciandaro, and Tabellini (1991) in the selection of characteristics, which are as follows: (i) formal CB responsibilities based on policy objectives; (ii) relationships between CBs and governments; (iii) procedures for appointing CB boards.
INDICATOR VARIABLES	(1) "Ultimate" monetary policy authority: (b) held only by the CB (**); (b/g) not held exclusively by the CB (*); (g) held entirely by the government (−). (2) Government officials on the board: absence of government officials (with or without voting rights) on the board. (3) Appointments to the board: over half of board members are elected without government involvement. [There is an asterisk for items (2) and (3) if the variable is applicable; one or two asterisks for item (1).]
AGGREGATION METHOD	Simple sum of asterisks obtained + 1 (min = 1, max = 5). [The overall "policy independence" index grows as the level of independence rises.] Score of 1: Australia and Canada; score of 2: France, Italy, the United Kingdom, and Sweden; score of 3 for Belgium, Japan, and the United States; score of 4 for the Netherlands; score of 5 for Germany and Switzerland.

Source: Authors' elaborations.

Appendix IV Summary of base indicators of de facto independence

AUTHORS	Alex Cukierman (1992).
TYPE	De facto index of political independence. Name of index: TOR (turnover rate of governors).
SAMPLE	Period: 1950–1989. Countries: 19 OECD countries and 39 less developed or developing countries.
CHARACTERISTICS ANALYZED	Cukierman uses a rather elementary formula for the CB governor turnover rate, largely owing to the absence of simple indicators that make it possible to measure the extent to which the degree of actual CB independence diverges from legal independence across countries. The author's opinion, which is frequently cited in later literature, is that at least above a certain threshold, a higher turnover rate of the CB governor indicates a lower level of CB independence. This argument seems to primarily refer to less developed countries where it is safer to assume that practice may more frequently differ from the letter of the law.
INDICATOR VARIABLES	The TOR variable is defined as the average annual number of turnovers at the head of the CB. TOR run from a minimum of 0.03 (with average term in office of 33 years) for Ireland to a maximum of 0.93 annual turnovers (with an average term in office of 18 months) for Argentina. Confirming what was stated above regarding less developed countries, turnover rates in those countries are more dispersed than for OECD countries. While for OECD countries the range is from 0.03 for Iceland to 0.20 for Japan and Spain, more than half of less developed countries exceed this maximum, with the range varying from 0.13 for Malaysia to 0.93 for Argentina. A high turnover rate seems to point to low independence when the actual term in office of the CB governor is shorter than the actual term of the executive branch. If the average term of a governor is four years, the critical threshold of the turnover rate should be between 0.2 and 0.25.
AUTHORS	Alex Cukierman (1992).
TYPE	Measure of de facto independence through responses of qualified staff to a questionnaire sent to various CBs. Political and economic indicator. Name of index: QVAU (simple); QVAW (weighted).
SAMPLE	24 countries provided responses to the questionnaire, 10 of which were OECD countries. The implicit time frame of the questionnaire was 1980–1992.
CHARACTERISTICS ANALYZED	The questions asked in the questionnaire concern the following five issues: (i) legal aspects of CB independence; (ii) actual procedures followed when these differ from the legal norm; (iii) monetary policy instruments and institutional entities that control them; (iv) objectives and intermediate indicators; (v) final monetary policy objectives and their relative importance.

(Continued)

Appendix IV Continued

INDICATOR VARIABLES	The variables in question are: (1) *qto (tenure overlap with political authorities)*, consisting of the degree of overlap of the legal term in office of the government and CB. Ceteris paribus, if the legal term of office of the CB governor and board exceeds that of government, the CB is considered more independent. (2) *qll (limitations on lending in practice)*. This variable measures the actual magnitude of limitations on CB loans to government and the method in which the limitations are applied in practice. (3) *qrc (resolution of conflicts)*. This variable measures how conflict resolution is dealt with in practice and to the advantage of the CB. (4) *qbcb (who determines the budget of the CB?)*. This question aims at determining the actual degree of CB independence in decisions concerning its budget. (5) *qsp (who determines the salaries of high CB officials and the allocation of CB profits?)* aims at verifying who is charged with determining the compensation of CB officials and who decides on the allocation of profits. (6) *qst (are there quantitative money stock targets?)*, i.e., does CB has quantitative monetary targets, and to what extent does it adhere to them in practice? In other words, is CB able to focus its efforts on price stability in an unrestricted manner? (7) *qirt (are there formal or informal interest rate targets?)* asks whether CB has formal or informal targets set in terms of interest rates, and which therefore preclude a portion of CB's freedom to pursue price stability. (8) *qpps (what is the actual priority assigned to price stability?)*, i.e., what is the actual priority assigned to price stability? (9) *qsc (does the CB function as a development bank that grants credits at subsidy rates?)* measures degree to which the CB is required to provide loans at subsidy rates to both the private and public sectors.
AGGREGATION METHOD	As in the case of legal LVAU/LVAW, Cukierman follows a two-stage process. On the first level, variables (4) and (5) are combined with equal weight into a single financial independence item, *qfi*. The same process is used for variables (6) and (7) to obtain the item *qit*, summarizing both intermediate targets. At this stage the number of variables is reduced from nine to seven. As in the legal indicators, the second and final aggregation level is aimed at obtaining two alternative independence indices that reflect responses to the questionnaire. In order to obtain the simple index (QVAU), Cukierman performs a simple arithmetic mean of the numeric values obtained for each of the seven variables left after the first aggregation process. QVAW is obtained by using an average in which the same variables shown above have different weights; here again the author stresses the subjectivity in the selection of the latter (Cukierman 1992: 389):

Combined variable	Weight assigned
Qto (tenure overlap)	0.10
Qll (limitation on lending)	0.20

Qrc (resolution of conflicts)	0.10
Qfi (financial independence)	0.10
Qit (intermediate targets)	0.15
Qpps (priority to price stability)	0.15
Qsc (subsidized credits)	0.20
	1

AUTHORS Alex Cukierman, Steven B. Webb (1995).

TYPE De facto independence index formed as an index of CB vulnerability to political instability.

SAMPLE 67 countries (20 OECD countries and 47 developing economies), for the period 1950–89, sub-divided into two: Bretton Woods period (1950–71), and subsequent period (1972–89).

CHARACTERISTICS ANALYZED INDICATOR VARIABLES The index is a specification of Cukierman (1992) TOR. It represents an attempt to understand how political cycles relate to governor turnover rates at different stages of economic development and in different regimes. CB governor turnover rate is calculated at several time intervals departing from a political transition. After empirically proving that changes at the head of a CB that can be defined as purely political are those that occur within six months of a government change, and after calculating the annual frequency of political changes in each country, the authors define their indicator of CB vulnerability to political instability in each country as the percentage of political transitions that were immediately followed by the replacement of the CB governor:

$V(i) \equiv$ Number of replacements of CB governor within i months of a political transition/Number of political transitions (where $i = 1, 6$).

The complement of this measure to the total turnover rate is defined as non-political turnover of CB governors. The following table provides an overall framework of the differences among economic groups, various political regimes and relevant time intervals.

(Continued)

Appendix IV Continued

Economic groups considered	Vulnerability		Annual frequency of political changes
	Within six months	*Within one month*	
Total sample	0.24	0.12	0.27
Industrial countries	0.10	0.05	0.32
Developing countries	0.35	0.18	0.24
Industrial countries			
Only democratic economies	0.10	0.04	0.32
Mixed economies	0.12	0.12	0.33
Developing countries			
Only authoritarian economies	0.22	0.17	0.14
Only democratic economies	0.30	0.09	0.18
Mixed economies	0.39	0.20	0.30

Source: Authors' elaboration.

Appendix V Summary of empirical studies on de jure independence (The observations found in baseline studies are indicated at the beginning of each table to allow for a quicker review of similarities and differences; a dotted line separates base studies from the subsequent literature (this applies also to Appendix VI).)

Study	Measures used	Sample	Conclusions
Bade and Parkin (1977)	(BP) Index of political independence	12 OECD countries 1951–75	There is weak evidence that pursuing price stability as the only final policy objective is associated with achieving a lower level of inflation. It is shown that CBs that have a certain degree of independence are able to ensure a lower level of inflation, but not necessarily a low variability of monetary policy. In addition, the conduct of monetary policy does not seem to differ between independent CBs and those dominated by governments when all of the former's management is appointed by the executive branch.
Alesina (1988, 1989)	(AL) Index of political and economic independence	17 OECD countries 1973–86	Alesina observes that there is an inverse relationship between the degree of CB independence and average inflation, and indicates a weak correlation between the level of government spending as a percentage of GNP and the inflation rate based on the assumption that higher levels of government spending require higher levels of seignorage. Finally, by comparing the change in average inflation rates during government turnovers in selected countries, Alesina argues that when the CB is dependent, monetary policy has followed a more political path.
Grilli, Masciandaro, and Tabellini (1991)	(GMTP) index of CB political independence (objectives independence), (GMTE) index of CB economic independence (instruments independence), and (GMT) general independence index (sum of GMTP and GMTE)	18 OECD countries 1960–89	The authors argue that in general, an autonomous CB leads to low levels of inflation. At the same time, an independent CB does not seem to prevent excessive government deficits. On the other hand CB independence does not have a systematic impact on growth or the variability of real output, thus confirming the "free lunch" hypothesis.

(Continued)

Appendix V Continued

Study	Measures used	Sample	Conclusions
Cukierman (1992)	(LVAU) Simple index of political and economic independence, and (LVAW) the same index, but weighted	70 countries 1950–89	The overall contribution of individual groups of legal variables to the real currency depreciation rate in the entire sample is not statistically significant. By separating the two groups of countries, an increase in significance is not obtained even though this value is higher in industrial countries. In developed countries, the combined index exhibits a significantly negative coefficient, which does not occur for the sub-group of developing countries. "This may be due to a general norm of more adherence to the law in developed countries" (Cukierman 1992: 421).
Alesina and Summers (1993)	(AS) Index of political and economic independence constructed as the average of the general index GMT and the index AL	Same sample of 16 OECD countries used by Alesina (1988) 1955–88	The authors find a nearly perfect negative correlation between CB independence and both average inflation and its variability. There is no clear relationship between CB independence and the average (variance) real GNP growth, and comparison of the former with the average (variance) unemployment rate gives the same results. There are no long-term effects in the sample with respect to the relationship between CB independence and the level of real interest rates. However, the relationship is clearly negative if the variability of these rates is considered.
Eijffinger and Schaling (1993)	(ES) Index of policy independence	12 OECD countries as in Bade and Parkin (1977)	The authors do not use their index to calculate the impact of CB independence on inflationary and macroeconomic performance but to review the verisimilitude of the AL and BP measures.

		1960–89	inflation if its measure of "effective financial sector opposition to inflation" (FOI) is included as an additional explanatory variable. Posen emphasizes the existence of a causal relationship (rather than a mere association) between a high degree of FOI, a higher level of CB independence, and a lower average inflation rate that seems to move in this exact order.
Banaian, Burdekin, and Willett (1995)	LVAU, TOR, GMT, and their own index made up of a simple dummy variable	21 OECD countries 1971–88	The dummy variable (government's inability to override CB policy decisions) is statistically significant in explaining cross-country differences in inflation rates together with two control variables (deficit to GDP ratio, and trade openness), and provides better results than the other three indicators.
Fuhrer (1997)	LVAU and AS	70 countries 1950–89	No clear relationship between CB independence and the variable analyzed (inflation level and variability, growth, unemployment). The only significant relationship shows that growth and unemployment are negatively and positively correlated with CB independence. The statistical significance of the LVAU index with respect to inflation and inflation variability in the simple bivariate regressions (with the smaller Alesina and Summers, 1993, country sample) disappears once other cross-sectional attributes or variation over time in inflation determinants are controlled for.
de Haan and Kooi (1997)	Breakdown of GMT and LVAU into four measures: independence of CB board members and governor; monetary policy instruments independence; CB financing independence; level of conservatism assigned by law to CB	21 OECD countries 1972–79 and 1980–89	The results indicate that CB independence with respect to monetary policy instruments has a considerable impact on the inflationary performance (and the variability of inflation) of several countries, while the degree of legal conservatism and other aspects of independence have little or no influence. Neither independence nor the degree of conservatism exhibits any relationship with the variability of output.

(Continued)

Appendix V Continued

Study	Measures used	Sample	Conclusions
Campillo and Miron (1997)	LVAW	62 countries 1973–94	CB independence as proxied by Cukierman (1992) weighted LVAW index does not explain inflation when other control variables are added. The additional independent variables concern: time-consistency issues other than CB dependence (e.g., openness, political stability), fiscal aspects of optimal taxation and seignorage, the degree of the financial sector's aversion to inflation (FOI) and previous inflationary experience. Of these variables, those that seem optimal for explaining differing inflationary performance are the degree of trade openness, the ratio of debt to GDP, the level of the inflation tax in relation to conventional taxes, political instability, the income level, and (at least partially) previous inflationary experience.
Banaian, Burdekin, and Willett (1998)	LVAU	27 countries 1980–89	The analysis of 15 of the 16 LVAU components leads the authors to the conclusion that most of them (and thus, the combined index as well) have a relationship that is not statistically significant and/or positive (rather than negative) with the average level of inflation.
Crosby (1998)	LVAU	44 countries 1962–91	Crosby points at the lack of empirical evidence of positive correlation between output variability and CB independence (contrary to Rogoff's 1985 theoretical prediction): to explain such a missing link, the author hypothesizes that CB independence is endogenous to an economy's lower susceptibility to real shocks. To test this hypothesis Crosby regresses LVAU on the variance of the terms of trade (a proxy for the size of real shocks). Although the evidence is weakly consistent with this hypothesis, this doesn't seem sufficient to explain the lack of correlation between CB independence and output variability. One explanation is that delays in monetary policy transmission to the real economy make the discretionary monetary policy useless for reducing output variability.

85

Author	Indicators	Sample	Findings
Mangano (1998)	LVAU, GMT, AL, ES, TOR, and VUL	Same sample of 12 OECD countries for the six indicators 1980–89	When comparing GMT and LVAU in their nine common criteria, an interpretation spread of 30 percent is noted as well as a negligible weighting spread; when comparing the overall GMT and LVAU indices a criteria (i.e., difference in criteria considered relevant) spread of 40 to 45 percent arises. When comparing the rankings obtained using all six indices, it is shown that the degree of correlation among them is weak. By regressing these rankings on several macroeconomic performance variables it is found that in the case of average inflation, only GMT and AL exhibit significantly negative coefficients. Only ES has a statistically significant coefficient for inflation variability. Signs for growth are negative but never significant, and no significant relationship is observed for output variability.
Posen (1998)	LVAU	17 OECD countries 1950–89	Posen tests the existence of a CB independence-led credibility bonus by comparing CB independence, and private and public sector behavior reflecting such credibility. On the disinflationary credibility side (i.e., the theoretical ability of an independent CB to deflate with no unemployment or output costs) the author finds no evidence that a higher degree of CB independence implies lower costs of deflation by reducing the gap between inflationary expectations and reality. On the other hand, disinflations appear to cost more rather than less in countries with high CB independence; and it does not seem that greater CB independence significantly shortens the length of deflation episodes. Testing the link between CB independence and induced credibility in the labor market, it is shown that none of the several measures of wage rigidity used has a statistically significant relationship with CB independence. Finally, there is no trace of CB independence having the effect of restraining governments from using seignorage tax or engaging in electoral manipulation of economic policy.

(Continued)

Appendix V Continued

Study	Measures used	Sample	Conclusions
Cukierman and Lippi (1999)	LVAU	19 OECD countries 1980–94	The Calmfors-Driffill hump-shaped relationship between unemployment (inflation) and centralization in wage bargaining is, ceteris paribus, more likely to arise at low levels of CB independence. This relationship disappears and eventually becomes monotonically increasing as CB independence grows. In addition, the inflation-reducing impact that CB independence has on the economy is greater at intermediate levels of union centralization, while there is a significantly positive effect of CB independence on unemployment at low levels of bargaining centralization.
Lybek (1999)	A new legal indicator of CB independence and accountability, TOR and two indicators of reform progress	15 countries in the former ruble area 1995–97	The indicator is negatively correlated to inflation and positively to growth. TOR (used to proxy de facto independence) does not have any relationship with inflation or growth. No evidence that greater CB independence and accountability contributed to acceleration of reform process. Positive correlation between the index and the two indicators of progress in restructuring the economy suggests that strong political will towards reform can be complementary to CB independence in explaining the acceleration in economic modernization.
Franzese (1999)		18 OECD countries 1972–90	CB independence has greater anti-inflationary impact when the government is leftist, concentration of unions is high, the economy is less open, inflation abroad is high, the financial sector is small and there is little coordination in wage bargaining.

| Oatley (1999) | LVAW, TOR, GMTP, GMTE, GMT, AL, and 2 simplifications of AL (dummy variable for each level of independence; dummy variable to split CB with high independence from others) | 21 OECD countries 1970–90 | The hypothesis that CB independence reduces inflation holds even when economic/political-institutional control variables are added. Contrary to Campillo and Miron (1997), neither the fiscal situation nor the openness of the economy exhibits a strong relationship with inflation, but unemployment, the structure of the labor market and the government's political preferences provide good results. The five most complex of the eight indices fail to capture the theoretical negative relationship with inflation. The three simplest indices (in particular the dummy variable that divides CBs into two categories) are able to best explain international differences in inflation. |

Source: Authors' elaboration.

Appendix VI Summary of empirical studies on de facto independence

Study	Measures used	Sample	Conclusions
Cukierman (1992)	TOR (turnover rate of CB governors).	58 countries 1950–89	TOR negatively related to CB independence only above certain threshold (0.25 TOR per year), and its positive relationship with inflation is statistically significant only for the sub-group of developing countries.
Cukierman (1992)	(QVAU/QVAW) Simple/ weighted indices of political and economic independence based on a questionnaire	24 countries 1980–89	Most variables in the questionnaire show the expected negative sign. The most statistically significant are those concerning the existence of intermediate monetary policy targets and CB credit limitations. Overall contribution of the index in explaining real currency depreciation is not very significant.
Eijffinger, Van Rooij, & Schaling (1996)	Empirical CB independence index based on monetary policy reaction functions; compared with legal indices: AL, GMT, ES, and Bade & Parkin	10 OECD countries 1977–90	Index reflects differing upward pressures on money market rates and is obtained by estimating a country's individual effect within a reaction function of interest rates to inflation, growth and current account surpluses. Ranking of CBs, obtained through the empirical measurement of independence, coincides rather well with the legal measures considered.
Sikken and de Haan (1998)	LVAW, TOR, and VUL	30 developing countries 1950–94	Regressions of average surpluses on measures of CB independence do not provide any significant result. Regression of money growth on past and present fiscal deficits suggests that in most developing countries, deficits do not cause monetary expansions. On the other hand, regression of the growth rate of CB credits to the government on budget surpluses shows that in most countries in the sample a negative relationship exists. Monetary accommodation of fiscal deficits is significantly related with VUL and TOR.

Fry (1998)	New index rising with increased CB neutralization of its credit to government. Index compared to LVAU, TOR, and an index based on questionnaire	70 developing countries 1972–95	The author detects clear differences in monetary policy reaction functions when sample selection is based on fiscal, inflation, and growth attributes of countries; but that differences vanish when selection is based on the three codified measures. The work also concludes that large deficits and the use of the inflation tax and financial repression are associated with a lower degree of CB neutralization of increasing credit demands by the government. The more autonomous CBs are found in countries that report higher growth rates.
Akhand (1998)	LVAW, TOR, VUL, and NOR	62 countries 1960–89	Application of Levine and Renelt (1992) robustness test to the relationship between growth and CB independence, both legal and de facto. The results indicate a weak relationship.
de Haan and Kooi (2000)	TOR and new CB TOR measure based on information provided by IMF and CBs	82 developing countries 1980–89	New TOR, as well as Cukierman's TOR, explain inflation level and variability only for countries with high inflation. Posen's view that CB independence and inflation performance are caused by degree of "financial sector opposition to inflation" is not supported. No evidence that CB independence as proxied by TOR is significantly tied to growth.
Sturm and de Haan (2001)	TOR and their CB governor turnover rate developed on the basis of new sources	82 developing countries 1980–98	Once control variables are added, TOR is almost never statistically significant. In keeping with de Haan and Kooi (2000), in regressions in which the coefficient of TOR is significant, this result holds only if the sample includes countries with high inflation.

Source: Authors' elaborations.

2
Survey of Models and Indicators of Accountability

As discussed in Chapter 1, the standard policy response to the inflationary bias caused by discretionary monetary policy-making is the delegation of monetary policy to an independent institution. Directly linked and complementary to independence is the concept of accountability. Research on CB accountability is relatively recent and the literature is still evolving. Relatively few authors have focused on empirical measures of accountability, including Briault, Haldane, and King (1996), de Haan, Amtenbrink, and Eijffinger (1998), Bini-Smaghi and Gros (2000 and 2001), Stasavage (2003), and Siklos (2002). The literature we survey spans eight years, a period during which accountability indices have been refined. While there is still a lack of consensus among academics and practitioners, progress has been made in understanding the contributions of the different variables to a measure of CB accountability.

Responsibility and accountability

The definitions of "responsibility" and "accountability" overlap somewhat. A subject is "accountable for" something if he or she is bound in duty to account for his/her actions in an area for which he or she is "responsible." Similarly, an institution is accountable when it is able to give an account of its action, while it is responsible when it is entrusted by law with the fulfillment of a duty. Therefore the responsible subject can be called to order in case of omission or negligence in discharging its responsibilities. In particular, monetary policy is entrusted to the CB which, first, becomes responsible for it, and consequently, accountable for the actions performed subsequently. As we will see, our measure of CB accountability includes a sub-category called "responsibility" that measures the extent to which the CB is autonomously in charge of monetary policy. The variables in this sub-category represent the ideal link between our measures of CB independence and accountability. The level of accountability to which the CB is subject should be a function of the intensity of its responsibility or range of responsibilities. In turn, the extent and intensity of responsibility should depend on the CB's level of autonomy.

Responsibility

The first step is to identify an institution or a subject upon which to devolve a certain task or objective. This process is carried out through delegation, which requires the handover of well-defined responsibilities from the delegating to the delegated subject. In our case the object of delegation (i.e., the responsibility) is represented by monetary policy, the delegating subject is the government and the delegated entity is the CB. Bini-Smaghi and Gros (2000) define the process of tasks assignment as "ex ante control." This is a process through which a democratically elected body (parliament or government) defines the rules, principles, and standards under which an institution is held accountable.

Because the delegation of monetary policy concerns not a single subject but society in its entirety, a problem of definition of "objectives" arises. Who should decide monetary policy's final objectives? On the one hand we have the parliament, democratically elected; on the other hand we have the CB (or its board of directors), which is only indirectly elected (i.e., appointed) by people's representatives (i.e., parliament). While the first entity is formed to take decisions in conformity to the will of the people, the second can move away from the direct interest of society. The process of delegation of responsibilities therefore involves the resolution of an underlying conflict between creating a democratic deficit, in case it is the CB that sets the objectives of monetary policy, and turning the CB into a mere executor of the government's will.

Accountability

As outlined, the importance of accountability stems from the individual and collective costs attached to the choice of delegation, which may deliver a monetary policy-maker with different preferences than the rest of society. The awareness of these costs brings about the request of a formal mechanism of responsibility, as stated by Padoa-Schioppa and Randzio-Plath (2000):

> Accountability is an essential and constituent element of a democratic political order. In such an order, institutions and bodies with the

power to affect the lives and welfare of the community must be subject to the scrutiny of the citizens or of their elected representatives. This is particularly relevant for those policy fields – such as central banking – where decisions are consciously removed from the day-to-day influences of the political arena. Thus, accountability pertains to a civic and moral obligation inherent in the political order, and is not directly related to what could be termed the "economic order."[1]

As theory and empirical evidence show, the delegation of monetary policy to a conservative and independent CB brings about significant benefits in terms of lower inflation. Independence, however, means managing monetary policy without external conditioning and, therefore, independently from governmental or parliamentary pressures. The prevention of interference precludes the government from modifying or deviating from the objective of price stability. Higher levels of independence, however, require a higher level of CB accountability. The parliament and society at large must necessarily be informed through well-defined mechanisms, as they cannot interfere with the policy of the CB. As a result, accountability is particularly important on the operational side of the allocated responsibility. Accountability allows the other stakeholders to evaluate how the CB carries out its responsibilities. It allows society to assess whether the CB fulfills its mandate in the proper way, by publicly accounting for its actions to the delegating authority and making possible an evaluation based on the entrusted objectives. In a way, accountability displays the degree of "soundness" of the CB's behavior with respect to its mandate. In Padoa-Schioppa and Randzio-Plath (2000) this is defined as "ex post accountability."

"Accountable for what? Accountable to whom?"[2] Some features in the structure and behavior of the CB directly strengthen its accountability to society, others contribute to strengthen its accountability with respect to the objectives of monetary policy. Since monetary policy is carried out in the interest of society, the CB must account for its actions to an institution representative of society. To do this, the CB must continuously report to the delegating authority, that is, the parliament (or the government). It is therefore important to analyze the way in which the CB and the parliament (or the government) interact along the three phases of

---

[1] Padoa-Schioppa and Randzio-Plath (2000: 31).
[2] Padoa-Schioppa and Randzio-Plath (2000: 29).

the monetary policy process: decision, implementation, and assessment of results.

An additional aspect of accountability has to do with the relationship between expected and actual results. We start by presuming that, in the process of formulating objectives Pareto-efficient targets are selected using all available information at a specific time. Hence, CB performance can be assessed by comparing expected and actual targets, and the framework in which the CB operates is also important. As we will see, some frameworks inherently favor a higher degree of accountability: for instance, in the case of inflation targeting the reference benchmark (i.e., the target) against which the performance of the CB is evaluated is well known to the public. In other frameworks this may not be the case and it can be more difficult to find the appropriate benchmark.

The concept of accountability in the literature

The different definitions of accountability that are discussed in the empirical literature, and which are summarized in Table 2.1, are discussed in the following paragraphs.

Briault, Haldane, and King (1996): de jure and de facto accountability

The authors suggest that the concept of accountability, within a principal–agent relationship, can be seen from two different viewpoints.

Table 2.1 Accountability in the empirical literature

Authors	Meaning(s) of accountability		
Briault, Haldane, and King (1996)	Accountability	Ex ante accountability Ex post accountability	
de Haan, Amtenbrink, and Eijffinger, (1998)	Accountability	Objectives Transparency Responsibility	
Bini-Smaghi and Gros (2000 and 2001)	Democratic control	Ex ante control Accountability	Ex ante accountability Ex post accountability
Siklos (2002)	Accountability	Accountability on objectives Procedural accountability Information accountability	

Source: Authors' elaboration.

De jure accountability means that a formal contract between the CB and the government is entrenched in law (e.g., in statute). The definition requires the contract to specify not only the object of the responsibility, but also statements about assumption of responsibility, the reporting duties of the CB, and punishment in case of failure. De facto accountability means that the CB behaves in an accountable way, beyond the obligations imposed by law. This happens when the CB itself feels the necessity of accounting for and explaining its actions. The rise of the spontaneous communication of intents, objectives, or achieved results by the CB can strengthen its credibility and, therefore, influence expectations of the private sector:

> even a non-independent central bank could perceive advantages in explaining its actions, intentions and objectives as a means of influencing public expectations – and thus affecting the costs of delivering the central bank's goals; influencing the public's social welfare function – by educating the public about the benefits of price stability; and of enhancing the reputation and credibility of the central bank – by providing a means for it to be judged against the coherence and persuasiveness of its analysis.[3]

In this case we talk about de facto accountability because the CB is accountable to the public even in the absence of specific legal provisions.

Bini-Smaghi and Gros (2000): ex ante and ex post accountability

The authors distinguish ex ante from ex post accountability (besides accountability on procedures), whereby the former is defined as the act through which a democratically elected government outlines the duties for which the delegated institution must be accountable. The authors therefore refer to the accuracy of the objectives assigned to the CB. Ex post accountability, on the other hand, is what we usually mean by strictly defined accountability; it refers to the ways and instruments through which the CB externally accounts for its work. At the beginning of their work the authors also underline an important difference between accountability and democratic control:

> The concepts of democratic control and democratic accountability are often confused. Democratic control refers to the following three constraints on the exercise of government: Ex-ante control defines the

---

[3] Briault, Haldane, and King (1996: 11).

rules, standards and principles laid down in advance by a democratically elected body, to be followed by the accountable body in the exercise of its function; Accountability is the act of listening to criticism and responding to questions about the past and future behavior that may be put forward by a democratically elected body; Popular mandate refers to the attribution of power through democratic procedures.[4]

The concept of accountability is thus introduced within the broader concept of democratic control, and split into two tightly correlated components of ex ante control and accountability. The quality of accountability depends at first on the way in which ex ante control is put in place. The authors use two examples: if parliament determines the mandate of the CB with extreme accuracy, the performance of the CB can be evaluated very minutely; if, on the other hand, escape clauses are laid down in the phase of ex ante control, the CB can more easily justify possible deviations of its actions from mandated objectives.

de Haan, Amtenbrink, and Eijffinger (1998): three main features

In our view the concept of central bank accountability has three main features: (1) decisions about the ultimate objectives of monetary policy; (2) transparency of actual monetary policy; and (3) who bears final responsibility with respect to monetary policy.[5]

Accountability is affected by the way in which the final objectives of monetary policy are defined. It is asked whether it is right, in a democratic system, to leave the definition of the objectives of monetary policy in the hands of an independent institution which is not directly elected or subject to the direct control of a democratic institution. It is clear, on the other hand, that accurately defined objectives favor accountability by setting clear evaluation benchmarks. In the process of objectives or targets definition some factors are worth considering. A high number of objectives can make the evaluation of the CB more complex. The situation progressively improves when the number of objectives is reduced with the optimum being a single objective, such as price stability. A second relevant characteristic is clarity. Targets must be easily interpretable and, more importantly, unequivocal. The last characteristic concerns the

---

[4] Bini-Smaghi and Gros (2001: 2).
[5] de Haan, Amtenbrink, and Eijffinger (1998: 4).

quantification of the objectives. If objectives are quantifiable the CB can be assessed more accurately, thus raising its level of accountability.

Transparency is the second essential characteristic of CB accountability highlighted by the authors. It is considered as an integral part of accountability because, without the release of information by the CB, the stakeholders of monetary policy cannot evaluate its performance.

Transparency is a very important element of accountability. As Glastra (1997: 323) puts it: "Accountability requires that the central bank, at the very least explains and justifies its policies or actions, and gives account for the decisions made in the execution of its responsibilities." Whatever other arrangements concerning democratic accountability may exist, their scope is limited without transparency because information concerning the behavior of the central bank is crucial for the evaluation of its performance (see also Demertzis et al. 1998). As Alan Greenspan puts it: "In a democratic society all public policy making should be in the open, except when such a forum impedes the primary function assigned to an institution."[6]

The last feature of accountability concerns the final responsibility for monetary policy. This builds upon the ex ante and ex post relationship between the CB and the parliament. We are in the presence of an ex ante relationship when the policy-maker provides indications about policies undertaken to the parliament. This can be done by publishing documents in which the adopted measures are communicated and explained or by appearing directly before the parliament to report and debate. The practice of publicly reporting to the parliament can be either a precise provision of the statute, a voluntary decision of the CB or an explicit request of the government. When, on the other hand, we are in the presence of an ex post relationship, the initiative passes from the hands of the CB to those of the government or the legislature. The delegating institution controls the operations, evaluates the performance and the achieved objectives, and, when necessary, imposes penalties upon the monetary policy-maker. An example of penalty could be the coercive resignation of the governor in the case of missed achievement of the target. The last feature of the ex post relationship between the delegating authority and the CB is represented by the possibility of overriding the CB. The presence of an override clause raises the level of accountability of the CB only if the interference of the overriding institution (i.e., the government) occurs in strictly exceptional cases, explicitly set

---

[6] de Haan, Amtenbrink, and Eijffinger (1998: 5).

out in the law and does not interfere in the ordinary conduct of monetary policy.

Castellani (2002)

Castellani (2002) clearly distinguishes the idea of accountability from that of transparency: "We shed some light on the distinction between accountability, responsibility for policy-making (deeds), and transparency, the communication strategy adopted by the central bank (words)."[7] With respect to accountability Castellani states that the need for CB accountability originates from the fact that there is a difference between what society expects from the CB and what the CB actually does. This discrepancy, which can be caused by a lack of clarity on the delegated objectives or on central bankers' preferences, provides the rationale for a high level of CB accountability. To the author, as in the case of Padoa-Schioppa and Randzio-Plath (2000), CB accountability has a strong ex post component. As the performance of the CB can only be evaluated by the private sector and the government once the CB has acted, the CB itself will necessarily be accountable ex post, and at a time when information not available to the CB at the time of its decision may be available. This temporal mismatch may give rise to a negative evaluation of monetary policy, even though at the moment of formulation the policy was optimal. In the process of analysis of accountability this ex post component of accountability needs to be taken into account.

Siklos (2002)

Siklos makes use of the concept of accountability as it was presented in the work of de Haan, Amtenbrink, and Eijffinger (1998) and divides it into three categories: accountability on objectives (the clarity and precision with which the objectives of monetary policy are stated and/or communicated); procedural accountability (the degree and forms of communication of policy decisions and strategies to accomplish the stated objectives); and informational accountability (the extent to which the CB is required to answer for past decisions, the form such responses must take, and the nature of the bodies to whom the chief executive of the CB is responsible). Procedural accountability ensures that the actions and decisions of the CB are fair, tend to public welfare, and are not subject to external pressure. Within procedural accountability we can distinguish an ex ante and an ex post control, as defined above. Siklos' main contribution lies in the link he makes between accountability

---

[7] Castellani (2002: 4).

on objectives and procedural accountability. A high level of clarity in the definition of the objectives of monetary policy is not sufficient to guarantee a high level of accountability if the level of procedural accountability is not equally high, namely if there is no full and prompt communication of the undertaken actions. On the side of communication, then, what matters is not the quantity but rather the quality of information and its comprehensibility to the outside world.

Time inconsistency and accountability

We have seen that time inconsistency issues arise every time policymakers have an incentive, albeit a short-term one, to deviate from the announced policy. Different solutions to the time inconsistency problem in monetary policy have been proposed in which accountability, directly or indirectly, has an important role.

Delegating monetary policy to an independent central bank

Rogoff (1985) argues that the inflation bias is, at least partly, eliminated by delegating monetary policy to an autonomous central bank that is more conservative than the government. Accountability is a fundamental part of the delegation process. In fact an independent CB could have interests in contrast to those of the government (i.e., the delegating authority). This, as commented above, requires a high level of CB accountability. Accountability is, in sum, an essential pillar of the delegation process: it is difficult for an institution to be willing to delegate monetary policy if it has little possibility of checking how the delegated institution is operating.

Override

As already pointed out, Lohmann (1992) proposes to leave monetary policy under the control of an independent authority, but to couple this independence with a so-called escape clause. The idea consists in devolving monetary policy to a conservative central bank, as in Rogoff (1985), but give in parallel to the government the possibility to override the CB in the face of unusually important shocks. This escape clause has significant effects as it could influence the way the CB acts. For instance the CB could feel forced to pay much more attention to the will of the delegating authority, just to avoid being deprived of its powers. This is reflected in the idea of accountability presented in de Haan, Amtenbrink, and Eijffinger (1998), where the presence of an explicit override clause raises the level of ex ante accountability in monetary policy. Indeed this is not sufficient, a priori, to prevent the CB from behaving in a socially sub-optimal manner.

Contractual solution

Within the solution to the time inconsistency problem given by Svensson (1997) a principal–agent relationship appears. The principal (the government) not only delegates monetary policy but entrusts a precise target to the CB, which is defined in terms of inflation. The presence of a well-defined target represents the optimal benchmark for the evaluation of the performance of the CB. The presence of an inflation targeting mechanism inherently renders the policy-maker much more accountable.

Indicators and measures of accountability

In view of the several definitions of accountability, several sets of variables have been proposed for elaborating an index of CB accountability. One of the areas where differences are most marked is whether transparency is part of accountability or not. This conceptual difference translates in transparency variables being included or excluded from the indicator of accountability. The second issue one has to address is to assess whether the variables impact equally on accountability, or whether some of them should be given a higher (lower) weight. A widely adopted solution has been to weight all variables equally so as to reduce the potential for arbitrariness. The principal sources of information used by most of the authors are taken from the statute of the CB. Other features of the framework and environment in which the CB operates are also considered, for instance its relationships with the government. However, there is no standard modality of analyzing and coding such information so as to build a proxy for such an abstract concept, as the analysis of CB independence measures by Mangano (1998) pointed out.

Briault, Haldane, and King (1996)

In order to analyze the relationship between independence and accountability, the authors build an index of CB accountability that follows the logic of Eijffinger and Schaling's 1993 index of CB independence. The result is a measure composed of four variables in the form of questions (see Table 2.2).

The first variable ("Is the central bank subject to external monitoring by parliament?") refers to what can be defined as "democratic accountability." It is essential for elected representatives to be able to monitor

Table 2.2   Briault, Haldane, and King's accountability index

---

- Is the central bank subject to external monitoring by parliament?
- Are the minutes of meetings to decide monetary policy published?
- Does the central bank publish an inflation or monetary policy report of some kind, in addition to standard central bank bulletins?
- Is there a clause that allows the central bank to be overridden in the event of certain shocks?

Source: Authors' elaboration based on Briault, Haldane, and King (1996).

the activity of non-elected public institutions, enabling them to report to the electorate. The second and third variables (respectively, "Are the minutes of meetings to decide monetary policy published?" and "Does the central bank publish an inflation or monetary policy report?") refer to the concept of transparency and highlight the fact that a mechanism of external communication is in place, allowing monetary policy stakeholders to evaluate the performance of the CB. The last variable ("Is there a clause that allows the central bank to be overridden in the event of certain shocks?") refers to an override clause, which provides for high ex ante accountability, by allowing the government to limit CB independence under exceptional but precisely defined circumstances. However, this may influence the normal behavior of the CB and make it more accommodating.[8]

Bini-Smaghi and Gros (2000 and 2001) have criticized the excessive simplicity of the indicator. They argue that it is not detailed enough to capture the peculiarities of accountability: "In our view, these criteria are unsatisfactory. They oversimplify the process and thereby give an incomplete picture of the framework within which accountability is exercised." Another critique has been presented regarding the last variable which seems to belong to an indicator of CB independence rather than accountability: "the last criterion seems more appropriate for evaluating independence than accountability. The possibility of overriding the central bank is unrelated to ex-ante control and thus to accountability."[9]

de Haan, Amtenbrink, and Eijffinger (1998)

The authors propose a framework for assessing CB accountability based on thirteen variables (see Table 2.3) which look at the final objectives

---

[8] The authors apply this indicator to thirteen countries (see results in the synoptic Table 2.6 below).

[9] Bini-Smaghi and Gros (2001: 6).

Table 2.3 de Haan, Amtenbrink, and Eijffinger's accountability index

Ultimate objectives of monetary policy

1. Does the central bank law stipulate the objectives of monetary policy?
2. Is there a clear prioritization of objectives?
3. Are the objectives clearly defined?
4. Are the objectives quantified (in the law or based on document based on the law)?

Transparency of actual monetary policy

5. Must the central bank publish an inflation or monetary policy report of some kind, in addition to standard central bank bulletins/reports?
6. Are minutes of meetings of the central bank board made public within a reasonable time?
7. Must the central bank explain publicly to what extent it has been able to reach its objectives?

Final responsibility for monetary policy

8. Is the central bank subject to monitoring by parliament (is there a requirement, apart from an annual report, to report to parliament and/or explain policy actions in parliament)?
9. Has the government (or parliament) the right to give instructions?
10. Is there some kind of review in the procedure to apply the override mechanism?
11. Has the central bank possibility for an appeal in case of an instruction?
12. Can the central bank law be changed by a simple majority in parliament?
13. Is past performance a ground for dismissal of a central bank governor?

Source: Authors' elaboration based on de Haan, Amtenbrink, and Eijffinger (1998).

of monetary policy, with a view to assessing whether the objectives are accurately defined and if a hierarchy exists in case they are multiple. They express their basic idea as follows:

> Yet, the less a central bank is bound to specific objectives the more difficult it becomes to evaluate the bank's performance, since a suitable yardstick is missing. The evaluation of central bank performance is the central element of central bank accountability and a clearly stated objective is therefore essential.[10]

The second aspect analyzed refers to monetary policy transparency. To be accountable, the CB should communicate to stakeholders about inflation and monetary policy. The aim of this information is to make

---

[10] de Haan, Amtenbrink, and Eijffinger (1998: 11).

all stakeholders aware of the CB's actions, allowing them to comprehend and evaluate the decisions adopted. Transparency is significantly improved in all cases in which the CB publicizes the results achieved or the reasons for a divergence between achieved and expected results. Implicitly, the authors consider transparency to be an integral part of accountability, while others separate the two concepts.

The third aspect relates to the final responsibility for monetary policy. The authors analyze the relationship between the delegating and the delegated authority through six questions, by considering the procedures through which the two authorities interact, for instance the way in which the CB can appeal against a decision of the government. This responsibility aspect also includes the evaluation of CB performance and sanctions in case of failure. The twelfth variable ("Can the central bank law be changed by a simple majority in parliament?"), akin to an override clause, is considered an important mechanism that can lead the CB to behave in line with the preferences of the delegating authority.

Bini-Smaghi and Gros (2000 and 2001)

The index developed by Bini-Smaghi and Gros (2000 and 2001) differs from those presented so far because it has a different objective: "Our aim is not to create a numerical index, but rather to examine the ways and opportunities that central banks use to interact with public opinion, market participants and the other institutions in society."[11] Hence, the result is an indicator that highlights the specificities of each CB with regard to its interaction with public opinion, elected representatives, or financial markets. The authors develop a fifteen-variable index, as presented in Table 2.4.

The area of ex ante accountability includes five variables. Clear definition of the objective of price stability is considered to raise the level of accountability, as well as the announcement of an operational target, which allows markets to monitor the actions undertaken by the CB, and the announcement of an intermediate target, which allows the formation of expectations on future inflation on the basis of the observable variables at the time of the announcement. The presence of indicators for assessing monetary policy also allows markets to understand how the CB interprets inflation forecasts and how it will react in the case of a mismatch between the projected target and actual results. Therefore, it allows a better understanding of monetary policy operating procedures

---

[11] Bini-Smaghi and Gros (2001: 6).

Table 2.4 Bini-Smaghi and Gros' accountability index

Ex ante accountability

1. Clear definition of the objective of price stability
2. Announcement of the operational target
3. Announcement of intermediate target
4. Announcement of indicators for assessing monetary policy
5. Explanation of how monetary policy targets affect other policies and objectives

Ex post accountability

6. Publication of data on intermediate target or explanation of possible deviation
7. Publication of inflation forecast and deviation from target
8. Explanation of main policy measures (or absence thereof) and underlying reasons
9. Explanation of how these measures affect other policies
10. Regular (monthly, quarterly, yearly) public reports covering issues 1–8 above
11. Hearings in parliament with Q&A

Accountability procedures

12. Participation of government representative at meeting of the decision-making bodies (as observers)
13. Publication of summary minutes
14. Publication of detailed minutes
15. Publication of the votes of the members of the decision-making bodies

---

Source: Authors' elaboration based on Bini-Smaghi and Gros (2001).

before monetary policy is implemented. The last variable in the first sub-category follows the same logic: when the CB provides an explanation of how the targets of monetary policy affect other policies or objectives, it allows a better ex ante understanding of monetary policy procedures.

With regard to ex post accountability, the variables relate to the communication channels through which the CB publishes information regarding adopted monetary policy. They relate to the publication and explanation of data concerning targets, forecasts, or measures used and how these influence other policies. Ex post accountability includes all that relates to forecasts and outlooks. The publication of forecasts and deviations from the targets allows the stakeholders to formulate forecasts on the CB's future behavior.

The third group of variables refers to the set of operating procedures. These procedures include the publication of the way in which the instruments described in the previous sub-components are used. The procedures, therefore, also encompass all relationships between the government and the CB, such as the presence of government representatives at the meetings of the CB board. The publication of the minutes of board meetings and cast votes falls into this category. While the authors consider the possibility of an overlap between the various variables, they underline the importance of each variable for the accuracy of the assessment.

Stasavage (2003)

Stasavage builds a synthetic index of accountability with the aim of analyzing the linkages between transparency, democratic accountability, and the advantages of the delegation solution. The author relies on two variables. The first scrutinizes the presence in the CB law of a provision that clearly regulates the relationship of the CB with parliament, and requires the CB to report to parliament on monetary policy. The second variable investigates the presence of an override clause that positively influences the level of accountability of the CB.[12,13]

Siklos (2002)

Siklos builds a measure of accountability based on twelve variables (see Table 2.5). He acknowledges that some of them are exposed to critiques since they overlap with the concept of disclosure, but notes that it is not always easy to distinguish between the two concepts. His measure relies heavily on the clear and accurate definition of monetary policy objectives, as well as on the relationship between the delegated and the delegating authority, including a variable that scrutinizes the presence, within the CB law, of well-defined procedures that regulate the possibility of a conflict between the CB and the delegating authority. The appointment procedure for the members of the decision-making body is also analyzed in order to fully understand the relationship between the delegated and the delegating authorities.

---

[12] It is worth mentioning that the literature is not unanimous on the idea of a positive influence of the override clause on the level of accountability of a CB, on the grounds that it is best considered as a component of CB independence rather than accountability.

[13] Stasavage applies his index to a sample of 44 countries, and focuses on the relationship between accountability, transparency, and independence. He observes that 32 countries have a specific requirement for CB officials to testify before a national parliament on a regular basis. With regard to OECD countries, a similar proportion appears: 14 countries have provisions for parliamentary monitoring of CBs. With regard to the ability of the government to override a CB decision, he finds that this is the case for 12 of the 44 countries, including 5 of the 22 OECD CBs.

Table 2.5 Siklos' accountability index

Variables

1. Clarity of objective (de jure)
2. Quantification of objective (de facto)
3. Publication of an economic outlook

    (i)   in the form of explicit forecasts
    (ii) forecasts with assessment of risks
    (iii) general statement only

4. Publication of statement of accountability and ultimate responsibility for monetary policy
5. Conflict resolution procedures (de jure)

    (i)   definition of conflict
    (ii) procedures to resolve conflict
    (iii) clear outcomes in the case of failure to resolve conflict

6. Reporting mechanisms and procedures (dealing with policy)

    (i)   to minister
    (ii) to legislature
    (iii) other (for example, board)

7. Decision-making structure (de jure)

    (i)   by committee (size)
    (ii) CEO only

8. Gives explicit advice to government
9. Clear and detailed explanation of appointment procedures
10. Regular appearances before parliament (de jure/de facto)
11. Is the central bank subject to possible interference in the conduct of monetary policy? (de jure)
12. Who sets the objectives of monetary policy?

    (i)   none/government
    (ii) management
    (iii) set by statute
    (iv) joint CB/government

Source: Authors' elaboration based on Siklos (2002).

Accountability indices: comparison of empirical results

Table 2.6 summarizes the results (absolute and normalized values so as to allow a comparison between the indicators) of three indicators we have surveyed. The main conclusions are as follows:

- Briault, Haldane, and King (1996) find that CBs with relatively low anti-inflationary reputation achieve a good level of accountability, while low inflation countries have the opposite result. This might

Table 2.6 Summary of accountability values

	Briault et al., 1996	de Haan et al., 1998	Siklos 2002	Briault et al., 1996	de Haan et al., 1998	Siklos 2002
	Absolute values			*Normalized values*		
Australia	1,5	7	8,75	0,375	0,5385	0,7292
Austria	–	–	6,75	–	–	0,5625
Belgium	0	3	3,5	0	0,2308	0,2917
Canada	–	7	6	–	0,5385	0,5
Denmark	2,5	4	4,25	0,625	0,3077	0,3542
Finland	–	–	7,58	–	–	0,6317
France	1	6	6,92	0,25	0,4615	0,5767
Germany	0	3	8,83	0	0,2308	0,7358
Ireland	–	–	4,88	–	–	0,4067
Italy	1	4	4,88	0,25	0,3077	0,4067
Japan	1,5	6	9,5	0,375	0,4615	0,7917
New Zealand	3	10	10	0,75	0,7692	0,8333
Netherlands	0,5	5	7,75	0,125	0,3846	0,6458
Norway	–	–	6,67	–	–	0,5558
Portugal	–	–	7,38	–	–	0,615
Spain	2	7	8,67	0,5	0,5835	0,7225
Switzerland	0	2	6,75	0	0,1538	0,5625
Sweden	2	5	7,38	0,5	0,3846	0,615
UK	3,5	11	8,25	0,875	0,8462	0,6875
US	2	6	6,75	0,5	0,4615	0,5625
ECB	–	4	8,5	–	0,3077	0,7083

Source: Briault, Haldane, and King (1996); de Haan, Amtenbrink, and Eijffinger (1998); Siklos (2002), and authors' estimates.

indicate that the presence of an override clause, while increasing accountability, does reduce CB independence and its anti-inflationary stance. In our view this represents a limit of this index, as it creates a trade-off between independence and accountability.

- de Haan, Amtenbrink, and Eijffinger (1998) find low democratic accountability for the ECB, while the CBs in the United Kingdom and New Zealand get the highest scores. The high scores for the latter compared to the low score for the ECB might derive from the inclusion in the index of transparency variables that account for three out of thirteen variables.

- Siklos finds that New Zealand has the most accountable CB, immediately followed by Japan. The ECB gets a relatively high score, but lower than Austria's and Germany's. The US Fed, in contrast, gets a rather low accountability score.

- For all indices the best performer is New Zealand, which has been an early reformer in the direction of increased transparency and accountability. From the second position onward, the indices show significant discrepancies.

3
Survey of Models and Indicators of Transparency

Introduction

The importance of monetary policy transparency is now largely taken for granted – a far cry from Alan Greenspan's reported remark after his appointment as Chairman of the Federal Reserve Board in 1988: "I guess I should warn you, if I turn out to be particularly clear, you have probably misunderstood what I said." CBs around the world now wrestle with how to achieve better, rather than just more, transparency. This chapter investigates the long path followed by CBs, practitioners, and academics away from a position of opaque talk, towards transparency in monetary policy. The broad consensus that transparency is an integral part of a sound governance framework for CBs reflects the understanding that the success of monetary policy also depends on how the CB communicates its objectives, adopted measures, and achieved results to the public. Accurate and frequent communication is expected to enhance CBs' credibility and the confidence of the private sector over time. Hence, transparency is a necessary complement to independence.

The increased importance attached to transparency in the monetary policy process is reflected in the fact that nowadays most CBs have an external website and a commitment to external disclosure. More and more often, CBs release a large amount of information to their stakeholders whether it is required or done spontaneously. The advent of the internet has allowed the release of huge amounts of information at near-zero marginal cost to a global audience. Additionally, the IMF's *Code of Good Transparency Practices in Monetary and Financial Policies* has played a key role in promoting transparency in all areas of financial supervision and regulation, including CBs' activities.

The link between CB independence and the need for CB transparency is very strong: the delegating authority, by losing direct control over monetary policy, will only be able to monitor the functioning of the CB through the information that the latter decides to release. The CB, as we have observed in the case of time inconsistency, can use secrecy to its (short-term) advantage. The presence of mechanisms for the transmission of information and the communication of operating procedures to the public allows the private sector to understand monetary policy and formulate accurate expectations on the way the central bank acts.

Transparency in monetary policy includes the set of communication channels through which the CB provides information about its responsibilities and the ways they are carried out. Communications can include information about the way monetary policy is implemented and future policies, the publication of forecasts, the economic models employed in the decision-making phase, or the minutes of board meetings. However, it would be misleading to evaluate transparency on the basis of the amount of released information alone. The concept of CB transparency encompasses also features such as the accuracy, quality, truthfulness, and relevance of information.

Rationales for transparency

There are a number of reasons why CB transparency is an essential requisite of good central banking. We list a few of them in the following paragraphs.

Boost central bank credibility

When discussing the problem of time inconsistency, we have highlighted how credibility is essential in reducing the inflationary bias. The possibility to communicate externally the adopted decisions, objectives, and forecasts enhances the credibility of the CB. If the objectives and the adopted measures are accurately indicated, the private sector will be able to forecast the results of monetary policy, thus enhancing the credibility of the institution. By building trust through transparency, the CB is able to affect the economy: the private sector will know that, once announced, the CB will not have an incentive to deviate from the target. Credibility affects positively the behavior of the financial sector, and this in turn enhances economic performance.

Influence expectations

The CB can build trust by announcing its targets and communicating policies that are consistent with the achievement of those targets.

Economic agents will therefore believe the announcement and adapt their expectations accordingly. Transparency not only raises the level of credibility but also avoids credibility losses in case of failure. A CB that commits to communicating all adopted decisions, the motivations for preferring a certain measure over another, the economic variables that are taken into account in the decision process, and the economic forecasts, allows economic agents to understand the logic behind CB operations. Being aware of the whole monetary policy decision-making process, the public will continue to trust the CB even in cases of failure to fulfill the objectives. This happens because transparency allows the CB to be evaluated on the basis of its operations and not only on the basis of achieved results. Economic agents can discern whether the failure of the CB originates from a number of unpredictable factors or from incompetence.

Protect central bank independence

An independent CB which is also transparent has a higher chance of maintaining its independence compared with a non-transparent one. Communication allows any economic agent to evaluate adopted decisions and beyond. Transparency can show whether the CB has been subject to any pressure in the formulation of monetary policy. If, owing to a transparent framework, eventual pressures from the government become evident outside, the government will have to abstain from pressurizing the monetary policy-maker, as this would result in a clear negative interference in front of the electorate. It must be noted, however, that there could be other sources of pressure on the CB beyond the government. There are pressure groups that, through persistent requests, could have an impact on policy decisions. To minimize such pressures full transparency in the decision-making and voting mechanisms of the CB helps. If all the motivations and decisions related to a certain policy choice are made public, eventual pressures are more easily identifiable.

Strengthen the understanding of monetary policy

Transparency enhances the understanding of the ways in which the CB carries out monetary policy. The swift publication of the board's decisions allows the private sector to understand the logic of a decision. In normal situations, therefore, the CB can make it known externally how it interprets the signals from the economy. Therefore, economic agents will be able to foresee with a higher degree of accuracy the decisions that the CB will adopt as a reaction. This reduces the time between the reaction of the CB to the shock and the understanding of its action by the private sector, thereby accelerating monetary policy transmission.

Reduce informational asymmetries and uncertainty in financial markets

Greater availability of information means greater knowledge of the structure of the economic system and lower mismatch between public expectations and actual outcomes. Eusepi (2003) studies the impact of CB transparency on its performance and ability to influence economic stability; he notes that: "If market participants have access to some information about central bank actions, this can improve their forecasts and stabilize the economic system. Some degree of transparency and credibility might improve the private sector's learning process, affecting stability under learning."[1] For instance, a transparent CB should supply information explaining the monetary policy choices, and the inflation and output growth forecasts that are used in policy formulation. Under this definition, Eusepi finds that CB transparency has an important role in monetary policy transmission. In a world where monetary policy transmission is delayed, the presence of CB transparency plays a crucial role in the formation of private sector expectations, thereby helping to stabilize the economic system. Lack of transparency causes inability to formulate accurate forecasts on the part of the private sector, and undermines the credibility of the CB.

Also, Eusepi (2005) shows that in the presence of uncertainties concerning the future level of inflation or the CB's monetary policy strategy, a good degree of CB transparency makes optimal targeting robust also in the presence of expectations errors. Lack of transparency, instead, can lead to self-fulfilling expectations destabilizing the economic equilibrium and affecting welfare. The private sector is forced to formulate its own expectations on the basis of a narrow informational set and this brings about instability in the economic system. As a consequence a non-transparent CB can only stabilize private expectations by adopting a sub-optimal monetary policy rule. Hence, transparency is a critical aspect of the process of delegation of monetary policy to an independent institution.

Finally, transparency can reduce uncertainty about the CB's preferences. Eijffinger and Hoeberichts (2000) argue that transparency can clarify to the public the degree of inflation aversion of the CB. Transparency can therefore raise the level of accountability.

---

[1] Eusepi (2003: 2). The author defines transparency as the degree to which market participants can deduce the intentions of the CB.

Enhance market efficiency

If the private sector is confident that in the face of shocks the CB will swiftly publish the new data, it will be able to act accordingly. In the presence of shocks, the public will be able to quickly modify its investment choices thanks to the publications released by the CB. Another important psychological aspect relates to expectations. In the presence of shocks, the public knows that the central bank will behave consistently with previously adopted and communicated measures.

Eliminate government uncertainty on the performance of monetary policy

We have seen that in the delegation process, the government entrusts the responsibility of monetary policy to the CB which becomes responsible and accountable. Transparency is important from this viewpoint as it enables understanding the work of the CB through its communications, allowing the government to verify whether it carries out its tasks correctly. Hence, the government can quickly verify whether the central bank is fulfilling its obligations, being able, if necessary, to intervene in order to limit the risks caused by uncertainty or wrongdoing.

Enhance fiscal and monetary policy coordination

Greater transparency will give the government sufficient information regarding monetary policy conduct so that it can plan ahead its own fiscal operations without operational interference, and make this known to the public. This enhances the effectiveness of monetary and fiscal policy operations, while avoiding operational clashes or overlaps.

The concept of transparency in the literature

de Haan and Amtenbrink (2003) define transparency as the degree of real understanding of the monetary policy and decision-making process by external agents. As we have seen, we can also define the concept of transparency as the absence of informational asymmetry: in the presence of transparency the private sector and the CB will share nearly the same information. However, the concept of transparency, although less controversial than accountability, has various shadings in the literature.

Transparency and accountability

The concept of transparency is sometimes included in the definition of accountability. There is a division between those who consider transparency as a prerequisite of accountability and those who support the opposite idea (i.e., transparency is only a consequence of the accountability process). In our opinion transparency has to be considered separately from (although connected to) accountability. Since the CB should be accountable and must pursue precise objectives, transparency is instrumental to achieve these objectives better and/or faster. The objectives will be more easily met (for instance, via their impact on expectations formation) by communicating to the public which are the targets and which are the actions undertaken to meet them. The effects of transparency go well beyond accountability and impact markets' efficiency. de Haan, Amtenbrink, and Eijffinger (1998) consider transparency to be one of the three fundamental components of a good level of CB accountability because, in their opinion, there would be no accountability without transparency. They define transparency as a prerequisite for accountability, and without transparency it would not be possible to evaluate the performance of the CB. Briault, Haldane, and King (1996) also consider transparency to be a critical part of accountability; the second ("Are the minutes of meetings to decide monetary policy published?") and third variables ("Does the central bank publish an inflation or monetary policy report?") in their index (see Table 2.2) refer to transparency.

The publication of the minutes of board meetings and the presence of inflation and monetary policy reports are part of that set of information that a transparent CB takes care to communicate. The idea is that fast and clear external communication by the CB is an essential prerequisite of accountability. Within this index of accountability half of the variables represent aspects that could be isolated in a separate index of transparency.

Characteristics of transparency

Transparency in monetary policy can be defined as the amount of information that is released by the CB in relation to the monetary policy decision process: "Transparency of monetary policy can be defined as the extent to which central banks disclose information that is related to the policy-making process."[2] However, this definition has the limit of being uni-dimensional, as it only considers the quantity of information released by the CB. We have already pointed out that what matters is not (only) the quantity but the quality of information: "In a world where . . . cognitive limits matter, more information and greater detail does not by

---

[2] Eijffinger and Geraats (2002 [2004: 2]).

itself translate into greater transparency and better understanding, nor does it necessarily lead to more efficient decision-making."[3]

Winkler (2000) proposes a more complete definition of the aspects of CB transparency: "A different view of transparency: clarity, honesty and common understanding."[4] The problem of excess information is quite common in practice and for this reason Winkler introduces the concept of "optimal" quantity of information, i.e., the level at which the benefit of information equals the cost associated with the search for, and analysis and interpretation of this information. The author defines this concept as "informational efficiency." Winkler therefore enriches the definition of transparency by including three aspects of the information transmission process. Beyond informational openness the author takes into account clarity, informational efficiency, and honesty.

- The first characteristic, the degree of informational openness, concerns the amount of information that the CB commits to provide.
- The second characteristic concerns the clarity of information. Information must be clear and allow critical analysis at multiple levels. Before being communicated the information need to be rationalized, as the fundamental requisite is public understanding. Information will have to be grouped, filtered, organized, and finally published; at the same time the CB should avoid communicating information in ambiguous ways, with the consequence of complicating its interpretation.
- The third characteristic centers on the communication process that must be founded on a common language which has to be comprehensible by both parties: the communicating party and the receiving one. The problem is not only with what language is adopted but with the technical jargon, which has to be adapted to the targeted audience.
- The fourth and last characteristic refers to honesty. The information the CB commits to release must be fully reliable and correspond exactly to that circulating internally. This means that there should not be modification or omission which could hamper the interpretation of information. Transparency must be led by the sincere interest in the public's better understanding of the monetary policy process. If we consider a CB that publishes the macroeconomic models it uses, it is essential that those models are exactly the same as those

---

[3] Winkler (2000: 18).
[4] Winkler (2000: 18).

used internally in the decision-making process. Therefore, honesty is considered a key characteristic of transparency.

Waller and de Haan (2004) emphasize the importance of the quality of information as opposed to the quantity of information. They develop an indicator of CB transparency through a sample of seven countries. The results obtained by the authors significantly differ from those obtained by the previous literature, and this discrepancy is explained through the presence of the quality of information.[5]

Aspects of transparency in the policy-making process

Geraats (2000) distinguishes various aspects of CB transparency depending on the phase of the monetary policy process (see also Eijffinger and Geraats 2002 [2004, 2006]). Such a division has the advantage of deepening the concept of transparency depending on its domain. However, the large number of aspects complicates the definition and usage of a quantitative indicator.

Political transparency

Political transparency refers to the degree of openness of the CB regarding its objectives. This requires the presence of explicit and formally expressed objectives, and the presence of a hierarchy among them. The CB must clearly define its objective and, in case of a plurality of objectives, it must assign a clearly defined hierarchical order. Objectives' quantification and conflict resolution among objectives also fall within this aspect of transparency. The definition of objectives, as we have seen, plays an important role also in the analysis of CB accountability: in the presence of a single and clearly defined objective it is easier for the CB to be accountable; the more precise the definition of the CB objective, the more accountable the CB will be. Similarly, the more rigorously defined are its objectives, the more transparent the CB will be.

---

[5] The authors state that: "A possible cause for the low score on perceived transparency may be found in the quality of the information being provided . . . Failure to present public statements and reports on monetary policy issues with appropriate content could undermine the credibility of central banks and result in corresponding behavior by the financial markets, thereby negatively influencing the outcome of monetary policy. The focus of disclosure should be on the materiality and relevance of the information that is being provided to the public. The objective of transparency would for example not be met by the release of reports that offer contradictory assessment" (Waller and de Haan 2004: 20–1).

Economic transparency

Economic transparency concentrates on the information used in the assessment of monetary conditions and includes all the information the CB uses in order to formulate its monetary policy. This comprises all the economic indicators that allow the construction of economic forecasts or the estimation of the impact of a future decision on the economy. This last type of forecast assumes a fundamental role in the presence of a lag between the implementation of monetary policy and its effects on the economy. The publication of internal forecasts allows other economic agents to formulate their own forecasts on the same information set as the CB, and with the same or different hypotheses. The transmission of this information enables understanding of the CB's policy stance and a reduction in the temporal gap between monetary policy announcements, implementation, and effects.

Procedural transparency

Procedural transparency refers to the way in which monetary policy decisions are adopted. The publication of the board meeting minutes and votes falls into this area. This allows a closer evaluation of the decision-making process from a procedural point of view, by enabling the public to observe whether decisions have been taken in compliance with the correct procedure and without external pressures. The publication of the minutes allows the public disclosure of how a consensus is reached amongst the members of the CB executive body. Within this area we also find publications related to the monetary rule(s) and strategy pursued by the CB. The publication of a strategy document has the advantage of placing every adopted measure within a defined strategic framework, thereby allowing the public to evaluate the procedural and economic adequacy of any given action.

Policy transparency

Policy transparency is described as "prompt announcement of policy decisions"[6]; it refers to the immediate and timely announcement of the adopted decisions. The announcement must include an explanation of the decision and an indication on prospective monetary policy actions. This type of communication is important as it allows addressing monetary policy decision as part of a larger strategic plan instead of stand-alone actions.

---

[6] Eijffinger and Geraats (2002 [2004: 3]).

Operational transparency

Operational transparency refers to the implementation of monetary policy actions, and includes the analyses related to the evaluation of past errors and the possible mismatches between achieved and proposed results. It takes also into account all possible causes that may have resulted in a failure, such as macroeconomic changes or the presence of unforeseen shocks that may have impacted the transmission mechanisms. Operational transparency coincides with the widely diffused practice of accounting for policy actions and eventual failures. The link between operational transparency and accountability, and the possibility of formulating a judgement on monetary actions is now apparent. As we will see, the indicator developed by Eijffinger and Geraats tries to address each one of these aspects.

Indicators and measures in the literature

General observations

The measurement of transparency allows an accurate analysis of CB behavior and comparisons with peers and an analysis of the role of transparency in the monetary policy process and its relationship with autonomy and accountability. The construction of an index of transparency involves the selection of a certain number of variables that must be sufficient to define in a satisfactory manner how the CB communicates its action, although at times the choice of one variable over another hides different definitions of transparency (i.e., in certain cases transparency variables are included in indices of accountability). Additionally, one needs to define an appropriate weighting scheme for the variables. All these aspects inevitably involve a degree of subjective judgement.

Transparency based on the amount of information released is one aspect of the concept best susceptible to quantification. Obviously, the existence and the number of parliamentary auditions are more easily quantified than, for example, the clarity and quality of released information. Therefore, the quantity of released reports, their periodicity, and the adopted instruments will have to be measured. However, in as much as this uni-dimensional definition of transparency falls short of a complete description of transparency, it is important to analyze the instruments and the communication channels.

CBs have several communication instruments, with differing degrees of importance. There are various media through which information can be released as well as various languages with which the CB can communicate its actions to the rest of the world. One first consideration deserves some attention: the internet has become the primary channel through which a CB can publicize its action internationally. Therefore it is fundamental that this information is internationally intelligible; this means that beyond the national language, information should always be provided in one internationally known language, possibly used by practitioners and the public alike.

The information can also be classified on the basis of its domain or periodicity. It is important to strike the right balance and find the right hierarchy for information on different aspects of CB communications. As anticipated, periodicity has a significant weight. The time frequency (daily, weekly, monthly, quarterly, or annual communications) with which the information is released is very important. Each particular type of information should be associated with a specific periodicity, depending on its particular characteristics. Obviously, a daily report on the conduct of monetary policy would be inappropriate, as would a single annual publication of the minutes of board meetings. Each topic must have an appropriate release schedule in order to contribute to CB transparency, where "appropriate" often depends on the usual practices and code of behavior in the field.

Siklos (2002)

As in the case of the accountability indicator, Siklos proposes a measure of transparency which includes eleven variables (Table 3.1) concerning the supply of information; variables that evaluate the understanding of monetary policy; variables related to procedural transparency; and also variables that hardly relate to the concept of transparency and would better fit in an index of CB autonomy or responsibility. Variable 8 (special recognition of the role of financial system stability), for example, impacts CB responsibility: in the case of a positive answer, the CB will also be entrusted with financial system stability supervision. As we have seen, Siklos has worked out an index of accountability as well as the index of transparency considered here. According to Siklos, transparency is strongly linked to accountability for two reasons: (i) transparency is necessary to make the CB accountable, as it provides the essential means to evaluate CBs performance; and (ii) transparency pinpoints the limits of accountability by highlighting the presence of interferences.

Eijffinger and Geraats (2004)

As we have seen, Geraats (2000) distinguishes five different features of CB transparency and Eijffinger and Geraats (2002 [2004]) build a

Table 3.1   Siklos' transparency index

Variables

---

1. Publication of minutes of central bank meetings
2. Key assumptions in generating outlook
3. Publication of committee voting record
4. Regular information published about how monetary policy decisions are made and their justification
5. Operational instrument of monetary policy
   (i)   single
   (ii) multiple
6. Instrument independence?
7. Are monetary policy and operational objectives the same?
8. Special recognition of the role of financial system stability (de jure)
9. Economic modeling procedures:
   (i)   publicly available
   (ii) described or discussed but complete details not provided
   (iii) no information provided
10. Forms of communication (public or private)
    (i)   statements or reports on inflation/monetary policy
    (ii) reports, bulletin on activities
    (iii) regular speeches
    (iv) economic research
    (v)   annual report/retrospective analysis
11. Publication of a monetary policy strategy and/or limits of monetary policy

---

Source: Authors' elaboration based on Siklos (2002).

five-category index. Each category is characterized by three questions, each assigned a maximum score of 1 (Table 3.2).

The methodology used to obtain scores on single variables combines an independent analysis of available information with a direct feedback by the CB. As a first step, the information published by the CB and the other available resources is analyzed. Then, the resulting score and the description of the methodology are sent to the CB for cross-checking of the data and eventual potential revision of the score. Subsequently CBs' answers are considered to finalize the estimation of the assigned scores.

Stasavage (2003)

The publication of economic forecasts represents for Stasavage a good indicator of CB transparency. At a first glance, however, the author finds that almost all CBs in the sample (i.e., 36 out of 44) do publish some sort of economic forecast. Therefore the presence of a published forecast must be qualified at a deeper level. To do this, the author constructs

Table 3.2   Eijffinger and Geraats' transparency index

Variables and areas

Political transparency
(a) Is there a formal statement of the objective(s) of monetary policy, with an explicit prioritization in case of multiple objectives?
(b) Is there a quantification of the primary objective(s)?
(c) Are there explicit institutional arrangements or contracts between the monetary authorities and the government?

Economic transparency
(a) Are the basic economic data relevant for the conduct of monetary policy publicly available?
(b) Does the CB disclose the formal macroeconomic model(s) it uses for policy analysis?
(c) Does the CB regularly publish its own macroeconomic forecasts?

Procedural transparency
(a) Does the CB provide an explicit policy rule or strategy that describes its monetary policy framework?
(b) Does the CB give a comprehensive account of policy deliberations (or explanations in case of a single central banker) within a reasonable amount of time?
(c) Does the CB disclose how decisions on the level of its main operating instrument/target were reached?

Policy transparency
(a) Are decisions about adjustments to the main operating instrument or target promptly announced?
(b) Does the CB provide an explanation when it announces policy decisions?
(c) Does the CB disclose an explicit policy inclination after every policy meeting or an explicit indication of likely future policy actions (at least quarterly)?

Operational transparency
(a) Does the CB regularly evaluate to what extent its main policy operating targets (if any) have been achieved?
(b) Does the CB regularly provide information on (unanticipated) macroeconomic disturbances that affect the policy transmission process?
(c) Does the CB regularly provide an evaluation of the policy outcome in light of its macroeconomic objectives?

Source: Authors' elaboration based on Eijffinger and Geraats (2002 [2004]).

an index composed of four variables (Tables 3.3 and 3.4), which are all centered on the publication of an economic forecast: the first two allow isolating the CBs that do not publish any forecast from those that limit the forecast to a synthetic announcement, say, on future inflation. Variables 3 and 4 allow assessing whether the CB engages in more articulated

Table 3.3   Stasavage's transparency index

Questions (variables)

1. What is the form of publication of forecasts? Is it in words only, or is it presented in terms of numbers?
2. Does the central bank publish forward-looking analysis in standard bulletins on at least an annual basis?
3. Are risks to the forecast published, and if so in what form?
4. Is there a discussion of past forecast errors, and if so is this a standard feature of discussion?

Source: Authors' elaboration based on Stasavage (2003).

Table 3.4   Stasavage's transparency scores

OECD countries		Other countries	
France, Austria, Denmark, Greece	0	Poland, Cyprus, Hungary, Bahamas	0
	1	Egypt, Hong Kong	1
Germany, Belgium, Finland, Spain	2	Fiji, Thailand, Korea, Malaysia, Barbados, Israel, Sri Lanka, Malta	2
Japan, Australia	3	Mexico, China, Ecuador, South Africa	3
Switzerland, Italy, Sweden, Norway, USA, Ireland, Netherlands, Portugal, UK, New Zealand, Canada	4	Singapore, Chile, Czech Rep., Slovakia	4

Source: Authors' elaboration based on Stasavage (2003).

forecasts. If a discussion on past forecast errors (be it standardized or not) is provided, the CB is even more positively evaluated.

de Haan and Amtenbrink (2003)

The authors build an indicator that centers upon the information supplied and the activities undertaken by the CB, and formulate fourteen questions, divided into three groups including (i) clarity, prioritization, definition, quantification, and scheduling of objectives; (ii) strategy in announcing interest rates decisions and inflation forecasts; and (iii) strategy of communication (Table 3.5). For the authors, transparency turns out to be a strategic activity through which the CB enhances the public's ability to understand policy decisions.

Table 3.5   de Haan and Amtenbrink's index of transparency

Variables and areas

Objectives
  1. Clear objectives
  2. Clear priorities
  3. Clear definition
  4. Clear time horizon
  5. Quantification

Strategy
  6. Announcement of strategy
  7. Interest rate decision immediately announced and always explained
  8. Inflation forecast

Communication strategy
  9. Parliamentary hearings
 10. Frequency of reports
 11. Meeting schedule
 12. Press conferences/press releases
 13. Publication of minutes
 14. Publication of individual votes

Source: de Haan and Amtenbrink (2003).

The score attached to each variable is different, with more and less important weights depending on the importance assigned to each of them. Beyond that, positive answers can have different scores depending on the degree of quality of the released information.

Comparison between measures

Table 3.6 summarizes the comparative results for the three indicators we have surveyed. The main conclusions are as follows:

- Siklos (2002) reports the highest transparency by the CB in the United Kingdom, followed by the United States. New Zealand and Canada are third in the rank with a high transparency score. Noteworthy is the low score for the ECB.
- de Haan and Amtenbrink (2003) obtain results that are slightly different from Siklos' results, especially for the ECB. The latter has a high score, significantly higher than the US Fed and the Bundesbank. The Bank of England is the most transparent. However, if all questions had the same weight, the ECB would be the most accountable CB.

Table 3.6　Summary of transparency values

	Siklos (2002)	de Haan and Amtenbrink (2003)	Eijffinger and Geraats (2002 [2004])
Australia	6.5	–	8
Austria	2.7	–	–
Belgium	0.5	–	–
Canada	9.5	16	10.5
Denmark	2.5	–	–
Finland	5.5	–	–
France	2.5	–	–
Germany	8	10	–
Ireland	4.7	–	–
Italy	5	–	–
Japan	8.5	–	8
New Zealand	9.5	16	13.5
Netherlands	7.5	–	–
Norway	6	–	–
Portugal	4.5	–	–
Spain	7	–	–
Switzerland	7.5	–	7.5
Sweden	10	–	12
UK	10.5	17	12.5
US	10	11	10
ECB	6	15	10

Source: Authors' elaboration based on Siklos (2002); de Haan and Amtenbrink (2003); Eijffinger and Geraats (2004).

- Eijffinger and Geraats (2002 [2004]) obtain maximum scores for New Zealand, the United Kingdom, and Sweden, followed by Canada, the ECB, and the US Fed. Countries with an inflation targeting regime have high transparency scores.

Conclusions

Our survey of the literature shows that a consensus on how to measure CB transparency has not yet been reached among academics and practitioners, although in the last decade progress has been made in this direction. In particular, different measures have been proposed in the literature on the basis of the various definitions which have been favored. Noteworthy is the fact that some indices of transparency regard it as a component of CB accountability. In addition, these indicators have been applied only to small samples of CBs; this does not allow the assessment of their suitability for different groups of CBs. Finally, these indices have almost always been applied to advanced economies. In conclusion, the literature has yet to reach a consensus regarding the separation between accountability and transparency, and additional empirical research has to be done, considering the still limited empirical applications to non-advanced economies; this will be examined in the following chapters.

4
Indicators of Independence, Accountability, and Transparency

None of the studies on CB independence, accountability, and transparency that are surveyed in Chapters 1 to 3 has attempted to analyze worldwide trends. In an effort to fill this gap, and drawing on the advances we have described, we propose indicators of CB independence, accountability, and transparency, which we will apply to a sample of CBs in countries at different stages of economic development (advanced economies, emerging market economies, and developing countries) and from all geographic areas. In this chapter we define the indicators of CB independence, accountability, and transparency that are used in Chapters 5 to 7, by drawing on the literature discussed earlier.

Methodology for assessing central bank independence

General considerations

Our assessment of CB independence draws on the methodologies developed by GMT (1991) and the methodology used by Cukierman (1992), as described in Chapter 1, which we briefly recall here. Both methodologies focus on an analysis of de jure CB independence. GMT (1991) surveys CB legislation with a view to building two additive measures of CB independence, one focusing on political features, the other focusing on economic and financial features. Cukierman (1992) looks at the provisions in CB legislation with regard to the CB's chief executive officer; policy formulation by the CB and its objectives; and the limitations on CB lending to the government.

The GMT (1991) index

By defining *political independence* as the ability to select the final objectives of monetary policy, GMT (1991) assigns to the CBs one point for

Table 4.1 Detailed GMT independence index

Independence index		Value
Political independence		**8**
Procedures regarding the appointment of the central bank governor and board		
(1) Central bank governor not appointed by the government	Yes	1
(2) Central bank governor appointed for more than five years	Yes	1
(3) Central bank board not appointed by the government	Yes	1
(4) Central bank board appointed for more than five years	Yes	1
Relations between the central bank and the government		
(5) Government representatives not required to participate in the board	Yes	1
(6) Government approval not required for formulation of monetary policy	Yes	1
Formal responsibility of the central bank in monetary policy formulation		
(7) Price stability is one of the primary objectives of monetary policy	Yes	1
(8) Legal provisions strengthen central bank position if conflict with government	Yes	1
Economic independence		**8**
Conditions for granting direct central bank credit to the government		
(1) Direct credit is not automatic	Yes	1
(2) Direct credit bears market rates	Yes	1
(3) Direct credit is temporary	Yes	1
(4) Direct credit is subject to quantitative limits	Yes	1
(5) Central bank does not participate in primary market of government securities	Yes	1
Level of central bank's control over its monetary instruments		
(6) Central bank's policy rate is set autonomously by the central bank	Yes	1
(7) Banking supervision:		
– not assigned to the central bank	Yes	2
– shared with another agency	Yes	1
Total independence		**16**

Source: Authors' elaboration based on GMT (1991).

each of the eight satisfied criteria, as shown in Table 4.1. The assessment focuses on three main areas: (i) the appointment procedure and tenure of the CB board; (ii) the functional relationships that link the CB to the government; and (iii) the CB's formal responsibility in the conduct of monetary policy. The first of the three areas aims at verifying whether the law provides for autonomous procedures in the appointment of the CB's decision-making bodies, and whether such bodies enjoy fairly long terms of office. The second area measures the level of institutional independence of the CB's decision-making body as well as its autonomy in monetary policy formulation. Finally, the third area verifies the adherence of the CB's formal mission to the objective of monetary stability and the absence of an outright override power of the government.

The second sub-index of *economic independence* aims at measuring the CB's independence in the selection of instruments. It focuses on the following areas: (i) the degree of availability of CB credit to the government; and (ii) the nature of monetary instruments over which monetary authorities have full control. The first area evaluates whether CB credit to the executive branch is subject to appropriate limitations in quantity and terms, in order to restrain government influence on short-term base money creation. The second area evaluates whether the CB has direct control over the policy rate and has limited responsibility in banking supervision.

The Cukierman (1992) index

As discussed in Chapter 1, among reviewed legal indicators, the measure by Cukierman (1992) is one of the most comprehensive, and the one based on the broadest sampling. It is made up of sixteen variables, many of which are equivalent to those analyzed by GMT (1991), grouped in four main areas:

- The *chief executive officer* area contains proxies for (i) the length of the term of office of the governor, (ii) the entity delegated to appoint him/her, (iii) the provisions for his/her dismissal, and (iv) his/her ability to hold another office;
- The *policy formulation* area contains proxies for (v) the entity responsible for formulating monetary policy, (vi) the rules concerning the resolution of conflicts between the CB and the government, and (vii) the degree of the bank's participation in formulating the government budget;
- The *objectives of the central bank* area includes proxies for (viii) the provisions of charters regarding primary monetary objectives and the relative role of monetary stability;
- The final *lending limitations* area contains proxies for (ix) advances and (x) securitized lending, (xi) the authority that has control over the conditions of lending, (xii) the width of the circle of potential borrowers from the CB, (xiii) the types of limitations on loans, where limits exist, (xiv) the maturity of possible loans, (xv) the limitations on interest rates applicable to these loans, and (xvi) prohibitions on CB participation in the primary market for government securities.

Table 4.2 Matrix of central bank samples and indexes

Sample (no. of central banks)	Full index	Narrow index
All central banks (163)	• End 2003	–
GMT sample (18)	• End 1980s	
	• End 1980s–end 2003 evolution	–
Cukierman sample (50)	–	• End 1980s
		• End 2003
		• End 1980s–end 2003 evolution

Assessment procedure and sampling

Our assessment of CB independence at the end of the 1980s is based on the original GMT index for the eighteen OECD CBs analyzed in GMT (1991), hereafter referred to as the *full index*; and the Cukierman (1992) data converted into the GMT index for fifty additional CBs assessed in that paper, hereafter referred to as the *narrow index*. Assessments of the evolution of CB independence over time (from end-1980s to end-2003) for these two samples are also based on the *full* and *narrow* indices, respectively, with a view to ensuring maximum comparability. Finally, our assessment of CB independence at the end of 2003 for the full sample of 163 CBs relies on the *full index*. The matrix presented in Table 4.2 summarizes the different samples and indexes that are used in this exercise. To ensure comparability we standardize results by dividing the absolute values by the maximum potential score. Due to the method we use to transpose Cukierman's data into the *narrow index*, some qualification is warranted regarding our assessment of independence evolution over time. The narrow index is a sub-set of eleven variables, with ten of those in Cukierman matching the same sub-set of ten variables contained in the *full index*, and the eleventh one from Cukierman substituting one in GMT (Table 4.3).

Methodology for assessing central bank accountability and transparency[1]

In Chapters 2 and 3, we presented several indicators of accountability and transparency from the existing literature, which all have inherent merits and limitations. While Siklos' indices can be considered as the

---

[1] Alberto Brovida contributed to this section.

Table 4.3 Cukierman versus GMT conversion table

GMT (1991) variable	Cukierman (1992) variable	Definition	Cukierman's score (1992)	Conversion to GMT scale
Political indicator				
(1) Governor not appointed by government	*App*: Who appoints the CEO?	CEO appointed by CB board	1	1
		CEO appointed by a board composed of members of executive branch, parliament, and the CB board	0.75	1
		CEO appointed by legislative branch	0.5	1
		CEO appointed by executive branch	0.25	0
		CEO appointed by one or two members of executive branch	0	0
(2) Governor appointed for more than 5 years	*Too*: Term of office of CEO in years	Greater than or equal to 8	1	1
		Between 8 and 6	0.75	1
		Equal to 5	0.5	0
		Equal to 4	0.25	0
		Less than 4	0	0
(5) No mandatory involvement of government in board	*Off*: Is CEO allowed to hold another office	CEO prohibited by law from holding other office in government	1	1
		CEO not allowed to hold any other office in government unless authorized by executive branch	0.5	0
		Law does not prohibit CEO from holding another office	0	0
(6) Government approval not required in formulating monetary policy	*Monpol*: Who formulates monetary policy?	CB alone has this authority to formulate monetary policy	1	1
		CB participates in formulation of monetary policy together with government	0.66	0
		CB participates in formulation of monetary policy in an advisory capacity	0.33	0
		Government alone formulates monetary policy	0	0

(7) Central bank is required to pursue monetary stability as one of its primary objectives	Obj: Objectives of CB	Price stability mentioned as the only or major goal, and in case of conflict with government CB has final authority to pursue policies aimed at achieving this goal	1	1
		Price stability mentioned as the only goal	0.8	1
		Price stability mentioned along with other objectives that do not seem to conflict with price stability	0.6	1
		Price stability mentioned with a number of potentially conflicting goals	0.4	1
		CB charter contains any objectives for CB	0.2	0
		Some goals appear in charter but price stability not one of them	0	0
(8) Legal protections exist to strengthen the central bank's position in event of conflict with the government	Conf: Government directives and resolution of conflict	CB has final authority over issues clearly defined in the law as CB objectives	1	1
		Government has final authority only over policy issues that have not been clearly defined as CB goals or in case of conflict with CB	0.8	1
		In case of conflict final decision up to a council whose members are from CB, legislative branch, and executive branch	0.6	1
		Legislative branch has final authority in policy issues	0.4	1
		Executive branch has final authority in policy matters, but subject to due process and possible protest by CB	0.2	0
		Executive branch has unconditional authority over policy	0	0

Excluded variables

Excluded variables

(3) Board not appointed by government

(4) Board is appointed for more than five years

(Continued)

Table 4.3 Continued

GMT (1991) variable	Cukierman (1992) variable	Definition	Cukierman's score (1992)	Conversion to GMT scale
	Diss: Provisions for dismissal of CEO *Adv*: Is CB given an active role in formulation of government's budget?			
Economic indicator				
(1) Direct credit is not automatically extended to the government	*Lla*: Limitations on advances	Advances to government prohibited	1	1
		Advances permitted but subject to limits in terms of absolute cash amounts or to other types of relatively strict limits (e.g., up to 15% of government revenues)	0.66	1
	Lls: Limitations on guaranteed loans to the government	Advances subject to relatively accommodative limits (e.g., advances can exceed 15% of government revenues or are specified as fractions of government expenditures)	0.33	1
		No legal limits on advances; their quantity subject to periodic negotiations between government and CB	0	0
		Specification of levels identical to those for advances		
(2) Direct credit provided at market interest rates	*Lint*: Limitations on interest rates	Interest rate on CB loans must be at market rate	1	1
		Interest rate on CB loans cannot be lower than a certain floor	0.75	0
		Interest rate on CB loans cannot exceed a certain ceiling	0.5	0
		No explicit legal provisions regarding interest rate on CB loans	0.25	0
		Law stipulates no interest rate charge on government's borrowing from the CB	0	0

is explicitly temporary	loans	...on months	1	1
		Maturity of CB loans limited to a maximum of one month	0.66	1
		Maturity of CB loans may go above one year	0.33	1
		No legal upper bounds on the maturity of CB loans	0	0
(4) Direct credit subject to limitations on amount	Ltype: Types of limit when such limit exists	Limit specified as absolute cash amount	1	1
		Limit specified as percentage of CB capital of other liabilities	0.75	1
		Limit specified as percentage of government revenues	0.5	1
		Limit specified as percentage of government expenditure	0.25	1
		No limit (NA)[1]	0	0
(5) CB does not participate in primary market for government securities	Lprm: Prohibitions on lending in primary market	CB prohibited from buying government securities in primary market.	1	1
		CB not prohibited from buying government securities in primary market	0	0

Excluded variables

(6) CB sets discount rate autonomously

(7) Banking supervision is not the responsibility of central bank, or is not responsibility of CB alone

Excluded variables

Ldec: Who decides control of term of lending?

Lwidth: How wide is the circle of potential borrowers from CB?

[1] This last definition is not present in the original Cukierman (1992) index; it is added to account for the case of absence of formally explicit quantitative limits on CB loans.

Source: Authors' elaborations based on GMT (1991) and Cukierman (1992).

synthesis of the literature, the definition and scope of some of the criteria that are used lack clarity. In this section we build two new indicators in an attempt to correct these imperfections. For that, we define "modules," that is key aspects of transparency and accountability; then we identify several criteria under each module.

General considerations

In our work we attempt to avoid the overlap between accountability and transparency, while relying on the main inputs from the earlier literature. We rely in particular on Siklos (2002) as a starting point in view of the following factors: (i) Siklos' work is based on measures of transparency and accountability encompassing the fundamental milestones of previous works on the topics; (ii) the indices are recent; (iii) Siklos is one of the few authors that have jointly developed two indices, therefore considering the interrelations between accountability and transparency, and avoiding a confusion found in some research between transparency and accountability (i.e., de Haan, Amtenbrink, and Eijffinger 1998); and (iv) the measures by Siklos are detailed and take into account a high number of characteristics, allowing us to eliminate some of them without diminishing too much the explanatory power of the original measures.[2] Tables 4.4 and 4.5 summarize our assessment of Siklos' criteria and their classification according to our own modules; the following paragraphs elaborate on our definition of CB accountability and transparency.

Accountability index

One fundamental aspect of CB accountability that we consider has to do with the basic assumption whereby a CB cannot be considered accountable if it is not responsible for its actions. Therefore, responsibility is a foundation of accountability. Moreover, accountability can be analyzed from two different points of view: accountability *for* the duties entrusted to the CB by the delegating authority (government or parliament), and accountability *towards* the delegating authority itself. The first instance is defined as accountability with respect to the objectives, the second as ex post accountability. Thereafter, CB accountability is quantified through ten criteria, expressed in the form of questions that in turn are grouped

---

[2] The reduction in the number of variables is motivated by the fact that some variables do not seem consistent with the concepts they describe, or due to lack of information in a number of developing countries.

Table 4.4 Siklos' accountability index: observations and reclassification

Siklos' criteria	Observations	Reclassification
1. Clarity of objective (de jure)	Change in formulation ("Clarity on final objective of de jure objective of monetary policy") We answer the question with three alternatives (i) Multiple objectives without prioritization (ii) Clear prioritization of multiple objectives (iii) Single and clearly defined objective	Accountability on objectives
2. Quantification of objective	No changes	Accountability on objectives
3. Publication of an economic outlook: (i) in the form of explicit forecasts (ii) forecasts with risk assessment (iii) general statement only	No changes	Accountability on objectives
4. Publication of statement of accountability and ultimate responsibility for monetary policy	Not retained because of lack of clarity	
5. Conflict resolution procedures: (i) definition of conflict (ii) procedures to resolve conflict (iii) clear outcomes in the case of failure to resolve conflict	No changes	Ex post accountability
6. Reporting mechanisms and procedures dealing with policy): to minister; to legislature; other (e.g., board)	No changes	Ex post accountability
7. Decision-making structure: by committee (size); CEO only	No changes	Governance responsibility
8. Gives explicit advice to government	Not retained because of lack of clarity	
9. Clear and detailed explanation of appointment procedures	No changes	Responsibility of governance
10. Regular appearances before parliament (de jure/de facto)	No changes	Ex post accountability
11. Is the CB subject to possible interference in the conduct of monetary policy? (de jure)	No changes	Responsibility
12. Who sets the objectives of monetary policy: none/govt.; management; set by statute; joint CB/govt.	Substituted with a similar question with a different underlying economic logic	Responsibility

Source: Authors' elaboration from Siklos (2002).

Table 4.5 Siklos' transparency index: observations and reclassification

Siklos's criteria	Observations	Reclassification
1. Publication of minutes of central bank meetings	No changes	Procedural transparency
2. Key assumptions in generating outlook	No changes	Economic transparency
3. Publication of committee voting record	No changes	Procedural transparency
4. Regular information published about how monetary policy decisions are made and their justification	No changes	Operational transparency
5. Operational monetary policy instrument: (i) single; (ii) multiple	Not retained because of lack of clarity (the connection between this characteristic and transparency is not clear)	
6. Instrument independence?	Not retained because of lack of clarity (instrument independence more appropriate in an independence index)	
7. Are monetary policy and operational objectives the same?	Not retained because of lack of clarity	
8. Special recognition of the role of financial system stability (de jure)	Not retained because it is more appropriate in an independence index	
9. Economic modeling procedures: (i) publicly available (ii) described or discussed but complete details not provided (iii) no information provided	No changes	Economic transparency
10. Forms of communication (public/private): (i) statements or reports on inflation/monetary policy (ii) reports, bulletin on activities (iii) regular speeches (iv) economic research (v) annual report/retrospective analysis	No changes	Operational transparency
11. Publication of a monetary policy strategy and/or limits of monetary policy	No changes	Economic transparency

Source: Authors' elaboration from Siklos (2002).

under four main modules: (i) responsibility; (ii) accountability on objectives; (iii) ex post accountability; and (iv) governance responsibility.

The first module (responsibility) assesses whether the CB has the exclusive task of monetary policy-making and is the only responsible agency. This depends upon the existing relationships between the CB and other institutional subjects, such as the government or the legislature. The interference of the delegating institution in the conduct of monetary policy, be it formal or de facto, reduces the autonomy of the CB and therefore its responsibility. Therefore, as an entity cannot be held accountable for a duty which is entrusted to another, responsibility emerges as a fundamental prerequisite for a CB to be accountable.

The second module (accountability with respect to objectives) signals the presence (or absence) of clearly defined objectives that the CB has to pursue and meet. The objectives of monetary policy, therefore, become the benchmarks against which the performance of the CB must be evaluated. All features that enhance the clarity and accuracy of objectives, such as the hierarchical ranking of the different objectives or their quantification, raise the level of accountability of the delegated institution with respect to these objectives.

The third module (ex post accountability) captures the strength of reporting procedure to parliament and/or government. In the absence of such reporting procedures no type of democratic accountability is in place. This is why the presence of procedures granting ex post accountability is essential for a CB to be accountable.

The fourth module (governance responsibility) gives indications about the CB functioning mechanisms in carrying out monetary policy. The concept of responsibility considered here differs from the one related to the first category, and is synonymous with behavioral soundness. This category concerns both the collegiality of the decision-making process and the appointment and dismissal procedures at the CB.

Transparency index

As pointed out earlier, transparency represents the CB's ability to reduce informational asymmetry to the advantage of the private sector. This means the ability to make the adopted monetary policy clear and understandable to the general public. To communicate and be fully transparent the CB should have a set of established procedures and publish an extensive range of documents. We measure transparency through nine criteria grouped under three modules as follows: (i) operational transparency; (ii) economic transparency; and (iii) procedural transparency.

Operational transparency concerns the instruments used and the procedures followed by the CB to disclose and publicize the decisions and initiatives adopted. In this category we will find a set of criteria concerning the publications designed to reduce the level of informational asymmetry among the general public, that is the specific publications focusing on inflation and monetary policy, and those more generally oriented to economic research. All these publications should ultimately serve to publicize strictly operational aspects of monetary policy, namely those connected to its implementation.[3]

Economic transparency concerns all publications disclosing the macroeconomic rationale that shapes monetary policy. In this category we will find the publication of economic models, specific outlooks and long-term strategies adopted and pursued by the CB.

Procedural transparency refers to the disclosure of information concerning the decision-making process at the board level. In this subcategory we will find two variables, the first concerning the publication of the board's meeting minutes, the second relating to the publication of the votes cast by every board member on each decision.

Detailed index of accountability

Table 4.6 summarizes the components of our index of accountability. Each variable has a potential maximum score of 1; in the case of multiple choice questions, a different value is assigned to the answers based on our evaluation of their contribution to accountability.

Responsibility

The first question has to do with the responsibility for setting and announcing the intermediate objectives of monetary policy. The more autonomous the CB in setting its intermediate objectives, the more the CB will be accountable for the related outcome. The variable has four possible answers, according to the degree to which the CB is responsible.

The CB acts in the interest of the community by pursuing a single or a plurality of final monetary policy objectives, which are normally established by law. The CB is directly responsible for achieving such a set of objectives, but interference that reduces its operational autonomy will reduce its degree of responsibility. As intermediate objectives are instrumental to the fulfillment of the final objectives, to be held accountable

---

[3] Operational transparency is the feature most affected by a country's level of income and development.

Table 4.6 Detailed accountability index

Modules	Value		Max. score
Responsibility			2
(1) Who sets the objectives of monetary policy?			1
(i) Central bank	Yes	1	
(ii) Central bank and government jointly	Yes	0.66	
(iii) Set by statute	Yes	0.33	
(iv) None/government	Yes	0	
(2) Is the central bank subject to possible interference?	No/Yes	1/0	1
Accountability on objectives			3
(3) Clarity on final objective of monetary policy (de jure)			1
(i) Single and clearly defined objective	Yes	1	
(ii) Clear prioritization of multiple objectives	Yes	0.5	
(iii) Multiple objectives without prioritization	Yes	0	
(4) Quantification of objective (de facto)	Yes/No	1/0	1
(5) Publication of an economic outlook			1
(i) In the form of explicit forecasts	Yes	1	
(ii) Forecasts with assessment of risks	Yes	0.66	
(iii) General statement only	Yes	0.33	
(iv) No economic outlook	Yes	0	
Ex post accountability			3
(6) Reporting mechanisms and procedures (dealing with policy)			1
(i) To minister	Yes	0.33	
(ii) To legislature	Yes	0.33	
(iii) Other (for example, board)	Yes	0.33	
(7) Regular appearances before parliament (de jure – de facto)	Yes/No	1/0	1
(8) Conflict resolution procedures (de jure)			1
(i) Definition of conflict	Yes	0.33	
(ii) Procedures to resolve conflict	Yes	0.33	
(iii) Clear outcomes in the case of failure to resolve conflict	Yes	0.33	
Governance responsibility			2
(9) Decision-making structure (de jure)			1
(i) By committee	Yes	1	
(ii) CEO only	Yes	0.5	
(10) Clear and detailed explanation of appointment procedures			1

Source: Authors' elaborations.

on the latter the CB needs to have the power to set the former. There-fore, only a CB that sets its intermediate objectives autonomously can be considered responsible (hence accountable) for monetary policy.

We have seen that the literature has not reached a consensus when it comes to identifying the link between accountability and independence; the relationship depends upon the definition of accountability that is used and some authors even identify a trade-off between accountability and independence. In our measure of accountability, an increase in the CB's ability to define its objectives raises its level of responsibility in monetary policy conduct.

Let us analyze the four possible answers to the question of who bears responsibility for the intermediate objectives of monetary policy:

- **The CB.** Consistent with our rationale above, we attribute the max-imum score when the CB autonomously determines its intermediate objectives.
- **The CB and the government jointly.** Quite often the CB determines its operating objectives jointly with the minister of finance, as a repre-sentative of the government. From a theoretical perspective this could be justified by the tight link existing between monetary and fiscal policy. Therefore, the possibility of a joint decision could result in higher efficiency. This positive aspect, however, does not resolve a fundamental issue: if the decision is adopted or the announcement is made jointly by the government and the CB, the responsibility can-not be univocally assigned. It follows that the assigned score is lower compared to the preceding case.
- **Set in the CB's law.** In this case, the formal responsibility for the determination of the objectives falls on the legislator. This, however, does not exclude the possibility of the CB acting as a consultant in the determination of the objectives. Therefore, we assign a positive, albeit low, value.
- **None or the government.** A null score is assigned when it is not possible to determine the existence of intermediate objectives or to understand who has responsibility for setting them. The score would also be zero when the operating objective is imposed upon the CB by the government.

The second question focuses on the possibility, from the legal point of view, for an institution other than the central bank to interfere in the formulation of monetary policy. Any interference would inevitably reduce the responsi-bility of the CB in the process of formulation of monetary policy. Clearly, the concept of interference is quite wide, and we have already signaled the tight link between independence and the variables proxying responsibility, and the corollary that only a fully independent CB can be held (fully) responsible for its actions. This variable explicitly focuses on the interference that can reduce the level of independence of the CB and in turn reduce its accountability.

From the theoretical definition of responsibility it follows that an institution is fully responsible for its actions only if it is autonomous in its implementation. Consequently, for the category of responsibility, we label as interference all external pressure in the formulation of monetary policy.[4] The answer to the second question is positive, and the score null, when (i) a member or a directly nominated representative of the government with voting right sits on the board of the CB (even more so when the representative has the power to lead the board's monetary policy); and (ii) the decisions on the CB's monetary policy are subjected to the approval of the government.

Accountability on objectives

We have already explained that an institution can be considered accountable only if the objective possibility of evaluating the performance of its duties against a clear and well-defined benchmark exists, hence the need for clarity regarding the final objective(s) of the CB, which will serve as reference benchmark(s). Against this background, the third question aims at evaluating whether the final objectives of monetary policy are clearly defined by law and whether, in the case of multiple objectives, there is a clear hierarchical ranking.

Question three deals with the final objective of monetary policy. As already discussed, price stability is a well-accepted final objective of monetary policy. In many laws, however, we find a multitude of additional objectives, including support for economic growth, fostering economic development, the defense of the external value of the currency, and the maintenance of financial stability. While in the case of price stability the quantification of the objective is an easy task, it is difficult to quantify results with regard to the other objectives. On that basis, our index

---

[4] Responsibility as defined here is different from the mechanisms of ex post supervision by the government, which are set as a safeguard clause in the general interest. These ex post controls are considered under the category of ex post accountability. If the government can override CB decisions only in exceptional cases, clearly defined by law to safeguard the general interest, there may not be any reduction in effective independence. The presence of an override clause, on the other hand, can raise the level of accountability.

contemplates three possible answers to question three: (i) we assign the maximum score when a single objective is indicated; (ii) we assign a positive score of one half in case the law indicates a multiplicity of objectives, but in a well-defined hierarchical order; and (iii) a null score is assigned in case the law sets multiple objectives without providing any indication about their hierarchical ranking.

The fourth question deals with the quantification of the final objective. For a successful evaluation of the CB it is necessary to scrutinize the presence of quantifiable final and intermediate objectives so as to be in a position to assess the performance of the CB. When a quantified operating objective exists a positive score of one is assigned. Otherwise, a null score is assigned.[5]

Objectives quantification is a fundamental requirement of some monetary frameworks, in particular inflation targeting frameworks, but also exchange rate or monetary aggregate targeting frameworks in as much as they involve an explicit statement of intermediate objectives. The presence of a quantified objective significantly facilitates performance evaluation; however, to raise the level of CB accountability, the intermediate target must be known to the public: it must be clearly stated and explained by the CB. Hence, this variable reflects aspects of accountability and transparency. If the monetary policy process relies on instruments that enhance transparency, the accountability on objectives also benefits from them. Imagine two frameworks, both featured with a quantified operating target. In the first case the CB neglects an attentive and timely public communication of the objective and the related adopted measures, while in the second case the opposite occurs, and the CB adopts various instruments to communicate target-related information to the public. Undoubtedly, the second CB turns out to be the most accountable.

The fifth question deals with the publication of an economic outlook on the state of the economy. The underlying assumption is that the publication of such a document allows the general public, the government, and the parliament to foresee and evaluate the policy of the CB. In particular, the private sector can understand on which forecast the CB has based its policy measures. The publication of an economic outlook therefore has three advantages: (i) it makes the monetary policy process more transparent

---

[5] This variable tells us whether an intermediate target, against which the outcomes of monetary policy are benchmarked, exists. Differently from the first variable, which concerns the responsibility of the monetary policy-maker, this variable focuses exclusively on the quantification of the objectives.

and accountable, by eliminating or reducing the informational asymmetry between the CB and the private sector; (ii) it facilitates the evaluation of monetary policy and makes the CB more responsible with respect to its objectives and towards society; and (iii) it broadens the time horizon in which monetary policy is carried out, by providing a longer-term perspective, which allows the private sector to formulate its expectations and strategies in a longer horizon.

While the intermediate objective is a benchmark that allows the evaluation of the current effect of past policies, the outlook shifts the comparison between present and future, by allowing evaluation of the present policy of the CB against the future macroeconomic scenario. Monetary policy is determined on the basis of the information set available to the CB at a certain point in time; however, as the outlook represents part of this information, if the economic expectations of the CB differ from those of the private sector, doubts may arise about the Pareto efficiency of monetary policy. Four possible answers are assigned to the variable, each scored on the basis of the quality of the information released. The higher the accuracy of the information the higher the score:

- **Publication of explicit forecasts**. The maximum score of one is assigned when the CB publishes detailed indications about its future economic forecasts, by clarifying for instance the expected trend of certain fundamentals: inflation, employment, and GDP, among others. To assign the maximum score it is not necessary to find a publication entitled "economic outlook" on the website; the score of one is also assigned when, for instance, a document such as the annual report contains a section entirely dedicated to the economic forecast.
- **Publication of forecasts with assessment of risks**. A score of 0.66 is assigned for forecasts with assessment of risks. In this case the information is generally less accurate compared to the case of explicit forecasts but nevertheless the forecast is broadly complete. In these cases forecasts typically take a conditional "what if" form and are linked to scenarios with certain likelihood and certain risks. As in the previous case the publication of a stand-alone "economic outlook" is not binding.
- **Publication of general statement only**. A lower positive score of 0.33 is assigned in case the forecast only consists of a general statement. CBs that publish a document in which the outlooks and the expected policy actions are only stated in broad terms, fall into this category. The information released by the CB is still forward-looking but nonetheless is less specific so it has less value to the public.

- **No economic outlook is published**. In the absence of any type of forecast by the CB a score of zero is assigned. The private sector is deprived of any basis for the formulation of expectations and ex post evaluation of official forecasts.

Ex post accountability

The sixth question deals with reporting mechanisms and procedures. Ex post accountability has to do with the CB's duty of reporting directly to parliament or the government. To be considered accountable, it is necessary for a CB to have reporting procedures, which are essential to publicly account for the measures adopted and actions taken. To provide a score for this variable, the laws that regulate the institutional relationships between the CB and the other bodies of the state (which sometimes have a constitutional rank) must be scrutinized. Different procedures may be in place. The most common procedure is to send to the delegating institution a number of reports on the conduct of monetary policy at pre-specified dates. Another widespread procedure consists of a certain number of periodic meetings between the chairman of the CB board and government representatives or parliamentary commissions. We identify the three possible answers to question 6, each of them having an equal score of 0.33, as follows:

- **Reporting to the legislature**. A parliamentary reporting procedure is the first direct indication of "democratic responsibility." The legislature enjoys a higher level of importance within the index compared to the other institutional entities, as is recalled also in the seventh variable.
- **Reporting to ministers**. The relationship between the CB and the ministries of finance (or the Treasury) is also relevant given the linkages between monetary and fiscal policy, as a way to enhance monetary and fiscal policy coordination.
- **Reporting to other bodies**. If the CB reports to bodies other than the above mentioned (e.g., cabinet, head of state) the level of accountability is clearly enhanced.

Question seven focuses on appearances before parliament. The previous question focused solely on the formal side of parliamentary reporting arrangements. The present variable, on the other hand, refers jointly to the de facto and de jure relationship between the CB and the legislature. An example of this relationship is, for instance, the presentation of a report by the head of the CB before parliament at least once a year, as is the case in the United States. In the presence of a tangible relationship between parliament and the CB a score of one is assigned; in the opposite case a null score is assigned.

Question eight investigates conflict resolution mechanisms. It refers to the presence in the law of procedures for the resolution of conflicts between the CB and the government. The presence of such procedures can significantly raise the level of accountability as they allow foreseeing, even in difficult situations, how the relationship between the delegating and the delegated authority will evolve. The reasons that can lead to a conflict are fundamentally two: (i) divergences about monetary policy measures to be adopted (e.g., stance vis-à-vis the exchange rate); and (ii) missed fulfillment of set objectives on the part of the CB. The coding of a set of possible cases or conflict resolution procedures may help solve the problem even before a conflict emerges. The effects, in terms of responsibility and accountability, differ according to the type of conflict.

In the event of contrasting opinions on policy, conflict resolution procedures usually help to clarify the allocation of responsibilities with respect to monetary policy and make the CB more accountable by favoring its evaluation. In this case, the expression "definition of conflict" means that the possibility of a disagreement between the CB and the government must be defined. The "procedure to resolve conflict" is the course followed in the relationship between the CB and the government in case a conflict arises. Finally, by "clear outcomes in the case of failure to resolve conflict" we mean the last resort procedures that have to be adopted in case the conflict is not resolved. This usually involves the possibility for one of the two subjects or for a third one (e.g., a parliamentary commission) to have the last word at the end of the conflict resolution procedure.[6]

On the other hand, when the conflict arises upon the missed fulfillment of a CB objective, the case is slightly different. Conflict definition and resolution procedures must necessarily be in place in this case; if not, the presence of objectives and intermediate targets for the CB loses its meaning. Clear outcomes in case of failure to resolve the conflict also enhance the accountability of the CB. The presence of a charge upon the CB in the case of failure to fulfill an objective raises its accountability, by providing incentives to honor its responsibilities. Undoubtedly,

---

[6] The index of CB political independence presented in this book evaluates positively only the case of legal provisions that strengthen the position of the CB in case of conflict.

a CB would not have an incentive to achieve its objectives if the missed fulfillment of one of them was not regulated. Ex post accountability is essential to give the CB the right incentives. If the CB does not achieve its target, it should bear a cost that would restore its behavioral incentives. A CB that does not meet its target and does not get penalized has no incentive to reach its final objectives, and consequently could follow a sub-optimal path.

In the case of conflict resolution procedures that can raise the level of accountability of the CB, the index specifies three, equally weighted, cases, each one describing a phase of the conflict resolution procedure: definition, resolution, and outcome in case of failure.

- **Definition of conflict**. The law must provide for the case of failure in the achievement of the objectives in a sufficiently accurate way.
- **Procedures to resolve conflict**. The charter must include a set of procedures allowing conflict resolution between the CB and the government. If, for instance, the CB was not able to meet its targets, a system to report before parliament on such failure should be set.
- **Clear outcomes in the case of failure to resolve conflict**. In case the conflict resolution procedure fails, the law must provide for a clear and unambiguous final settlement of the dispute.

An override clause can be set as one of several possible conflict resolution procedures. Under given conditions such a clause can raise the level of CB accountability. As we have shown through the index of CB independence, an override clause has a negative impact on the level of autonomy of the CB. We have also seen, however, that de Haan, Amtenbrink, and Eijffinger (1998) see the presence of this override clause as an essential requisite of the democratic accountability of the CB. The authors define three relational aspects of CB accountability: the CB's relationships with the legislature, appointment and resignation procedures, and override clauses. This last aspect considers the possibility for the government to replace the CB as the monetary policy-maker in certain extreme and clearly defined cases, as an important accountability instrument. It has to be noted that an override clause can enhance accountability only if there is complete transparency in its enforcement. When the conditions for the enforcement of the override clause are accurately defined by law, possible interference by the government outside the occurrence of a conflict is avoided and the independence of the CB is preserved in the ordinary conduct of business. In this case the government can intervene only when certain exceptional conditions occur.

Governance responsibility

Question nine looks at the decision-making structure of the central bank. The organizational structure of the CB that defines the decision-making framework is usually included in the CB charter, and typically two models can be adopted: (i) decisions are adopted on a collective basis by a committee/board; (ii) decisions are taken by the chairman of the board/committee alone. From the viewpoint of accountability the first option is preferable on the grounds that a single-headed decision-making process makes governance responsibility a personal responsibility, and this reduces the accountability of the CB. Therefore, we assign the higher score when decisions are taken by a committee and a score of 0.5 when decisions are taken by one person.

Question ten investigates the presence of clear appointment procedures. The law must be clear on this front; for instance, a charter that only states that the CEO must be appointed by the government, without specifying any further personal requirement and the procedures for dismissal, is not accurate enough. The conditions and procedures applying to the appointment, the term of office, and the dismissal of board members should be clearly stated, so that undue interference in the composition of the board of the CB can be avoided and the individuals in charge can have full responsibility.

Detailed index of transparency

Table 4.7 summarizes the components of our index of transparency, composed of eight variables, grouped into three modules: operational transparency, economic transparency, and procedural transparency.

Operational transparency

Operational transparency consists of making the CB operations publicly available. To this end, the CB commits to providing to the public a set of documents aimed at reporting its activity, or specific measures adopted. The CB can communicate through a plurality of instruments and channels. The higher the number of instruments used the higher the operational transparency of the CB.

The first question focuses on the forms of communication. The presence of these instruments of communication on the CB website significantly raises its level of transparency, since they enhance the public's awareness and understanding of monetary policy by reducing the informational asymmetry with the CB. There is no uniform classification for these documents across the various websites: the vast majority of CBs provide an extensive set of information. However, this information is not

Table 4.7   Detailed transparency index

Modules	Value		Max. value
Operational transparency			**4.5**
1. Forms of communication (public or private):			2.5
(i) Statements or reports on inflation/monetary policy	Yes/No	0.5–0	
(ii) Reports, bulletin on activities	Yes/No	0.5–0	
(iii) Regular speeches	Yes/No	0.5–0	
(iv) Economic research	Yes/No	0.5–0	
(v) Annual report/retrospective analysis	Yes/No	0.5–0	
2. Regular information published about how monetary policy decisions are made and their justification	Yes/No	1/0	1
3. Official website:			1
(i) English website frequently updated	Yes	1	
(ii) English website not frequently updated	Yes	0.66	
(iii) No website available in English	Yes	0.33	
(iv) No website	Yes	0	
Economic transparency			**3**
4. Publication of monetary policy strategy and/or limits of monetary policy	Yes/No	1/0	1
5. Key assumptions in generating outlook	Yes/No	1/0	1
6. Economic modeling procedures:			1
(i) Publicly available	Yes	1	
(ii) Described or discussed but complete details not provided	Yes	0.5	
(iii) No information provided	Yes	0	
Procedural transparency			**2**
7. Publication of minutes of central bank meetings	Yes/No	1/0	1
8. Publication of committee voting record	Yes/No	1/0	1

Source: Authors' elaborations.

necessarily structured in the same way across CBs, nor included in standardized documents. The only document that follows more or less the same scheme across different CB is the annual report. We consider five means of communication, carrying a score of 0.5 point:

- **Statements or reports on inflation/monetary policy**. These include general declarations on future monetary policy stance, or statements and explanations on the adopted measures. In some cases the explicit object of the report concerns the evolution of inflation in the reference time frame and the document is generally labeled an "inflation report." A "monetary program," on the other hand, is a forward-looking document containing indications about prospective conduct of monetary policy.

- **Reports, bulletin on activities.** Their main characteristic is the relatively high frequency of publication (i.e., weekly, monthly, or bi-monthly). The document we referred to for the assessment of this criterion is typically called a "monthly bulletin," and is generally available on the CB website, but we also take into account quarterly publications when the information they contain is comprehensive.
- **Regular speeches.** This criterion refers to whether written dispatches of the speeches made by the governor or his/her deputies on behalf of the monetary authority are regularly published. Clearly the frequency of speeches can vary substantially between CBs. However, the presence of a dedicated section on the website, containing written copy of the speeches, is adopted here as the satisfactory condition.
- **Economic research.** A large part of CB publications consists of economic research, often published as "working papers" or "policy papers" on the website. The sole presence of a research department within the CB is not necessarily sufficient for our assessment. To answer positively to this criterion the effective presence of substantial research work is needed. Beyond working papers, we judged sufficient the presence of a series of analyses on the country's economic situation, its policy stance, or the recurrent presentation of economic models.
- **Annual report/retrospective analysis.** This criterion refers to the backward-looking statement most often frequently called an "annual report." This instrument usually describes monetary policy measures adopted during the previous year and introduces important considerations about monetary policy strategies. It is often an extensive document describing the past situation, the monetary measures adopted, and usually also estimates of future policy developments. The annual report emerges as one of the main instruments for democratic accountability, as most of the CB laws mandate its publication and transmission to parliament and the government.

Question two evaluates the presence of a detailed explanation of policy measures that have been adopted. As we have seen, this is critical to achieve full transparency and enables the private sector to comprehend the CB's modus operandi. More precisely, we assess whether the CB promptly publishes adopted operational decisions, such as designed actions or decisions on short-term inter-bank interest rates, one of the most common CB operational instruments. This variable looks at high-frequency publications, most likely fortnightly or weekly documents. A score of one is assigned when the CB regularly publishes its decisions and the related justifications. If none of these apply or in case of mis-specification a null score is assigned.

Question three investigates the existence and format of an official website for the central bank. The use of the internet significantly enhances the possibility for the CB to be transparent. Through online publication it can communicate worldwide and without the need for paper support, allowing the recipients to access the information from virtually anywhere. The website has therefore become an essential communication tool for transparency purposes. Difficulties may arise in some developing countries, where efficient telecommunication infrastructures may still be lagging behind. These technological issues, however, do not entail any shortfall for our assessment:

- **English website frequently updated**. Most of the CBs that we have analyzed have developed a frequently updated English website. The use of the English language undoubtedly raises the level of transparency, as it allows the CB to communicate internationally. The assigned score in this case is the maximum of one.
- **English website not frequently updated**. Some CBs do not provide a complete English version of their websites, and not all publications may be translated. In some cases the website is in English, but infrequently updated. For instance, when looking for regular publications (monthly, quarterly, or annual) sometimes we find only a "coming soon" announcement. In these cases a lower score of 0.66 is assigned.
- **No website available in English**. A small number of CBs provide no English website or most of the publications are not translated. In these cases the score assigned is 0.33.
- **No website**. A null score is assigned in case of complete absence of a website.

Economic transparency

Question four deals with the publication of a specific document in which the main characteristics of the strategies adopted by the central bank are discussed. The information must be objective, and specifically must appear within an ad hoc issue or a dedicated chapter and not be indirectly inferred from other documents. A more refined way of communicating monetary policy's strategies and limits is to publish them in a dedicated section of the website.[7] We assign a score of one, when the CB publishes such information and a null score in the opposite case, or where this information does not have a dedicated space.

Question five deals with the publication of an economic outlook. Differently from the variable dedicated to the publication of an economic outlook in the index of accountability, this variable refers to forecasts of a specific object. Within any monetary framework there is a specific object or macroeconomic variable on which the CB is expected to publish a forecast. The principal reference document here is the "inflation outlook," a forecast document exclusively dedicated to inflation. This criterion has a direct effect on transparency: through the publication of an inflation outlook, the CB strongly enhances the level of information available to the public and reduces informational asymmetries, by directly influencing private sector expectations. In the presence of a specific forecast document such as the inflation outlook, we assign a positive score of one. In the opposite case we assign a null score of zero.

Question six investigates the publication of economic models. Publication allows the private sector to understand on which grounds the CB calculates its forecasts, its policy measures, and their macroeconomic effects. These models represent a very powerful communication tool, even though they are rarely publicized in their completeness. The possibility of understanding on which economic foundations the action of the CB is founded significantly enhances its transparency. Given that this type of information is generally not readily available, we assign the maximum score of one when there is complete publication. A score of 0.5 is assigned when economic models are described or discussed, but complete details are not provided.[8]

Procedural transparency

In the category of procedural transparency we examine whether the methodology used in the decision-making process by the executive bodies of the CB is publicized. We consider the official documents whose publication is indicated in the central bank charter.

---

[7] For instance, the Lithuanian CB publishes an ad hoc document explaining both the strategies and the limits of its monetary policy. This document is entitled "Monetary Policy of the Bank of Lithuania." The Nicaraguan CB on the other hand provides such information in a separate section of its website, which it also signals within a dedicated chapter of the annual report.

[8] To assess this variable it may be necessary to search the various economic and not-recurrent publications on the CB official websites, looking for explicit economic modeling.

Question seven investigates the publication of minutes of central bank meetings. The minutes of executives' meetings are official documents that contain the statements of board members and the decisions adopted by the management of the CB. The publication of the minutes of board meetings, in which the procedures followed in the decision-making process are disclosed, allows the private sector both to understand the process in detail and sometimes to be informed about the decisions adopted in a timely manner. This represents a very powerful communication tool when it is published shortly after decisions are adopted. To assess this variable both the complete publication of the official minutes and the simple reporting of the adopted decisions are held as equally valid, and are assigned the score of one. When none of these items are found a null score is assigned.

Question eight focuses on the central bank decision-making process. We examine whether the votes cast by the board members on each resolution are publicized, which can significantly enhance transparency. As of now, only a very small number of CBs publish the voting records.

5
Global Trends in Central Bank Governance

This chapter[1] discusses global trends in CB governance based on the indicators of independence, accountability, and transparency presented in Chapter 4, and which are applied to CBs from advanced countries, emerging markets, and developing countries. Our analysis is based on the levels of CB independence, accountability, and transparency observed in the recent period. Furthermore, we analyze the evolution of CB independence over time (i.e., since the late 1980s) on the basis of measurements reported in GMT (1991) and Cukierman (1992). Given that such measurements do not exist for the other pillars of CB governance (i.e., transparency and accountability) an analysis of their evolution over time is not possible.

Global trends in central bank independence

Although several studies have documented recent trends in CB independence for groups of countries, no analysis of worldwide trends has yet been carried out.[2] To fill this gap we calculate indexes of de jure independence for 163 CBs, representing 181 countries, as of end-2003, and we construct comparable indices for a sub-group of 68 CBs as of the end of the 1980s. The cross-country and time-series dimensions of this new dataset enable us to draw several important lessons from global trends in CB independence over the past couple of decades. The snapshot of independence at the end of the 1980s is based on GMT and Cukierman

---

[1] Daniele Siena contributed to the sections on CB accountability and transparency.
[2] Lybek (1999) focuses on the Baltic states, Russia, and other countries of the Former Soviet Union; Jácome (2001) and Jácome and Vásquez (2005) focus on Latin America and the Caribbean; and Arnone, Laurens, and Segalotto (2006b) focus on OECD countries and a sample of emerging markets and developing countries. See also Arnone, Laurens, Segalotto, and Sommer (2008).

data for 68 CBs. Scores at the end of 2003 are based on our reading of legal documents for 163 CBs covering 181 countries. Table 5.1 provides an overview of independence scores for country groups by income levels, including advanced economies, emerging market economies, and developing countries. We also identify CBs which operate in the context of a monetary union.

Our assessment of CB independence at the end of the 1980s is based on the index for the 18 OECD countries analyzed in GMT (1991), and the Cukierman (1992) data converted into the GMT index for 50 additional countries. Our assessment of CB independence at the end of 2003 relies on the GMT index (i.e., *full index*, see Chapter 4). To ensure comparability we standardize results by dividing the absolute values by the maximum potential score. Due to the method we use to transpose Cukierman's data into the GMT index (see Chapter 4), some qualification is warranted regarding our assessment of CB autonomy evolution over time, given the assumption made to transpose Cukierman's index into the GMT index (see Table 4.3 in Chapter 4).

Central bank independence in the late 1980s

Our snapshot of CB independence in the late 1980s is based on the results of GMT (1991) and Cukierman (1992) for CBs in advanced economies, and Cukierman (1992) for CBs in emerging markets and developing countries. For all country groups, overall independence was rather low (i.e., below 0.50) at that time, with economic independence being generally greater than political independence (Figure 5.1). Advanced economies exhibited the highest scores of overall independence. However, countries in the Euro area showed levels of political and economic independence significantly lower than those in the other advanced economies. Developing countries exhibited slightly higher scores of overall independence than emerging market economies. However, excluding economies in transition, levels of independence in those two groups were comparable.

Central bank independence as of end-2003

Comparison by income groups

The indices of independence have sharply increased from their late 1980s levels, but with notable cross-country differences. On average, independence averages across the main income groups now exceed 0.50, with CBs in advanced economies achieving greater independence than those

Table 5.1 Scores of central bank independence in the late 1980s and 2003

Central banks (number of CBs)	Late 1980s (narrow index Cukierman sample) (full index GMT sample)			2003 (narrow index)			2003 (full index)		
	Political	Economic	Overall	Political	Economic	Overall	Political	Economic	Overall
All income levels									
All CBs (163)	NA	NA	NA	NA	NA	NA	0.49	0.68	0.59
GMT sample (18)	0.36	0.59	0.48	NA	NA	NA	0.74	0.81	0.77
Cukierman sample (50)	0.28	0.39	0.33	0.52	0.82	0.66	0.42	0.73	0.57
Advanced economies									
All CBs (28)	NA	NA	NA	NA	NA	NA	0.70	0.81	0.75
GMT sample (18)	0.36	0.59	0.48	NA	NA	NA	0.74	0.81	0.77
Cukierman sample (7)	0.33	0.21	0.28	0.67	0.89	0.77	0.64	0.86	0.75
ESCB (13)	NA	NA	NA	NA	NA	NA	1.00	0.78	0.89
Emerging markets									
All CBs (32)	NA	NA	NA	NA	NA	NA	0.56	0.75	0.65
Cukierman sample (22)	0.27	0.38	0.32	0.56	0.87	0.70	0.47	0.75	0.61
Developing countries									
All CBs (103)	NA	NA	NA	NA	NA	NA	0.41	0.63	0.52
Cukierman sample (21)	0.27	0.45	0.35	0.42	0.75	0.57	0.29	0.67	0.48
Monetary unions (3)[1]	NA	NA	NA	NA	NA	NA	0.54	0.79	0.67

[1] BCEAO, BEAC, and ECCB.

Source: GMT (1991), Cukierman (1992), and authors' detailed estimates presented in the appendix tables at the end of this chapter.

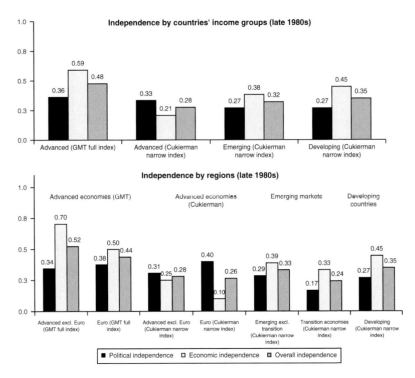

Figure 5.1   Independence scores in the late 1980s
Source: Authors' elaborations.

in emerging markets and developing countries (Figure 5.2). That said, CBs from all income groups levels can be found among the group with the highest and lowest scores: some advanced countries in the Asia and Pacific region score low relative to their peers, especially due to limited political independence (Figure 5.2), and a relatively large number of emerging and developing countries have CBs with some of the highest levels of independence (Table 5.2).

CBs of countries in transition have reached independence scores that are comparable with, and sometimes even higher than, scores of advanced economies. Transition economies have taken advantage of political changes to adopt CB frameworks reflecting best practices in advanced economies. In the case of Baltic and Central European countries, the proximity of the European Union together with the process of establishing the Euro zone with the highly independent ECB have

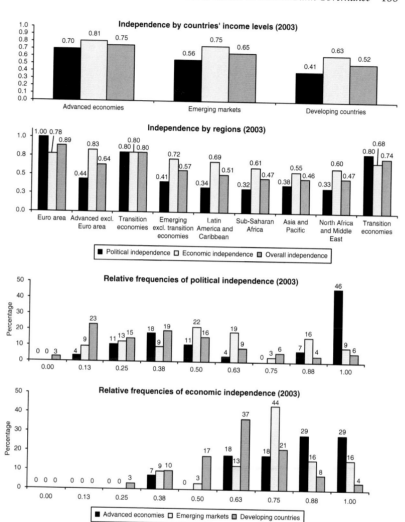

Figure 5.2 Independence scores in 2003
Source: Authors' estimates.

strengthened incentives for making CBs highly independent. Interestingly, CBs of monetary unions exhibit independence that is significantly greater than the average of their income group. The average of the CBs in the European System of Central Banks (ESCB) is close to the maximum level of independence. In the group of developing countries, the

Table 5.2 Central bank independence: ranking of individual central banks (2003)

Advanced	Emerging	Developing
Highest (scores at least equal to 0.80) ECB, Switzerland, Sweden, Luxembourg, France, Finland, Belgium, Austria, Spain, Netherlands, Germany, Portugal, Italy, Ireland, Greece	Latvia, Hungary, Bulgaria, Croatia, Czech Rep., Poland, Estonia, Lithuania, Slovenia, Turkey	Ecuador, Bosnia Herzegovina, Kyrgyzstan, Macedonia, Algeria, Armenia, El Salvador, Tajikistan, Ukraine
High (scores between 0.79 and 0.70) United States, Norway, Iceland, Denmark	Argentina	Albania, Bolivia, Georgia, Kazakhstan, Moldova, Mongolia
Medium (scores between 0.69 and 0.45) United Kingdom, Canada, Australia, Korea, Cyprus	Chile, Indonesia, Malta, Mexico, Peru, Romania, Venezuela, Brazil, Philippines, Slovakia, China, India, Malaysia, Morocco, Pakistan	BCEAO, BEAC, Costa Rica, Timor-Leste, Tunisia, Turkmenistan, Uzbekistan, Afghanistan, Azerbaijan, ECCB, Guatemala, Guinea Rep., Iraq, Madagascar, Papua New Guinea, Serbia Mont., Uruguay, Aruba, Cambodia, Dominican Rep., Nicaragua, Rwanda, Sierra Leone, Sri Lanka, Uganda, Cape Verde, Colombia, Eritrea, Ethiopia, Ghana, Guyana, Haiti, Honduras, Lebanon, Liberia, Mauritius, Nepal, Palestine, Paraguay, Saudi Arabia
Low (scores below 0.45) New Zealand, Japan, Singapore, Hong Kong	Russia, Thailand, Egypt, Israel, Jordan, South Africa	Bahrain, Belarus, Bermuda, Botswana, Comoros, Kenya, Lesotho, Libya, Macau, Mozambique, Netherlands Antilles, Nigeria, Syria, Trinidad & Tobago, UAE, Vietnam, Yemen, Zambia, Zimbabwe, Barbados, Belize, Burundi, Cayman Islands, Fiji, Iran, Jamaica, Laos, Malawi, Maldives, Myanmar, Namibia, Panama, Solomon Islands, Suriname, Tanzania, Vanuatu, Angola, Bahamas, Bhutan, Cuba, Kuwait, Oman, São Tomé Príncipe, Sudan, Tonga, Seychelles, Bangladesh, Qatar

three regional CBs (BCEAO, BEAC, and ECCB) also show independence levels that are considerably higher in both dimensions of independence than those of their peers. Noteworthy is the dichotomy in the political independence scores across countries. As discussed above, advanced economies (especially in Europe) and transition economies have, with some notable exceptions, politically autonomous CBs. By contrast, many developing countries have low scores regarding political independence (see next sub-section), and the cross-country dispersion of economic independence is much lower.

Independence sub-components

What are the main reasons for cross-country differences in the CB independence scores? Most of the differences in political independence are related to the legal provisions for appointing governing bodies of CBs (Table 5.3). In developing countries, governments often continue to be involved in the selection of CB boards and the tenures tend to be short (criteria 1–4); the government is generally represented on the board (criterion 5); and CBs have a limited legal protection in the event of a conflict with the government (criterion 8). Cross-country differences for the other sub-components of political independence are smaller; interestingly, most CBs have adopted monetary stability as one of their primary objectives (criterion 7). However, in many countries, governments continue to be involved in the monetary policy implementation (criterion 6).

Table 5.3 Performance on sub-components of the political independence index (2003)

Country group	Governor & central bank board (%)			Relationship with government (%)			Objectives (%)	
	(1)	*(2)*	*(3)*	*(4)*	*(5)*	*(6)*	*(7)*	*(8)*
Overall sample	34	40	31	38	47	54	95	50
Advanced economies	57	71	57	64	75	64	96	75
Emerging markets	41	44	44	50	47	63	97	63
Developing countries	26	30	20	27	40	49	94	39

Note: percentage of CBs satisfying the criteria: CB governor appointed without government (govt.) involvement (1); appointed for more than 5 years (2); CB board (CBB) appointed without govt. involvement (3), for more than 5 years (4); no mandatory participation of govt. representatives in CBB (5); no govt. approval needed for monetary policy formulation (6); monetary stability is one of CB's primary objectives (7); legal protection strengthens CB position in event of conflict with govt. (8).

Source: Authors' estimates from detailed data presented in the appendix tables.

Table 5.4   Performance on sub-components of the economic independence index (2003)

Country group	Monetary financing of government (%)					Scope of operations (%)		
	(1)	*(2)*	*(3)*	*(4)*	*(5)*	*(6)*	*(7)*	*(7 bis)*
All central banks	91	66	93	91	59	88	23	18
Advanced economies	93	89	93	93	89	100	18	57
Emerging markets	97	75	97	94	81	94	25	19
Developing countries	89	56	91	90	44	94	24	7

Note: The table shows the percentage of CBs satisfying the criteria: no automatic CB credit to govt. (1); when available credit is at market rates (2); temporary (3); for limited amount (4); CB does not bid in primary market for govt. securities (5); CB sets policy rate (6); CB shares supervisory responsibilities (one point) (7), or no responsibility (two points) (7 *bis*).

Source: Authors' estimates from detailed data presented in the appendix tables.

With regard to economic independence at the end of 2003 (Table 5.4), few governments, even in developing countries, have automatic access to the CB credit (criterion 1); when available, the interest rate charged by the CB is often close to the market rates[3] but practices differ especially in developing countries (criterion 2). Many CBs in developing countries are allowed to participate in the primary markets for government securities (criterion 5). This clearly represents an inflation risk but, as discussed below, this arrangement can reflect the insufficient development of financial markets in some countries. On the positive side, most CBs set their policy rates freely (criterion 6), and with the exception of advanced economies, the majority of CBs have retained their key role in banking supervision (criterion 7 *bis*).

Regional patterns

Looking across geographical regions, CBs in Europe have the highest independence scores in terms of both economic and political independence, even after disaggregating the scores by income groups (Table 5.5, row EUR). In the group of emerging markets, overall independence is the lowest in the Middle East and Central Asia (MCD) and sub-Saharan Africa (AFR) regions. Among developing countries, the differences in independence across geographical regions are not particularly large; however, the

---

[3] For example in the United Kingdom, the interest rate charged on government overdrafts is the CB's Bank Rate plus a premium which is negotiated between the Debt Management Office and the Bank of England.

Table 5.5   Regional patterns in central bank independence (end-2003)

Region	Political independence				Economic independence				Overall independence			
	All	*Adv.*	*Emer.*	*Dev.*	*All*	*Adv.*	*Emer.*	*Dev.*	*All*	*Adv.*	*Emer.*	*Dev.*
AFR	0.33	–	0.25	0.33	0.60	–	0.63	0.61	0.46	–	0.44	0.47
APD	0.35	0.27	0.44	0.34	0.60	0.67	0.67	0.55	0.47	0.47	0.55	0.44
EUR	0.79	0.85	0.73	0.79	0.80	0.84	0.81	0.68	0.80	0.85	0.77	0.73
MCD	0.45	–	0.25	0.48	0.63	–	0.63	0.64	0.54	–	0.44	0.56
WHD	0.40	0.50	0.54	0.36	0.73	0.88	0.83	0.69	0.56	0.69	0.69	0.52
All	0.49	0.70	0.56	0.41	0.68	0.81	0.75	0.63	0.59	0.75	0.65	0.52

Source: Authors' estimates from detailed data presented in the appendix tables.

CBs in Asia and Pacific (APD) and sub-Saharan Africa (AFR) regions rank the lowest on average.

Developments in central bank independence over time

Trends by countries' income levels

Over the last couple of decades average scores of CB independence for our global sample of 163 CBs have increased significantly: overall independence has about doubled. Its economic component continues to be significantly ahead of the political one.[4] Advanced economies have continued to strengthen their independence over the period for the most part due to higher levels of political independence. That said, political independence still lags somewhat behind the scores for economic independence.[5] In the group of emerging markets, overall independence has more than doubled and has surpassed independence in the advanced countries in the late 1980s. The measures of economic and political independence show similar levels of improvement, with the former remaining higher than the latter.[6] Finally, changes in CB independence

---

[4] Assessment based on independence scores for the Cukierman sample in the late 1980s and the global sample at the end of 2003. Since the scores for the Cukierman and global samples are similar at the end of 2003, the Cukierman sample can be a good proxy for the global independence scores in the late 1980s.

[5] For the late 1980s, the average CB independence score for advanced economies is approximated using the GMT sample of eighteen CBs in the OECD area. Note that the scores based on the GMT sample at the end of 2003 are close to those obtained for the complete sample of twenty-eight advanced economies.

[6] Similarly as in the case of global CB independence, we proxy the average independence scores of emerging markets for the late 1980s using the Cukierman sample.

in the group of developing countries are harder to assess given data limitations. Based on independence scores from the Cukierman sample (which represents about 20 percent of developing countries), political independence has improved only marginally and remains low. However, political independence increased to some extent according to the "narrow" definition of our independence index. On balance, our reading of the data is that political independence in developing countries is much lower than in emerging markets and advanced economies, although it is not possible to quantify the evolution of political independence over time. The picture emerging from the data is clearer with regard to economic independence: it has increased significantly over the period.

To assess the evolution of CB independence over time it is useful to transform the data into the four-quadrant framework of GMT (1991) (Figure 5.3). For all country groups, one can observe a general shift of the plotted observations upward and to the right, which confirms the broad-based strengthening in both economic and political independence. The shift is more uniform in the case of advanced economies, as most observations have become crowded in the top right quadrant. Regarding emerging markets and developing countries, the data also show an upward shift to the right (i.e., independence has increased), but the dispersion of observations is higher than for advanced economies. That said, it is interesting to note that scores for emerging market and developing countries at the end of 2003 are more concentrated and located to the right than was the case for advanced economies in the late 1980s, confirming the earlier finding that, at the end of 2003, developing and emerging market economies have achieved a level of independence higher than the one attained by advanced economies in the late 1980s. Finally, most of the cross-country differences are due to the differences in political independence.

Regional trends

The increase in CB independence is a worldwide phenomenon: CBs in all regions of the world have been granted increased political and economic independence (Table 5.6). But the increase in independence has been uneven among regions. CBs in Europe (EUR) have gained greatly in terms of both economic and political independence. In the Western hemisphere (WHD), much of the progress has been focused in the area of economic independence. By contrast, CBs in sub-Saharan Africa (AFR) and Middle East and Central Asia (MCD) regions have seen relatively modest gains in their independence over the past couple of decades.

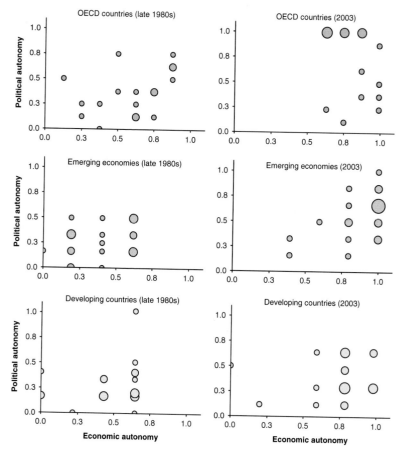

Figure 5.3 Trends in the distribution of central bank independence (late 1980s and 2003)

Source: Authors' estimates based on GMT sample for OECD countries; Cukierman sample for emerging markets and developing countries. The dot size represents the number of central banks.

Lessons from global trends

Building on the literature that highlights its macroeconomic benefits, CBs have been granted higher independence irrespective of the country's income level, although those in advanced economies continue to enjoy greater independence than those in emerging markets and developing countries. However, at the end of 2003, all country groups exhibit a

Table 5.6   Regional trends in central bank independence (1980s–2003)[1]

Region	Political		Economic		Overall	
	1980s	*2003*	*1980s*	*2003*	*1980s*	*2003*
AFR	0.17	0.37	0.52	0.72	0.33	0.53
APD	0.21	0.54	0.41	0.73	0.30	0.63
EUR	0.32	0.79	0.27	0.98	0.30	0.88
MCD	0.25	0.40	0.36	0.68	0.30	0.53
WHD	0.36	0.50	0.36	0.88	0.36	0.67
All	0.28	0.56	0.38	0.84	0.32	0.68

[1] Average independence scores are based on Cukierman sample and the "narrow" independence index.

Source: Authors' estimates from detailed data presented in the appendix tables.

higher level of independence than that reached by advanced economies in the late 1980s.

The vast majority of CBs have been mandated to set price stability as one of the objectives of monetary policy. In addition, most CBs have autonomy with respect to setting the policy rate and are not required to extend direct credit to the government.

There is divergence among CBs on the issue of financial supervision (see Chapter 7). Many CBs in emerging markets and developing countries have retained their key role in supervisory activities; in addition, CBs in a few large advanced countries have also retained some form of involvement in financial supervision. In fact, it is not infrequent for CB laws to prescribe the soundness of the financial system as an objective that is subordinated to medium-term price stability.

Participation in currency unions has helped to enhance autonomy, both among advanced economies (as in the case of the European System of Central Banks – ESCB) and developing countries (Central Bank of West African States – BCEAO; Bank of Central African States – BEAC; and the Eastern Caribbean Central Bank – ECCB). In the group of developing countries, this is because participation has been beneficial for financial market development, which in turn had been a prerequisite for the elimination of direct CB credit to the government (or CB participation in the primary market for government securities).

A number of emerging market and developing countries continue to strengthen their instrument autonomy. However, looking forward, the main challenge will be to boost political autonomy, mainly by ensuring that CB governing bodies are appointed without much political interference and for longer terms.

Global trends in central bank accountability and transparency

We apply the indices of accountability and transparency presented in Chapter 4 to 98 CBs representing 109 countries thus allowing a global assessment of trends in CB accountability and transparency (see appendix tables). Our assessment of accountability is mostly based on an analysis of CBs' laws; our assessment of transparency relies mostly on the analysis of CBs' websites, both on the basis of the methodology presented in Chapter 4.[7] In some cases, we supplement the information from these sources with information from the IMF's Financial Stability Assessment Program (FSAP) when available CB resources were not sufficient to assess one or more variables, or alternatively when their interpretation lacked clarity. From a methodological point of view, we start by analyzing CB accountability because it provides insights as regards transparency, in particular regarding the type of documents that may be found in CBs' websites which are relevant to transparency. Regarding transparency, the simple presence of a document was not sufficient to give a positive value on the relevant aspect; the quality and the effectiveness of documents and publications were also analyzed.[8] All the data collection work has been carried out in the first quarter of 2006 and only annual documents not published before 2004 were considered valid. More than three years of delay in the publication of a CB annual report led us to consider it as a missing publication.

Accountability scores

Overall results

Two main comments can be made regarding Table 5.7, which provides a distribution of countries within four ranges of accountability. First, CBs in emerging market economies exhibit relatively high levels of accountability, with the highest score reached by the Slovenian CB. The first six highest individual scores are also among this group of countries, as well

---

[7] Information from websites released in English, Spanish, French, and Italian was taken into consideration.

[8] For instance, a monthly bulletin that indicates short-term interest rates but does not provide a satisfactory explanation of underlying policy choices would not be rated positively on the transparency variable number 2.

Table 5.7 Central bank accountability: ranking of individual central banks

Advanced	Emerging	Developing
Highest (scores at least equal to 0.80)		
	Argentina, Czech Republic, Hungary, Peru, Slovenia, South Africa, Venezuela	Armenia, Guatemala
High (scores between 0.79 and 0.70)		
Sweden, Spain, Portugal, Netherlands, Germany, France, ECB, Austria, Switzerland, Greece, United States	Estonia, Slovakia, Romania, Indonesia, Bulgaria, Lithuania, Chile, Philippines, Poland, Pakistan	Albania, Mongolia, Bolivia, Uruguay, Georgia, Madagascar, BEAC
Medium (scores between 0.69 and 0.45)		
Japan, New Zealand, Italy, Ireland, Finland, Belgium, Korea, Australia, Canada, Denmark, Norway, United Kingdom, Singapore, Iceland	Mexico, Latvia, Russia, Brazil, Turkey, Malaysia, Croatia, Jordan, India	El Salvador, Botswana, Namibia, Bangladesh, Sierra Leone, Colombia, Kyrgyzstan, Costa Rica, Sri Lanka, Tanzania, Moldova, Kenya, Honduras, Ecuador, Uganda, Ukraine, Nigeria, BCEAO, Croatia, Paraguay, Belarus, Tunisia, Kazakhstan, Zambia, Ghana, Nicaragua, Algeria, Bahrain
Low (scores below 0.45)		
	Thailand, China, Israel, Morocco, Egypt	United Arab Emirates, Lebanon, Mozambique, Iran, Syria, Saudi Arabia

Source: Authors' estimates from detailed data presented in the appendix tables.

as seven out the nine countries with CBs with the highest scores (i.e., at least equal to 0.80 for a maximum standardized score of 1). Second, it is also noteworthy that several CBs in developing countries are among the CBs which have high scores of accountability (i.e., above 0.70). As we have noted with regard to CB independence, recently drafted legislation in these groups of countries tends to reflect the advances in best practices. As to advanced countries, it is noteworthy that none of the CBs are among the group with the highest scores. On the other hand, CBs in Western Europe exhibit relatively higher scores than their peers in other geographic areas. Finally, while the bulk of the CBs in advanced economies rank in the upper half of the sample, CBs in developing countries are more concentrated in the second half and CBs in emerging countries exhibit a greater dispersion. The average CB accountability scores for advanced economies and emerging markets are close (Figure 5.4) but there is a marked drop for developing countries.

Sub-components of accountability

Regarding performance of the components of accountability (Figure 5.4), CBs in the three income levels exhibit similar average levels of ex post accountability and governance responsibility. Accountability on objectives in developing countries, however, has a lower average score compared to advanced economies and emerging markets. This component also shows the sharpest differences between the most and the least accountable CBs. Given that this component includes variables (de facto quantification of objectives and publication of an economic forecast) for which legislation must be supplemented with other information, such as official websites, and that the preparation and publication of this information has a cost, this may be a constraint for some CBs in developing countries.

Accountability without the responsibility component

The responsibility component of accountability could significantly and adversely influence overall accountability, especially for some CBs in advanced economies (e.g., Canada and the United Kingdom). Therefore, we analyze overall accountability once that component is excluded. When we eliminate the "responsibility" component, the ranking of top CBs does not change substantially (Slovenia retains the first position, and five emerging market CBs are joined by Bulgaria and Pakistan to occupy the first seven positions). CBs in some advanced economies show the most marked improvement in ranking following the elimination of the

166

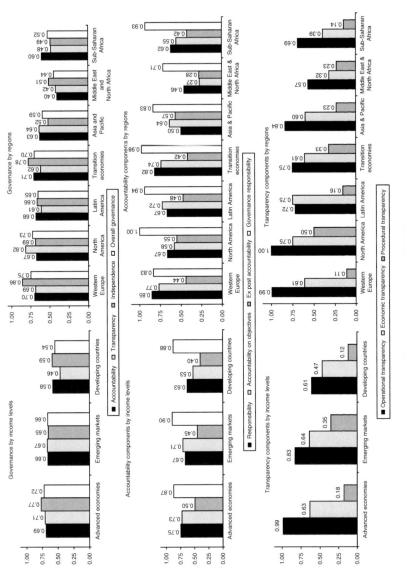

Figure 5.4 Transparency, accountability, and overall governance scores (2006)
Source: Authors' estimates. All scores are standardized to a maximum value of 1.

responsibility component of accountability (i.e., New Zealand, Norway, Korea, and Australia). This result suggests that CBs in advanced economies are less likely to have modified their legislation in the recent period (except for CBs in country members of the ESCB whose charters have been recently amended) and, therefore, may not have incorporated in their legislation the most recent advances regarding the practice of CB accountability. In contrast, CBs in emerging market economies are most likely to have benefited from those advances. This is confirmed by the fact that the largest downgrades within the new ranking are with CBs in emerging markets. Finally, it is noteworthy that the hierarchy of scores of accountability without the responsibility component remains the same when countries are grouped by income levels, advanced countries having the most accountable CBs and developing countries the least accountable ones. We conclude that the responsibility component does not distort the overall picture of CB accountability.

Accountability by regions

Regarding accountability by regions (Figure 5.4) transition countries score best, followed by Western Europe and Latin America; North America is only fourth. Middle East and North Africa are the regions with the weakest performance. The performance of transition economies can be attributed to the fact that new legislation was recently introduced, in the context of the transition process, as in the case of the two top performers (Slovenia and Hungary) which modernized their framework in the context of the EU accession process. Similarly, Figure 5.4 shows accountability components averages by regions. Western European CBs lead in the area of responsibility and accountability on objectives, but have the lowest scores on governance responsibility. The Asia and Pacific region scores best for ex post accountability, and North America for governance responsibility; CBs in transition economies, despite displaying the highest average accountability score, obtain a very low score on ex post accountability, immediately followed by the Middle East and North Africa.

Transparency scores
Overall results

Intuitively, one expects transparency to increase with economic development. In addition, democratic regimes are more common among advanced and emerging economies than among less developed countries. Therefore, the incentives structure in advanced economies should favor transparency. Three observations can be made from Table 5.8,

Table 5.8 Central bank transparency: ranking of individual central banks

Advanced	Emerging	Developing
Highest (scores above 0.8) United Kingdom, United States, Sweden, Norway	Hungary, Czech Republic, Thailand, South Africa, Slovenia	Guatemala
High (scores between 0.79 and 0.70) Switzerland, New Zealand, Japan, Canada, Singapore, Iceland	Slovakia, Latvia, Estonia, Chile, Brazil, Turkey, Romania, Poland, Philippines, Venezuela	Albania, Colombia
Medium (scores between 0.69 and 0.45) Korea, Spain, Portugal, Netherlands, Italy, Ireland, Greece, Germany, France, Finland, ECB, Belgium, Austria, Australia, Denmark	Mexico, Peru, Pakistan, Lithuania, Israel, Indonesia, Argentina, Russia, Jordan, India, Croatia, Malaysia, Bulgaria	Uruguay, Sri Lanka, Kenya, Nigeria, Bolivia, BCEAO, Costa Rica, El Salvador, Kyrgyzstan, Kazakhstan, Botswana, Bangladesh, BEAC, United Arab Emirates, Uganda, Tunisia, Ghana, Bahrain, Armenia, Nicaragua, Ecuador
Low (scores below 0.45)	Morocco, China, Egypt	Tanzania, Mozambique, Mongolia, Belarus, Algeria, Moldova, Georgia, Paraguay, Honduras, Zambia, Sierra Leone, Namibia, Saudi Arabia, Madagascar, Ukraine, Syria, Iran, Lebanon

Source: Authors' estimates from detailed data presented in the appendix tables.

which distributes countries within four ranges of CB transparency: (i) while CBs in developing countries are not well represented among the highest scores, those in emerging markets are as well represented as are those in advanced economies; (ii) as expected, the top half of the ranking is occupied for the greatest part by advanced and emerging markets, while developing countries are clustered in the lower half. As pointed out, external communication is costly, both in relation to the production of information and the construction of a dissemination system. Therefore advanced economies may find it easier to fulfill transparency criteria over other groups of countries, particularly developing countries; and (iii) average scores by income levels (Figure 5.4) confirm our findings, although the difference between advanced and emerging economies is rather small, contrary to the difference with developing countries.

Sub-components of transparency

Average scores by sub-components (Figure 5.4) show that operational transparency is the highest rated component for all groups of countries, while the lowest is for procedural transparency, with limited dispersion among income levels. However, noteworthy is the significantly higher average score for CBs in emerging markets with regard to procedural transparency, reflecting the more widespread practice of disseminating at least the minutes of CB board meetings. Among advanced economies, the CBs that most seem to lack procedural transparency are those in continental Europe.

Transparency by regions

With respect to transparency (Figure 5.4) North America is the region with the highest average transparency followed by Western Europe; next we find Asia, transition economies, and Latin America. The Middle East and North Africa regions have the lowest levels of transparency, with sub-Saharan Africa slightly above. The operational component is the highest for all groups of CBs; the economic component, while lower, has the highest convergence of practices; and the procedural component records the lowest average scores, with Western European CBs having the lowest scores.[9] Economic transparency, on the other hand, shows a different picture: Latin America shares the lead with North America, which is the best also in procedural transparency, leading to the highest scores in all

---

[9] Only 25 percent of CBs in advanced economies (and developing countries) fulfill at least one of the features of procedural transparency, against 65 percent for emerging economies.

components of transparency in North America (in particular due to the highest score by the US Federal Reserve on procedural transparency).

Relationships between independence, accountability, and transparency

Our assessment of the relationships and correlations between the indices of independence, accountability, and transparency is based on our sub-sample of 98 CBs. Our results, which are summarized in Table 5.9, do not imply causality but are useful tools to navigate the three pillars of CB governance and their sub-components.

Accountability and transparency

As shown in Figure 5.5 and in Table 5.9, our values for CB total account-ability and total transparency are closely and positively related, and the correlation is significant: overall, CBs which enjoy a high level of accountability also exhibit a high level of transparency. In particular, the correlation is stronger between the sub-components of accountabil-ity on objectives and economic transparency (0.66). As already discussed in Chapter 4, accountability on objectives signals the presence of clearly defined objectives that the CB has to pursue and meet; economic transparency refers to CB publications disclosing the macroeconomic rationale that shape monetary policy. It is clear that well-defined and ranked objectives make it possible (although not necessary) for the CB to focus its research work and publish detailed information on the mone-tary strategy, medium-term outlook, and adopted economic assumptions and models. There are, however, a few outliers, with some countries hav-ing a high level of transparency while CB accountability is low.[10] Our result is in line with the relevant economic literature, in particular Sik-los (2002). However, the relationships are somewhat less uniform when CBs are divided by stages of development: in emerging economies and developing countries the regression line is positively sloped, whereas in advanced economies the relationship is negative (i.e., high trans-parency is not matched by a proportionately high accountability). One reason for that discrepancy is that it is relatively easier to enhance transparency rather than accountability, given that the former may be achieved by making documents available to the public, while the latter

---

[10] The CB of Thailand exhibits the fourth-highest level of transparency while its accountability is low. Similarly, the Bank of England enjoys a (high) level of transparency not matched by its level of accountability.

Table 5.9 Correlations between accountability, independence, and transparency

	Accountability				Transparency					Independence					
	Total	Advanced	Emerging	Developing	Total	Advanced	Emerging	Developing	Economic	Total	Political	Economic	Advanced	Emerging	Developing
Independence	0.51	0.52	0.51	0.40	0.31	−0.36	0.36	0.16	—	—	—	—	—	—	—
Political	0.49	0.62	0.51	0.36	0.20	−0.52	0.37	0.04	0.14	—	—	—	—	—	—
Economic	0.26	−0.11	0.33	0.20	0.32	0.25	0.21	0.27	0.32	—	—	—	—	—	—
Accountability	—	—	—	—	0.56	−0.32	0.60	0.54	—	0.51	0.49	0.26	0.52	0.51	0.40
Responsibility	—	—	—	—	0.20	−0.62	0.50	0.29	—	0.61	0.66	0.18	0.68	0.57	0.57
Objectives	—	—	—	—	0.57	0.05	0.52	0.52	0.66	0.37	0.29	0.31	0.35	0.39	0.20
Ex post	—	—	—	—	0.29	−0.26	0.18	0.28	—	0.01	0.04	−0.05	−0.37	−0.05	0.09
Governance	—	—	—	—	0.18	−0.08	0.32	0.20	—	0.19	0.14	0.18	−0.12	0.45	0.23
Narrow[1]	—	—	—	—	0.58	−0.35	0.52	0.53	—	0.31	0.26	0.23	−0.17	0.36	0.25
Transparency	0.56	−0.32	0.60	0.54	—	—	—	—	—	0.31	0.20	0.32	−0.36	0.36	0.16
Operational	0.44	0.18	0.27	0.37	—	—	—	—	—	0.25	0.22	0.16	0.17	0.08	−0.13
Economic	0.49	−0.36	0.64	0.50	—	—	—	—	—	0.26	0.14	0.32	−0.26	0.31	0.31
Procedural	0.19	−0.16	0.36	0.06	—	—	—	—	—	0.11	0.03	0.20	−0.32	0.39	0.17

[1] Narrow accountability is equal to total accountability minus the responsibility component.

Source: Authors' calculations.

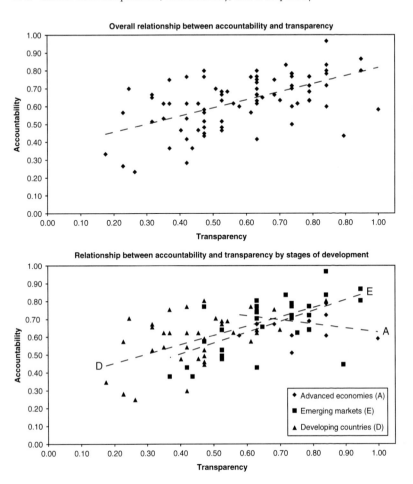

Figure 5.5   Relationships between accountability and transparency
Source: Authors' calculations.

typically involves changes to CB legislation. Advanced economies may have taken the opportunities offered by technological advancements and availability of resources to increase transparency, while on the other side showing lower willingness to apply the same efforts to their accountability frameworks. In contrast, the correlation in the case of developing countries and emerging economies is stronger (respectively 0.54 and 0.60), suggesting that on average CBs in these countries have achieved better simultaneous improvements of their accountability and transparency frameworks.

Accountability and independence

As already mentioned, our indicator of accountability includes an important component of independence which we have called *responsibility*, and we have underlined that the possible interference of the delegating subjects in the conduct of monetary policy can reduce CB independence, and with it its accountability. The basic idea is that no institution can really be called accountable for a responsibility that is entrusted to another subject: responsibility is a critical requirement for CB accountability. We analyze the correlation existing between our accountability index, which contains a number of independence criteria, and CB independence. Therefore, the expectation is that accountability and independence should be positively correlated, with a correlation decreasing once the responsibility component is omitted from the accountability index.

Figure 5.6 visualizes our results, and it shows a positive correlation between CB independence and overall accountability (including some of the criteria used to assess independence), with the regression line confirming our expectations. The overall correlation between the two indices is 0.51 and the dispersion is low except for a few outliers (i.e., South Africa and Bangladesh) which enjoy fairly high levels of CB accountability against low levels of CB independence. When looking at the correlation by stages of development, contrary to our observation in the case of transparency and accountability, the correlation between independence and accountability is increasing with the level of economic development, with significantly lower correlation in the case of CBs in developing countries (coefficient of 0.40) compared to CBs in emerging markets and advanced economies (respective correlation coefficients of 0.51 and 0.52).

Such a result helps clarify the debate in the literature discussed in Chapter 2 having to do with the lack of a consensus view regarding the relationship between CB independence and accountability. In particular, in some cases the literature stresses a potential trade-off between independence and accountability when CB independence includes both the concepts of positive and negative freedom. For instance, if independence involves the possibility for the CB not only to autonomously determine monetary policy (positive freedom, i.e., freedom to do something), but also independence in accounting for its own actions (negative freedom, i.e., freedom not to do something), the relationship between independence and accountability may turn out negative. It is interesting to note that such a trade-off does not seem to be occurring in our sample.

Figure 5.6 also visualizes the relationships between CB independence and narrow accountability (i.e., accountability minus the responsibility

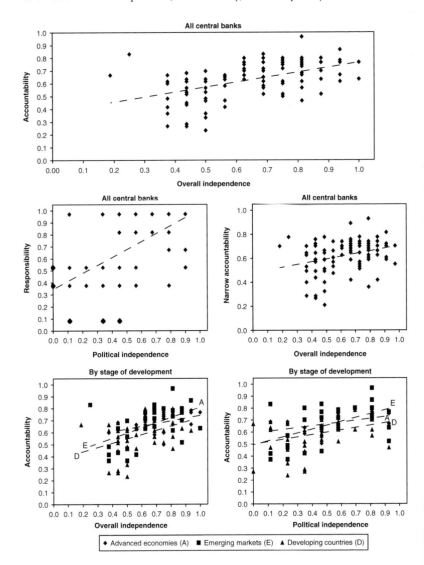

Figure 5.6   Relationships between accountability and independence
Source: Authors' calculations.

component). As expected, the correlation weakens significantly but remains positive: there is a sharp drop from 0.51 to 0.31. Dispersion of the observations also increases. These results bring about two important conclusions which help clarify the lack of consensus in the literature: first, the responsibility component of accountability is the component that displays the strongest correlation with independence; second, even after subtracting the responsibility component from the accountability index, we found no evidence of a trade-off between CB accountability and independence, contrary to what is sometimes highlighted in the literature.

With regard to the relationships between political independence and the responsibility component of CB accountability, Figure 5.6 shows that, based on our definition of responsibility (i.e., clear and detailed allocation of objective responsibilities among different institutions),[11] the correlation is significantly positive (0.66). This is consistent with expectations, given that government interference in monetary policy decisions would both hurt (and lower) responsibility and independence.

With regard to the relationships between the two sub-components of CB independence (i.e., political and economic independence) and CB accountability, we find results which are consistent with expectations. The correlation between accountability and political independence is higher than the correlation between accountability and economic independence (respectively 0.49 and 0.26). With regard to the relationship between accountability and political independence by stage of development, advanced economies enjoy the strongest relationship (correlation coefficient of 0.62), followed by emerging markets (correlation coefficient of 0.51), and developing countries (correlation coefficient of 0.36). Dispersion, however, particularly in the two latter cases is high.

Transparency and independence

The analysis of the correlations between CB transparency and independence allows us to address the problem of information asymmetries discussed in Chapter 2. Our findings, as shown in Figure 5.7, highlight that an overall correlation coefficient at 0.31 is positive but lower than the correlation between CB independence and accountability. Results for CBs by income levels are somewhat counter-intuitive (Figure 5.7). CBs in the group of emerging markets show a positive and modestly significant correlation of 0.36; CBs in developing countries show a very low correlation, although still positive, of 0.16. Such a result appears consistent with the idea that CBs in emerging markets have taken substantial actions to modernize both their independence framework *and* improve their transparency, while in developing countries a clear-cut

---

[11] As discussed in Chapter 3, our definition differs from that of de Haan, Amtembrink, and Eijffinger (1998).

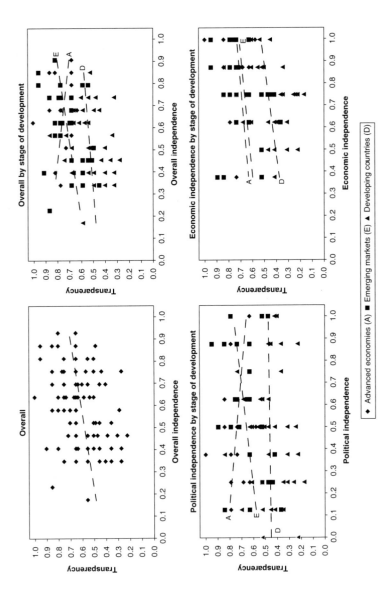

Figure 5.7   Relationships between transparency and independence
Source: Authors' calculations.

strategy has not emerged: some countries have given priority to updating their independence framework, while others have given priority to transparency. On the other hand, the negative correlation displayed by the group of advanced economies (−0.36) appears somewhat counterintuitive. It may reflect (similar to what we have observed regarding the correlation between CB accountability and transparency for CBs in such countries) the fact that it is relatively easier to enhance transparency than to enhance independence, given that the former may be achieved by making documents available to the public, while the latter typically involves changes to CB legislation. Our finding may also reflect the fact that when a CB has gained over the years a high level of credibility due to high de facto independence, there is less of a need to enhance its de jure independence.

In order to shed some light on the apparent inconsistency we have just found with regard to the correlation between independence and transparency in the case of CBs which operate in advanced economies, it is useful to assess the relationship between transparency and the two sub-components of independence. If our analysis is correct, we should find a negative correlation between transparency and political independence, and possibly a positive relationship between transparency and economic independence. That would reflect our hypothesis that CBs in advanced economies, while exhibiting high levels of economic independence, may enjoy levels of de facto political independence which are not reflected in legislation.

Results for advanced economies, as shown in Figure 5.7, are consistent with our expectations: we find significantly negative correlation between transparency and political independence (coefficient of −0.52), while the relationship turns positive when transparency is measured against economic independence (coefficient of 0.25). Even though the positive relationship is somewhat weaker and not necessarily significant, our results suggest that the negative relationship found between CB independence and transparency is driven by the level of political independence. On the other hand, in the case of CBs in emerging markets, we find correlation levels between transparency and economic and political independence which are comparable (correlation coefficient respectively of 0.21 and 0.37). This result suggests that CBs in those countries exhibit levels of de jure and de facto independence which are closely correlated. Finally, with regard to CBs in developing countries, we find a very weak, although positive, link between transparency and overall independence, and no correlation at all when transparency is measured against the political component of independence alone. The strength of the relationship improves slightly in the case of the economic sub-index of independence, even though the coefficient remains a low 0.27. As we mentioned above, this result suggests that a clear-cut strategy has not emerged yet for this group of countries as a whole, with some countries opting for improving transparency while others are opting for improving their independence framework.

Additional considerations

Our results reported in Table 5.9 show that, in the case of CBs in advanced economies, the general negative relationship observable between accountability and transparency entirely depends on the strong negative relationship between transparency and responsibility. Accountability for this group of CBs is also strongly and positively related to independence, which in turn depends almost entirely on the positive link between accountability and political independence. Finally, while a high level of CB accountability is found to be associated with a high level of CB political independence for CBs in all income levels groups, high levels of CB transparency tend to correspond to high levels of economic independence.

Conclusions

Overall, there is a positive and significant correlation between CB transparency and accountability: highly accountable CBs are also highly transparent. However, CBs in advanced countries show a negative link between these two dimensions of the CB pillars, pointing to some inertia in adjusting CB legislation with regard to accountability, while the practice of central banking, as reflected in the transparency component, has adjusted to the demands of market-based monetary policy. In other words, inertia in adjusting CB legislation may have slowed down the process towards high (de jure) accountability, while the process towards high (de facto) transparency has been significantly enhanced. Overall CB independence is positively and significantly correlated with accountability. Furthermore, CB accountability shows the strongest positive link with political independence. Finally, the relationship between CB transparency and independence is not as strong as the relationship observed in the case of independence and accountability. Furthermore, when looking at the relationship by stages of economic development, we find similar results to those obtained when assessing the relationships between CB transparency and accountability: CBs in advanced economies show a negative and significant correlation between their level of transparency and political independence, while we find the opposite regarding economic independence and transparency. Such a result also suggests inertia in adjusting CB legislation to the modern practice of central banking.

Global trends in central bank governance

Trends by stages of economic development and regions

Independence, accountability, and transparency are the three pillars which form the basis of the framework governing a CB and on which its governance should rest. Table 5.10 provides a distribution of countries within four ranges (i.e., highest, high, medium, and low) with regard to their overall CB governance performance, and Figure 5.4 above provides average scores for countries by stages of economic development. Four observations can be made: (i) the number of CBs having reached the highest level of governance is very small. Emerging market economies have a slightly higher representation in that category than advanced economies, and developing countries are not represented; (ii) most CBs in emerging market economies are ranked "medium" while those in advanced economies are equally represented in the "high" and "medium" categories; (iii) a majority of CBs in developing countries are ranked in the "low" category, but a significant number of them have reached a "medium" ranking; and (iv) a few CBs in advanced economies are lagging behind, as well as a few CBs in some large emerging market economies.

Regional average scores for overall CB governance were presented in Figure 5.4. CBs in Western Europe reach the highest average score for overall governance, closely followed by CBs in North America and in transition economies (average scores of at least 0.70). On the other end of the spectrum, CBs in the sub-Saharan African and Middle East and North Africa regions have the lowest scores (below 0.60), and CBs in the Latin America and Asia and Pacific regions have scores in between.

Relative deficit of accountability

CB accountability should be positively correlated to the level of independence of the CB: the more independent the CB, the higher should be its level of accountability; also, there would be no point in establishing accountability mechanisms for a CB with no autonomy from the government. We define three levels to characterize the lack of correspondence between independence and accountability (Table 5.11): high, when the index of accountability is below the index of independence (both indices being standardized to a maximum value of 1) by more than 0.25; low,

Table 5.10 Overall central bank governance: ranking of individual central banks

Advanced	Emerging	Developing
Highest (scores above 0.80)[1] ECB, Sweden, Switzerland	Hungary, Czech Republic, Slovenia, Latvia	
High (scores between 0.79 and 0.75)[1] Austria, France, United States, Germany, Netherlands, Spain, United Kingdom, Belgium, Finland	Estonia, Poland, Venezuela	Guatemala, Albania
Medium (scores between 0.74 and 0.60)[1] Portugal, Greece, Norway, Ireland, Italy, Canada, Denmark, Australia, Iceland, Japan, Korea, New Zealand	Chile, Romania, Slovakia, Argentina, Turkey, Lithuania, Peru, Bulgaria, Indonesia, Philippines, Brazil, Mexico, Croatia, South Africa, Pakistan	Bolivia, Armenia, Uruguay, Kyrgyzstan, El Salvador, Ecuador, Mongolia, BEAC, Costa Rica, BCEAO, Georgia, Colombia, Sri Lanka, Kazakhstan
Low (scores below 0.60)[1] Singapore	Thailand, Russia, Malaysia, India, Israel, China, Jordan, Morocco, Egypt	Moldova, Kenya, Tunisia, Algeria, Botswana, Nigeria, Uganda, Ukraine, Madagascar, Sierra Leone, Nicaragua, Honduras, Ghana, Tanzania, Belarus, Paraguay, Bangladesh, Bahrain, Namibia, United Arab Emirates, Zambia, Mozambique, Lebanon, Saudi Arabia, Syria, Iran

[1] Scores are the simple average of standardized scores with a maximum of 1.
Source: Authors' estimates from detailed data presented in the appendix tables.

Table 5.11 Relative deficit of accountability: ranking of central banks

Advanced	Emerging	Developing
High relative deficit of accountability (lower than −0.25)		
Belgium, Finland	Latvia, Croatia	Algeria, Ecuador, Saudi Arabia
Low relative deficit of accountability (between −0.25 and −0.01)		
Iceland, ECB, Switzerland, Austria, France, Sweden, Norway, Denmark, Ireland, Italy, Germany, Netherlands, Spain, United Kingdom, Greece, Portugal, United States	Turkey, Poland, China, Morocco, Bulgaria, Czech Rep., Lithuania, Hungary, Mexico, India, Estonia, Egypt	Kyrgyzstan, Ukraine, Kazakhstan, Syria, Tunisia, Lebanon, Mozambique, Moldova, El Salvador, BCEAO, Iran, Nicaragua, Costa Rica, Ghana, Armenia
Relative surplus of accountability (0 and higher)		
New Zealand, Canada, Australia, Korea, Singapore, Japan	Thailand, Brazil, Chile, Israel, Argentina, Malaysia, Indonesia, Romania, Philippines, Jordan, Peru, Slovakia, Venezuela, Slovenia, Russia, Pakistan, South Africa	United Arab Emirates, Georgia, Bahrain, BEAC, Bolivia, Mongolia, Uganda, Albania, Paraguay, Madagascar, Sri Lanka, Zambia, Sierra Leone, Belarus, Honduras, Uruguay, Nigeria, Colombia, Guatemala, Kenya, Tanzania, Botswana, Namibia, Bangladesh

Source: Authors' estimates from detailed data presented in the appendix tables.

when the difference is lower than 0.25 but remains negative; and nil, when the difference is positive. The first two levels reflect what we characterized as a relative deficit of accountability; the last case reflects what we characterized as a relative surplus of accountability.

Figure 5.8a to 5.8c, which plots countries into a four-quadrant framework, allows differentiating countries' performances vis-à-vis a potential deficit of accountability based on the level of CB independence. It visualizes the disparities between CBs according to the income level of the countries in which they operate. It is noteworthy that only a limited number of countries exhibit a high relative deficit of accountability, according to our definition.[12] However, it is somewhat unexpected to find a number of countries with a relative deficit of accountability among the group of advanced economies. This result is confirmed by looking at average levels of relative deficit/surplus of accountability by income groups: CBs in advanced countries have an average relative deficit of accountability which, although slightly lower, is similar to the level observed for developing countries, and higher than the level observed for emerging markets (Table 5.12). It is also somewhat unexpected to find a number of countries with a relative surplus of accountability. One of the reasons, in particular for advanced economies and emerging market economies for which CB independence is a well accepted pillar of CB governance, may be related to the fact that we use an index of de jure CB independence which does not capture fully de facto independence. In those cases, which encompass major CBs in Asia and the Pacific already identified as having a low level of de jure independence (Table 5.2), a relative surplus of accountability points to the need to upgrade CB legislation.

Relative deficit of transparency

CB transparency should be positively correlated to accountability as the exercise of accountability requires a high level of transparency. When looking at CBs' relative performance we define three levels to characterize the lack of correspondence between accountability and transparency (Table 5.13): high, when the index of transparency is below the index of accountability (both indices being standardized to a maximum value

---

[12] CBs in developing countries are clustered in the top two quadrants of Figure 5.8c, meaning that they have reached a high level of accountability but independence is lagging behind, although some CBs do not exhibit a deficit. CBs in emerging markets and advanced countries are clustered in the top right of Figures 5.8b and 5.8a, meaning that they have reached a high level of accountability and independence.

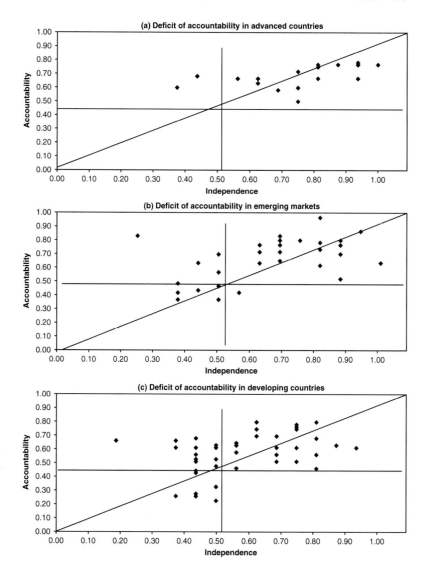

Figure 5.8 Relative deficit of accountability
Source: Authors' calculations.

of 1) by more than 0.25; low, when the difference is lower than 0.25 but remains negative; and nil, when the difference is positive. The first two levels reflect a relative deficit of transparency; the last case reflects what we characterized as a relative surplus of transparency.

Table 5.12   Average relative deficit/surplus of accountability and transparency

Country group	Average relative deficit/ surplus of accountability	Average relative deficit/ surplus of transparency
Advanced countries		
Surplus[1]	0.14	0.15
Deficit[2]	−0.15	−0.09
Emerging markets		
Surplus[1]	0.12	0.09
Deficit[2]	−0.13	−0.12
Developing countries		
Surplus[1]	0.11	0.04
Deficit[2]	−0.17	−0.17

[1] Simple average of the difference between accountability/transparency and independence/accountability for countries with a surplus of accountability/ transparency.
[2] Simple average of the difference between accountability/transparency and independence/accountability for countries with a deficit of accountability/transparency.
Source: Authors' calculations.

Figure 5.9a to 5.9c, which plots countries into a four-quadrant framework, allows differentiating countries based on their level of accountability. Contrary to what we have observed with regard to the relative deficit of accountability, CBs in advanced economies record the lowest average relative deficit and the average relative surplus of transparency is elevated. In contrast, CBs in developing countries are those for which the relative deficit of transparency is the highest and most widespread.[13] Such a result is consistent with the fact that transparency, in addition to facilitating the exercise of accountability, is also a prerequisite for CBs operating in the context of developed financial markets and relying on market-based monetary instruments, which tends to be less the case in developing countries.

The low relative deficit of transparency among CBs which operate in developed financial markets also suggests that market discipline has been a stronger driving force for the convergence of CBs towards well-balanced governance frameworks that one may call the "democratic discipline" (i.e., pressure to ensure a high level of accountability). Finally, the number of CBs which exhibit a relative deficit of transparency

---

[13] CBs in developing countries are clustered in the bottom right quadrant of Figure 5.9c meaning that they have reached a somewhat high level of accountability but transparency is lagging behind. CBs in emerging market economies and advanced countries are clustered in the top right of Figures 5.9b and 5.9a, meaning that they have reached a high level of accountability and transparency.

Table 5.13 Relative deficit of transparency: ranking of central banks

Advanced	Emerging	Developing
High relative deficit of transparency (lower than −0.25)		
	Bulgaria	Madagascar, Georgia, Namibia, Mongolia, Ukraine, Sierra Leone, Armenia, Honduras
Low relative deficit of transparency (between −0.25 and −0.01)		
ECB, Austria, France, Germany, Netherlands, Spain, Portugal, Greece, Belgium, Finland, Ireland, Italy, Australia, Denmark	Argentina, Peru, Indonesia, Slovenia, Russia, Lithuania, Venezuela, Malaysia, Pakistan, Estonia, Romania	Moldova, Zambia, Tanzania, BEAC, Paraguay, Ecuador, Lebanon, Botswana, Bolivia, El Salvador, Bangladesh, Belarus, Uganda, Kyrgyzstan, Costa Rica, Uruguay, Algeria, Albania, Tunisia, Iran, Syria, Nicaragua, Ghana
Relative surplus of transparency (0 and higher)		
Switzerland, Korea, Sweden, Japan, New Zealand, United States, Singapore, Canada, Norway, Iceland, United Kingdom	Mexico, Egypt, China, South Africa, Philippines, Slovakia, Poland, Jordan, India, Morocco, Chile, Hungary, Turkey, Czech Rep., Latvia, Brazil, Israel, Thailand, Croatia	Sri Lanka, Kazakhstan, Kenya, Bahrain, Saudi Arabia, United Arab Emirates, Guatemala, BCEAO, Nigeria, Colombia, Mozambique

Source: Authors' estimates from detailed data presented in the appendix tables.

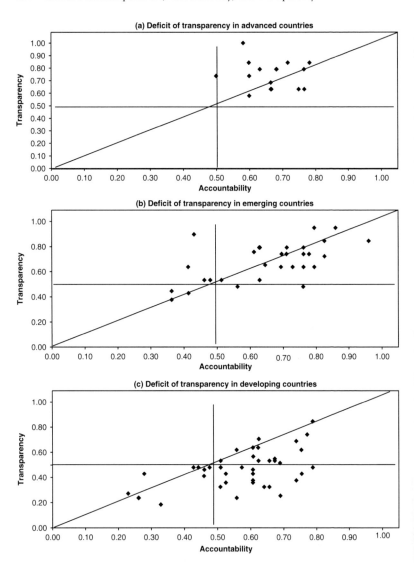

Figure 5.9   Relative deficit of transparency
Source: Authors' calculations.

is smaller than the number of those which exhibit a relative deficit of accountability. Such a result is consistent with the trend that has been noted by Laurens (2005) toward market-based instruments for the implementation of monetary policy.

Country

Full name	Code	Region[1]	Region[2]	Income level[3]
Afghanistan	AFG	PA	MCD	Developing
Albania	ALB	TR	EUR	Developing
Algeria	DZA	MN	MCD	Developing
Angola	AGO	SS	AFR	Developing
Argentina	ARG	LA	WHD	Emerging
Armenia	ARM	TR	MCD	Developing
Aruba	ABW	C	WHD	Developing
Australia	AUS	PA	APD	Advanced
Austria	AUT	EU	EUR	Advanced
Azerbaijan	AZE	TR	MCD	Developing
Bahamas	BHS	C	WHD	Developing
Bahrain	BHR	MN	MCD	Developing
Bangladesh	BGD	PA	APD	Developing
Barbados	BRB	C	WHD	Developing
BCEAO	BCEAO	SS	AFR	Developing
BEAC	BEAC	SS	AFR	Developing
Belarus	BLR	TR	EUR	Developing
Belgium	BEL	EU	EUR	Advanced
Belize	BLZ	LA	WHD	Developing
Bermuda		C	WHD	Developing
Bhutan	BTN	PA	APD	Developing
Bolivia	BOL	LA	WHD	Developing
Bosnia Herzegovina	BIH	TR	EUR	Developing
Botswana	BWA	SS	AFR	Developing
Brazil	BRA	LA	WHD	Emerging
Bulgaria	BGR	TR	EUR	Emerging
Burundi	BDI	SS	AFR	Developing
Cambodia	KHM	PA	APD	Developing
Canada	CAN	NA	WHD	Advanced
Cape Verde	CPV	SS	AFR	Developing
Cayman Islands		C	WHD	Developing
Chile	CHL	LA	WHD	Emerging
China	CHN	PA	APD	Emerging
Colombia	COL	LA	WHD	Developing
Comoros	COM	SS	AFR	Developing
Costa Rica	CRI	LA	WHD	Developing
Croatia	HRV	TR	EUR	Emerging
Cuba	CUB	C	WHD	Developing
Cyprus	CYP	E	EUR	Advanced
Czech Rep.	CZE	TR	EUR	Emerging
Denmark	DNK	E	EUR	Advanced
Dominican Rep.	DOM	C	WHD	Developing
ECB	ECB	EU	EUR	Advanced
ECCU	ECCU	C	WHD	Developing
Ecuador	ECU	LA	WHD	Developing
Egypt	EGY	MN	MCD	Emerging
El Salvador	SLV	LA	WHD	Developing
Eritrea	ERI	SS	AFR	Developing
Estonia	EST	TR	EUR	Emerging
Ethiopia	ETH	SS	AFR	Developing
Fiji	FJI	PA	APD	Developing
Finland	FIN	EU	EUR	Advanced
France	FRA	EU	EUR	Advanced
Georgia	GEO	TR	MCD	Developing
Germany	DEU	EU	EUR	Advanced
Ghana	GHA	SS	AFR	Developing

(Continued)

Appendix I Continued

Country					Country				
Full name	Code	Region[1]	Region[2]	Income level[3]	Full name	Code	Region[1]	Region[2]	Income level[3]
Greece	GRC	EU	EUR	Advanced	Liberia	LBR	SS	AFR	Developing
Guatemala	GTM	LA	WHD	Developing	Libya	LBY	MN	MCD	Developing
Guinea Republic	GIN	SS	AFR	Developing	Lithuania	LTU	TR	EUR	Emerging
Guyana	GUY	LA	WHD	Developing	Luxembourg	LUX	EU	EUR	Advanced
Haiti	HTI	C	WHD	Developing	Macau		PA	APD	Developing
Honduras	HND	LA	WHD	Developing	Macedonia	MKD	TR	EUR	Developing
Hong Kong		PA	APD	Advanced	Madagascar	MDG	SS	AFR	Developing
Hungary	HUN	TR	EUR	Emerging	Malawi	MWI	SS	AFR	Developing
Iceland	ISL	E	EUR	Advanced	Malaysia	MYS	PA	APD	Emerging
India	IND	PA	APD	Emerging	Maldives	MDV	PA	APD	Developing
Indonesia	IDN	PA	APD	Emerging	Malta	MLT	E	EUR	Emerging
Iran	IRN	MN	MCD	Developing	Mauritius	MUS	SS	AFR	Developing
Iraq	IRQ	MN	MCD	Developing	Mexico	MEX	LA	WHD	Emerging
Ireland	IRL	EU	EUR	Advanced	Moldova	MDA	TR	EUR	Developing
Israel	ISR	MN	EUR	Emerging	Mongolia	MNG	PA	APD	Developing
Italy	ITA	EU	EUR	Advanced	Morocco	MAR	MN	MCD	Emerging
Jamaica	JAM	C	WHD	Developing	Mozambique	MOZ	SS	AFR	Developing
Japan	JPN	PA	APD	Advanced	Myanmar	MMR	PA	APD	Developing
Jordan	JOR	MN	MCD	Emerging	Namibia	NAM	SS	AFR	Developing
Kazakhstan	KAZ	TR	MCD	Developing	Nepal	NPL	PA	APD	Developing
Kenya	KEN	SS	AFR	Developing	Netherlands	NLD	EU	EUR	Advanced
Korea	KOR	PA	APD	Advanced	Netherlands Antilles	ANT	C	WHD	Developing
Kuwait	KWT	MN	MCD	Developing	New Zealand	NZL	PA	APD	Advanced
Kyrgyzstan	KGZ	TR	MCD	Developing	Nicaragua	NIC	LA	WHD	Developing
Laos	LAO	PA	APD	Developing	Nigeria	NGA	SS	AFR	Developing
Latvia	LVA	TR	EUR	Emerging	Norway	NOR	E	EUR	Advanced
Lebanon	LBN	MN	MCD	Developing	Oman	OMN	MN	MCD	Developing
Lesotho	LSO	SS	AFR	Developing	Pakistan	PAK	PA	MCD	Emerging

Country	Code	Geo¹	IMF²	Status³
Palestine	PLW	MN	MCD	Developing
Panama	PAN	LA	WHD	Developing
Papua New Guinea	PNG	PA	APD	Developing
Paraguay	PRY	LA	WHD	Developing
Peru	PER	LA	WHD	Developing
Philippines	PHL	PA	APD	Emerging
Poland	POL	TR	EUR	Emerging
Portugal	PRT	EU	EUR	Advanced
Qatar	QAT	MN	MCD	Developing
Romania	ROM	TR	EUR	Emerging
Russia	RUS	TR	EUR	Emerging
Rwanda	RWA	SS	AFR	Developing
São Tomé Principe	STP	SS	AFR	Developing
Saudi Arabia	SAU	MN	MCD	Developing
Serbia Montenegro	SRB	TR	EUR	Developing
Seychelles	SYC	SS	AFR	Developing
Sierra Leone	SLE	SS	AFR	Developing
Singapore	SGP	PA	APD	Advanced
Slovakia	SVK	TR	EUR	Emerging
Slovenia	SVN	TR	EUR	Emerging
Solomon Islands	SLB	C	APD	Developing
South Africa	ZAF	SS	AFR	Emerging
Spain	ESP	EU	EUR	Advanced
Sri Lanka	LKA	PA	APD	Developing
Sudan	SDN	SS	MCD	Developing
Suriname	SUR	LA	APD	Developing
Sweden	SWE	E	EUR	Advanced
Switzerland	CHE	E	EUR	Advanced
Syria	SYR	MN	MCD	Developing
Tajikistan	TJK	TR	MCD	Developing
Tanzania	TZA	SS	AFR	Developing
Thailand	THA	PA	APD	Emerging
Timor-Leste	TLS	PA	APD	Developing
Tonga	TON	PA	APD	Developing
Trinidad Tobago	TTO	C	WHD	Developing
Tunisia	TUN	MN	MCD	Developing
Turkey	TUR	MN	EUR	Emerging
Turkmenistan	TKM	TR	MCD	Developing
Uganda	UGA	SS	AFR	Developing
Ukraine	UKR	TR	EUR	Developing
United Arab Emirates	ARE	MN	MCD	Developing
United Kingdom	GBR	E	EUR	Advanced
United States	USA	NA	WHD	Advanced
Uruguay	URY	LA	WHD	Developing
Uzbekistan	UZB	TR	MCD	Developing
Vanuatu	VUT	PA	APD	Developing
Venezuela	VEN	LA	WHD	Emerging
Vietnam	VNM	PA	APD	Developing
Yemen Rep.	YEM	MN	MCD	Developing
Zambia	ZMB	SS	AFR	Developing
Zimbabwe	ZWE	SS	AFR	Developing

¹ Geopolitical classification used in Figures 5.1, 5.2. PA: Asia & Pacific. TR: Economies in transition. MN: Middle East & North Africa. SS: Sub-Saharan Africa. LA: Latin America. C: Caribbean. EU: Euro area. E: Europe. NA: North America.

² IMF classification used in Tables 5.5, 5.6. AFR: Sub-Saharan Africa. APD: Asia & Pacific. EUR: Europe. MCD: Middle East & North Africa. WHD: Western Hemisphere.

³ Emerging markets include upper-middle income countries and some lower-middle income countries classified as such by *The Economist*, and countries with a sustained financial reform process. Developing countries include lower and lower-middle income countries, plus some with upper-middle/high income but with a level of financial sector development not matching their income.

Appendix II Independence: political scores for advanced economies (2003)

Country	Appointments				Relationships with the government		Constituting laws		Score	Standardized score
	(1)	(2)	(3)	(4)	(5)	(6)	(7)	(8)		
European Central Bank	Yes	Yes	Yes	Yes	Yes	Yes	Yes	Yes	8	1.00
Australia		Yes					Yes		2	0.25
Austria	Yes	Yes	Yes	Yes	Yes	Yes	Yes	Yes	8	1.00
Belgium	Yes	Yes	Yes	Yes	Yes	Yes	Yes	Yes	8	1.00
Canada	Yes	Yes					Yes		3	0.38
Cyprus					Yes		Yes	Yes	3	0.38
Denmark		Yes				Yes	Yes	Yes	4	0.50
Finland	Yes	Yes	Yes	Yes	Yes	Yes	Yes	Yes	8	1.00
France	Yes	Yes	Yes	Yes	Yes	Yes	Yes	Yes	8	1.00
Germany	Yes	Yes	Yes	Yes	Yes	Yes	Yes	Yes	8	1.00
Greece	Yes	Yes	Yes	Yes	Yes	Yes	Yes	Yes	8	1.00
Hong Kong				Yes	Yes		Yes		3	0.38
Iceland		Yes		Yes	Yes		Yes		4	0.50
Ireland	Yes	Yes	Yes	Yes	Yes	Yes	Yes	Yes	8	1.00
Italy	Yes	Yes	Yes	Yes	Yes	Yes	Yes	Yes	8	1.00
Japan		Yes					Yes		1	0.13

Country	(1)	(2)	(3)	(4)	(5)	(6)	(7)	(8)	Total	Ratio
Korea							Yes	Yes	2	0.25
Luxembourg	Yes	Yes	Yes	Yes	Yes	Yes	Yes	Yes	8	1.00
Netherlands	Yes	Yes	Yes	Yes	Yes	Yes	Yes	Yes	8	1.00
New Zealand			Yes		Yes		Yes		2	0.25
Norway	Yes	Yes	Yes		Yes		Yes		4	0.50
Portugal	Yes	Yes	Yes	Yes	Yes	Yes	Yes	Yes	8	1.00
Singapore						Yes	Yes	Yes	3	0.38
Spain	Yes	Yes	Yes	Yes	Yes	Yes	Yes	Yes	8	1.00
Sweden	Yes	Yes	Yes	Yes	Yes	Yes	Yes		7	0.88
Switzerland		Yes	Yes	Yes	Yes	Yes	Yes	Yes	7	0.88
United Kingdom					Yes	Yes	Yes		3	0.38
United States				Yes	Yes	Yes	Yes	Yes	5	0.63
Average										0.70
Satisfaction ratio	57%	71%	57%	64%	75%	64%	96%	75%		

Note: (1) governor appointed without government involvement; (2) governor appointed for more than five years; (3) CB board (CBB) appointed without government involvement; and (4) CBB appointed for more than five years; (5) no mandatory participation of government representatives in the CBB; (6) no government approval is required for formulation of monetary policy; (7) CB legally obliged to pursue monetary stability as one of its primary objectives; and (8) legal protections that strengthen the CB's position in the event of a conflict with government.

Source: Authors' estimates.

Appendix III Independence: political scores for emerging markets (2003)

Country	Appointments				Relationships with the government		Constituting laws		Score	Standardized score
	(1)	(2)	(3)	(4)	(5)	(6)	(7)	(8)		
Argentina		Yes		Yes	Yes	Yes	Yes	Yes	6	0.75
Brazil		Yes		Yes	Yes		Yes		4	0.50
Bulgaria	Yes	Yes	Yes	Yes	Yes	Yes	Yes	Yes	8	1.00
Chile				Yes	Yes		Yes	Yes	4	0.50
China		Yes		Yes			Yes		3	0.38
Croatia[1]	Yes	Yes	Yes	Yes	Yes	Yes	Yes	Yes	8	1.00
Czech Republic	Yes	Yes	Yes	Yes		Yes	Yes	Yes	7	0.88
Egypt							Yes		1	0.13
Estonia	Yes		Yes			Yes	Yes	Yes	5	0.63
Hungary		Yes	Yes	Yes	Yes	Yes	Yes	Yes	7	0.88
India						Yes	Yes		2	0.25
Indonesia			Yes		Yes	Yes	Yes	Yes	5	0.63
Israel							Yes		1	0.13
Jordan					Yes		Yes		2	0.25
Latvia	Yes	Yes	Yes	Yes	Yes	Yes	Yes	Yes	8	1.00
Lithuania	Yes		Yes	Yes	Yes	Yes	Yes	Yes	7	0.88
Malaysia	Yes						Yes		2	0.25
Malta					Yes	Yes	Yes	Yes	4	0.50

	(1)	(2)	(3)	(4)	(5)	(6)	(7)	(8)		
Pakistan	Yes					Yes	Yes		2	0.25
Peru		Yes			Yes	Yes	Yes		3	0.38
Philippines			Yes	Yes		Yes	Yes	Yes	3	0.38
Poland	Yes	Yes	Yes	Yes		Yes	Yes	Yes	5	0.63
Romania	Yes	Yes	Yes			Yes	Yes	Yes	7	0.88
Russia			Yes			Yes	Yes	Yes	5	0.63
Slovakia	Yes					Yes	Yes	Yes	4	0.50
Slovenia[1]	Yes	Yes	Yes	Yes		Yes	Yes	Yes	4	0.50
South Africa							Yes		7	0.88
Thailand		Yes	Yes	Yes	Yes		Yes		1	0.13
Turkey	Yes		Yes		Yes	Yes	Yes	Yes	4	0.50
Venezuela		Yes	Yes	Yes	Yes	Yes	Yes	Yes	5	0.63
Average										0.56
Satisfaction ratio	41%	44%	44%	50%	47%	63%	97%	63%		

[1] Indices for Croatia and Slovenia for the late 1980s are those of Yugoslavia at the time.

Note: (1) governor appointed without government involvement; (2) governor appointed for more than five years; (3) CB board (CBB) appointed without government involvement; and (4) CBB appointed for more than five years; (5) no mandatory participation of government representatives in the CBB; (6) no government approval is required for formulation of monetary policy; (7) CB legally obliged to pursue monetary stability as one of its primary objectives; and (8) legal protections that strengthen the CB's position in the event of a conflict with government.

Source: Authors' estimates.

Appendix IV Independence: political scores for developing countries (2003)

Country	Appointments				Relationships with government		Constituting laws		Score	Standardized score
	(1)	(2)	(3)	(4)	(5)	(6)	(7)	(8)		
Afghanistan					Yes	Yes	Yes	Yes	4	0.50
Albania		Yes	Yes	Yes		Yes	Yes	Yes	6	0.75
Algeria	Yes	Yes	Yes	Yes	Yes	Yes	Yes	Yes	8	1.00
Angola						Yes	Yes		2	0.25
Armenia	Yes	Yes	Yes		Yes	Yes	Yes	Yes	7	0.88
Aruba	Yes	Yes	Yes		Yes	Yes	Yes		6	0.75
Azerbaijan	Yes		Yes		Yes	Yes	Yes	Yes	6	0.75
Bahamas							Yes		1	0.13
Bahrain							Yes	Yes	2	0.25
Bangladesh									0	0.00
Barbados							Yes		1	0.13
BCEAO[1]	Yes	Yes		Yes			Yes		4	0.50
BEAC[2]	Yes					Yes	Yes	Yes	4	0.50
Belarus			Yes				Yes	Yes	4	0.50
Belize							Yes		1	0.13
Bermuda					Yes				1	0.13
Bhutan							Yes		1	0.13
Bolivia		Yes			Yes	Yes	Yes		4	0.50
Bosnia Herzegovina[4]	Yes	Yes	Yes	Yes	Yes	Yes	Yes	Yes	8	1.00
Botswana							Yes		1	0.13
Burundi					Yes	Yes	Yes		3	0.38
Cambodia						Yes	Yes	Yes	3	0.38
Cape Verde					Yes		Yes	Yes	3	0.38
Cayman Islands							Yes		1	0.13
Colombia							Yes		1	0.13
Comoros					Yes				1	0.13
Costa Rica				Yes		Yes	Yes	Yes	4	0.50

Cuba						Yes		Yes	3	0.38
Dominican Rep.	Yes					Yes			2	0.25
ECCB[3]	Yes				Yes	Yes	Yes	Yes	5	0.63
Ecuador		Yes	Yes	Yes	Yes	Yes	Yes	Yes	7	0.88
El Salvador			Yes	Yes	Yes	Yes		Yes	5	0.63
Eritrea		Yes				Yes	Yes	Yes	3	0.38
Ethiopia			Yes			Yes		Yes	3	0.38
Fiji						Yes		Yes	1	0.13
Georgia		Yes	Yes	Yes	Yes	Yes	Yes	Yes	7	0.88
Ghana						Yes	Yes	Yes	3	0.38
Guatemala						Yes	Yes	Yes	3	0.38
Guinea Republic	Yes		Yes			Yes	Yes	Yes	5	0.63
Guyana	Yes					Yes		Yes	2	0.25
Haiti	Yes	Yes			Yes			Yes	4	0.50
Honduras						Yes		Yes	1	0.13
Iran								Yes	0	0.00
Iraq			Yes		Yes	Yes	Yes	Yes	4	0.50
Jamaica	Yes					Yes		Yes	1	0.13
Kazakhstan	Yes	Yes	Yes			Yes	Yes	Yes	5	0.63
Kenya						Yes		Yes	1	0.13
Kuwait						Yes		Yes	1	0.13
Kyrgyzstan	Yes	Yes	Yes	Yes	Yes	Yes	Yes	Yes	8	1.00
Laos						Yes		Yes	1	0.13
Lebanon		Yes				Yes		Yes	2	0.25
Lesotho					Yes		Yes	Yes	2	0.25
Liberia				Yes	Yes	Yes	Yes	Yes	3	0.38
Libya	Yes					Yes		Yes	2	0.25
Macau	Yes	Yes	Yes			Yes		Yes	4	0.25
Macedonia[4]	Yes	Yes	Yes	Yes	Yes	Yes	Yes	Yes	8	0.50
Madagascar			Yes		Yes	Yes	Yes	Yes	4	1.00
Malawi						Yes	Yes	Yes	1	0.50
Maldives		Yes			Yes	Yes		Yes	3	0.13
										0.38

(Continued)

Appendix IV Continued

Country	Appointments				Relationships with government		Constituting laws		Score	Standardized score
	(1)	(2)	(3)	(4)	(5)	(6)	(7)	(8)		
Mauritius	Yes				Yes		Yes	Yes	4	0.50
Moldova	Yes	Yes	Yes	Yes		Yes	Yes		6	0.75
Mongolia	Yes	Yes	Yes	Yes	Yes	Yes	Yes	Yes	8	1.00
Mozambique	Yes				Yes		Yes		3	0.38
Myanmar					Yes		Yes		2	0.25
Namibia	Yes						Yes		2	0.25
Nepal						Yes	Yes	Yes	3	0.38
Netherlands Antilles		Yes		Yes			Yes		3	0.38
Nicaragua							Yes		1	0.13
Nigeria					Yes		Yes		2	0.25
Oman							Yes		1	0.13
Palestine				Yes	Yes		Yes		3	0.38
Panama		Yes			Yes	Yes	Yes		4	0.50
Papua New Guinea	Yes	Yes	Yes			Yes	Yes		5	0.63
Paraguay					Yes		Yes		2	0.25
Qatar							Yes		1	0.13
Rwanda		Yes			Yes	Yes	Yes		4	0.50
São Tomé &Príncipe						Yes	Yes		2	0.25
Saudi Arabia					Yes		Yes		2	0.25
Serbia Montenegro[4]	Yes		Yes			Yes	Yes	Yes	5	0.63
Seychelles							Yes		1	0.13
Sierra Leone					Yes	Yes	Yes	Yes	4	0.50
Solomon Islands							Yes		1	0.13
Sri Lanka		Yes		Yes		Yes	Yes		4	0.50

	1	2	3	4	5	6	7	8		
Sudan									0	0.00
Suriname							Yes		1	0.13
Syria		Yes					Yes	Yes	3	0.38
Tajikistan	Yes	Yes	Yes	Yes	Yes	Yes	Yes	Yes	8	1.00
Tanzania							Yes		1	0.13
Timor-Leste		Yes		Yes	Yes	Yes	Yes	Yes	6	0.75
Tonga					Yes		Yes		2	0.25
Trinidad and Tobago	Yes	Yes					Yes		3	0.38
Tunisia		Yes		Yes	Yes	Yes	Yes		5	0.63
Turkmenistan		Yes	Yes		Yes		Yes	Yes	5	0.63
Uganda			Yes		Yes		Yes	Yes	4	0.50
Ukraine	Yes		Yes	Yes	Yes	Yes	Yes	Yes	7	0.88
United Arab Emirates				Yes		Yes	Yes		3	0.38
Uruguay		Yes		Yes		Yes	Yes	Yes	5	0.63
Uzbekistan	Yes		Yes		Yes	Yes	Yes	Yes	6	0.75
Vanuatu							Yes		1	0.13
Vietnam		Yes		Yes			Yes		3	0.38
Yemen					Yes		Yes	Yes	3	0.38
Zambia					Yes		Yes	Yes	3	0.38
Zimbabwe					Yes			Yes	2	0.25
Average										0.41
Satisfaction ratio	26%	30%	20%	27%	40%	49%	94%	39%		

[1] BCEAO includes Benin, Burkina Faso, Côte d'Ivoire, Guinea Bissau, Mali, Niger, Senegal and Togo.

[2] BEAC includes Cameroon, Central African Republic, Chad, Republic of Congo, Equatorial Guinea and Gabon.

[3] ECCB includes Anguilla, Antigua-Barbuda, Dominica, Grenada, Montserrat, St. Kitts-Nevis, St. Lucia, and St. Vincent-the-Grenadines.

[4] Indices for Bosnia, Croatia, Slovenia, Serbia Montenegro and Macedonia for the late 1980s are those of Yugoslavia at the time.

Note: (1) governor appointed without government involvement; (2) governor appointed for more than five years; (3) CB board (CBB) appointed without government involvement; and (4) CBB appointed for more than five years; (5) no mandatory participation of government representatives in the CBB; (6) no government approval is required for formulation of monetary policy; (7) CB legally obliged to pursue monetary stability as one of its primary objectives; and (8) legal protections that strengthen the CB's position in the event of a conflict with government.

Source: Authors' estimates.

Appendix V   Independence: economic scores for advanced economies (2003)

Country	Monetary financing of public deficits					Monetary instruments		Score	Standardized score
	(1)	(2)	(3)	(4)	(5)	(6)	(7)		
European Central Bank	Yes	Yes	Yes	Yes	Yes	Yes	Yes/Yes	8	1.00
Australia	Yes	Yes	Yes	Yes	Yes	Yes	Yes/Yes	8	1.00
Austria	Yes	Yes	Yes	Yes	Yes		Yes/Yes	7	0.88
Belgium	Yes	Yes	Yes	Yes	Yes		Yes/Yes	7	0.88
Canada	Yes		Yes	Yes	Yes	Yes	Yes/Yes	7	0.88
Cyprus	Yes	Yes	Yes	Yes	Yes	Yes		6	0.75
Denmark	Yes	Yes	Yes	Yes	Yes	Yes	Yes/Yes	8	1.00
Finland	Yes	Yes	Yes	Yes	Yes		Yes/Yes	7	0.88
France	Yes	Yes	Yes	Yes	Yes		Yes/Yes	7	0.88
Germany	Yes	Yes	Yes	Yes	Yes		Yes	6	0.75
Greece	Yes	Yes	Yes	Yes	Yes			5	0.63
Hong Kong					Yes	Yes		3	0.38
Iceland	Yes	Yes	Yes	Yes	Yes	Yes	Yes/Yes	8	1.00
Ireland	Yes	Yes	Yes	Yes	Yes			5	0.63
Italy	Yes	Yes	Yes	Yes	Yes			5	0.63
Japan	Yes		Yes	Yes		Yes	Yes/Yes	6	0.75
Korea	Yes	Yes	Yes	Yes		Yes	Yes/Yes	7	0.88
Luxembourg	Yes	Yes	Yes	Yes	Yes		Yes/Yes	7	0.88

	(1)	(2)	(3)	(4)	(5)	(6)	(7)		
Netherlands	Yes	Yes	Yes	Yes	Yes		Yes	6	0.75
New Zealand	Yes	Yes	Yes	Yes		Yes		5	0.63
Norway	Yes	Yes	Yes	Yes	Yes	Yes	Yes/Yes	8	1.00
Portugal	Yes	Yes	Yes	Yes		Yes		5	0.63
Singapore	Yes	Yes	Yes					3	0.38
Spain	Yes	Yes	Yes	Yes	Yes		Yes	6	0.75
Sweden	Yes	Yes	Yes	Yes	Yes	Yes	Yes/Yes	8	1.00
Switzerland	Yes	Yes	Yes	Yes	Yes	Yes	Yes/Yes	8	1.00
United Kingdom	Yes	Yes	Yes	Yes	Yes	Yes	Yes/Yes	8	1.00
United States	Yes	Yes	Yes	Yes	Yes	Yes	Yes	7	0.88
Average									0.81
Satisfaction ratio (1 pt. in 7th crit.)	93%	89%	93%	93%	89%	57%	57%		
(2 pts. In 7th crit.)							18%		

Note: (1) no automatic procedure for government to obtain direct credit from CB; (2) when available, credit extended to government at market interest rates; (3) credit is temporary; (4) and for limited amount; (5) CB does not participate in primary market for public debt; (6) CB responsible for setting policy rate; and (7) CB has no responsibility to oversee banking sector (two points) or shares responsibility with other institutions (one point).

Source: Authors' estimates.

Appendix VI Independence: economic scores for emerging markets (2003)

Country	Monetary financing of public deficits					Monetary instruments		Score	Standardized score
	(1)	(2)	(3)	(4)	(5)	(6)	(7)		
Argentina	Yes	Yes	Yes	Yes	Yes	Yes		6	0.75
Brazil	Yes	Yes	Yes	Yes	Yes	Yes		6	0.75
Bulgaria	Yes	Yes	Yes	Yes	Yes	Yes		6	0.75
Chile	Yes	Yes	Yes	Yes	Yes	Yes	Yes	7	0.88
China	Yes	Yes	Yes	Yes	Yes	Yes		6	0.75
Croatia	Yes	Yes	Yes	Yes	Yes	Yes		6	0.75
Czech Republic	Yes	Yes	Yes	Yes	Yes	Yes	Yes	7	0.88
Egypt	Yes		Yes	Yes	Yes	Yes		5	0.63
Estonia	Yes	Yes	Yes	Yes	Yes	Yes	Yes/Yes	8	1.00
Hungary	Yes	Yes	Yes	Yes	Yes	Yes	Yes/Yes	8	1.00
India	Yes		Yes	Yes		Yes	Yes/Yes	6	0.75
Indonesia	Yes	Yes	Yes	Yes	Yes	Yes		6	0.75
Israel	Yes		Yes	Yes	Yes	Yes		5	0.63
Jordan	Yes		Yes	Yes		Yes		4	0.50
Latvia	Yes	Yes	Yes	Yes	Yes	Yes	Yes/Yes	8	1.00
Lithuania	Yes	Yes	Yes	Yes	Yes	Yes		6	0.75
Malaysia	Yes	Yes	Yes	Yes		Yes	Yes	6	0.75
Malta	Yes	Yes	Yes	Yes	Yes	Yes	Yes	7	0.88

Country	(1)	(2)	(3)	(4)	(5)	(6)	(7)	Score	Ratio
Mexico	Yes	Yes	Yes	Yes	Yes		Yes	6	0.75
Morocco	Yes	Yes	Yes	Yes	Yes		Yes	6	0.75
Pakistan	Yes	Yes	Yes	Yes	Yes			5	0.63
Peru	Yes	Yes	Yes	Yes	Yes	Yes	Yes/Yes	8	1.00
Philippines	Yes		Yes	Yes	Yes	Yes		5	0.63
Poland	Yes	Yes	Yes	Yes	Yes	Yes	Yes	7	0.88
Romania	Yes	Yes	Yes	Yes	Yes	Yes		6	0.75
Russia	Yes	Yes	Yes					3	0.38
Slovakia	Yes	Yes	Yes	Yes	Yes	Yes		6	0.75
Slovenia	Yes	Yes	Yes	Yes	Yes	Yes		6	0.75
South Africa	Yes	Yes	Yes					3	0.38
Thailand			Yes	Yes	Yes			3	0.38
Turkey	Yes	Yes	Yes	Yes	Yes	Yes	Yes/Yes	8	1.00
Venezuela	Yes	Yes	Yes	Yes	Yes	Yes	Yes	7	0.88
Average									0.75
Satisfaction ratio (1 pt. in 7th crit.)	97%	75%	97%	94%	81%	94%	25%		
(2 pts. In 7th crit.)							19%		

Note: (1) no automatic procedure for government to obtain direct credit from CB; (2) when available, credit extended to government at market interest rates; (3) credit is temporary; (4) and for limited amount; (5) CB does not participate in primary market for public debt; (6) CB responsible for setting policy rate; and (7) CB has no responsibility to oversee banking sector (two points) or shares responsibility with other institutions (one point).
Source: Authors' estimates.

Appendix VII Independence: economic scores for developing countries (2003)

Central banks	Monetary financing of public deficits					Monetary instruments		Score	Standardized score
	(1)	(2)	(3)	(4)	(5)	(6)	(7)		
Afghanistan	Yes	Yes	Yes	Yes	Yes	Yes		6	0.75
Albania	Yes	Yes	Yes	Yes	Yes	Yes		6	0.75
Algeria	Yes		Yes	Yes		Yes	Yes	5	0.63
Angola	Yes			Yes		Yes		3	0.38
Armenia	Yes	Yes	Yes	Yes	Yes	Yes		6	0.75
Aruba	Yes		Yes	Yes				3	0.38
Azerbaijan			Yes	Yes	Yes	Yes		4	0.50
Bahamas	Yes		Yes	Yes		Yes		4	0.50
Bahrain	Yes	Yes	Yes	Yes		Yes		5	0.63
Bangladesh	Yes		Yes			Yes		3	0.38
Barbados	Yes	Yes	Yes	Yes		Yes		5	0.63
BCEAO[1]	Yes	Yes	Yes	Yes	Yes	Yes	Yes	7	0.88
BEAC[2]	Yes	Yes	Yes	Yes	Yes	Yes	Yes	7	0.88
Belarus			Yes		Yes	Yes		3	0.38
Belize	Yes		Yes	Yes		Yes	Yes	5	0.63
Bermuda	Yes	Yes	Yes	Yes		Yes	Yes	6	0.75
Bhutan	Yes		Yes	Yes		Yes		4	0.50
Bolivia	Yes	Yes	Yes	Yes	Yes	Yes	Yes/Yes	8	1.00
Bosnia Herzegovina	Yes	Yes	Yes	Yes	Yes		Yes	6	0.75
Botswana	Yes		Yes	Yes	Yes	Yes	Yes	6	0.75
Burundi	Yes			Yes		Yes		3	0.38
Cambodia	Yes	Yes	Yes	Yes	Yes	Yes		6	0.75
Cape Verde	Yes		Yes	Yes	Yes	Yes		5	0.63
Cayman Islands	Yes	Yes	Yes	Yes		Yes		5	0.63
Colombia	Yes	Yes	Yes	Yes	Yes	Yes	Yes	7	0.88
Comoros	Yes	Yes	Yes	Yes	Yes	Yes		6	0.75
Costa Rica	Yes	Yes	Yes	Yes	Yes	Yes	Yes	7	0.88

Country									
Cuba	Yes	Yes	Yes			Yes		Yes	2	0.25
Dominican Republic	Yes	Yes	Yes	Yes	Yes	Yes	Yes/Yes		7	0.88
ECCB[3]	Yes	Yes	Yes	Yes	Yes	Yes			5	0.63
Ecuador	Yes	Yes	Yes	Yes	Yes	Yes	Yes/Yes		8	1.00
El Salvador	Yes	Yes	Yes	Yes	Yes	Yes	Yes/Yes		8	1.00
Eritrea	Yes	Yes	Yes	Yes		Yes			5	0.63
Ethiopia	Yes	Yes	Yes	Yes		Yes			5	0.63
Fiji	Yes	Yes	Yes	Yes		Yes			5	0.63
Georgia	Yes	Yes	Yes	Yes		Yes			5	0.63
Ghana	Yes	Yes	Yes	Yes		Yes			5	0.63
Guatemala	Yes	Yes	Yes	Yes	Yes	Yes	Yes		5	0.63
Guinea Republic	Yes	Yes	Yes	Yes		Yes			7	0.88
Guyana	Yes	Yes	Yes	Yes	Yes	Yes			5	0.63
Haiti	Yes	Yes	Yes	Yes		Yes			6	0.75
Honduras	Yes	Yes	Yes	Yes	Yes	Yes	Yes		4	0.50
Iran	Yes	Yes	Yes	Yes	Yes	Yes	Yes		7	0.88
Iraq	Yes	Yes	Yes	Yes	Yes				6	0.75
Jamaica	Yes	Yes	Yes	Yes		Yes	Yes		6	0.75
Kazakhstan	Yes	Yes	Yes	Yes		Yes	Yes/Yes		5	0.63
Kenya	Yes	Yes	Yes	Yes		Yes	Yes		7	0.88
Kuwait	Yes	Yes	Yes	Yes		Yes			6	0.75
Kyrgyzstan	Yes	Yes	Yes	Yes	Yes	Yes			4	0.50
Laos	Yes	Yes	Yes	Yes		Yes			6	0.75
Lebanon		Yes	Yes	Yes	Yes	Yes			5	0.63
Lesotho	Yes	Yes	Yes	Yes		Yes	Yes		6	0.75
Liberia	Yes	Yes	Yes	Yes		Yes			5	0.63
Libya	Yes	Yes	Yes	Yes		Yes			5	0.63
Macau	Yes	Yes	Yes	Yes	Yes	Yes	Yes		5	0.63
Macedonia	Yes	Yes	Yes	Yes	Yes	Yes	Yes		3	0.38
Madagascar	Yes	Yes	Yes	Yes	Yes	Yes	Yes		6	0.75

(Continued)

Appendix VII   Continued

Central banks	Monetary financing of public deficits					Monetary instruments		Score	Standardized score
	(1)	(2)	(3)	(4)	(5)	(6)	(7)		
Malawi	Yes	Yes	Yes	Yes		Yes		5	0.63
Maldives	Yes		Yes			Yes		3	0.38
Mauritius	Yes		Yes	Yes		Yes		4	0.50
Moldova	Yes	Yes	Yes	Yes	Yes	Yes		6	0.75
Mongolia	Yes		Yes	Yes		Yes		4	0.50
Mozambique	Yes		Yes	Yes		Yes		4	0.50
Myanmar	Yes	Yes		Yes		Yes		4	0.50
Namibia	Yes		Yes	Yes		Yes		4	0.50
Nepal	Yes	Yes	Yes	Yes		Yes		5	0.63
Netherlands Antilles	Yes		Yes	Yes		Yes		4	0.50
Nicaragua	Yes	Yes	Yes	Yes	Yes	Yes	Yes/Yes	8	1.00
Nigeria	Yes		Yes	Yes	Yes	Yes		5	0.63
Oman	Yes		Yes	Yes		Yes		4	0.50
Palestine	Yes		Yes	Yes	Yes	Yes		5	0.63
Panama						Yes	Yes/Yes	2	0.25
Papua New Guinea	Yes	Yes	Yes	Yes		Yes		5	0.63
Paraguay	Yes	Yes	Yes	Yes	Yes	Yes		6	0.75
Qatar	Yes					Yes		2	0.25
Rwanda		Yes	Yes	Yes	Yes	Yes		5	0.63
São Tomé &Principe			Yes	Yes		Yes		3	0.38
Saudi Arabia	Yes		Yes	Yes	Yes	Yes	Yes	6	0.75
Serbia Montenegro	Yes		Yes	Yes	Yes	Yes		5	0.63
Seychelles	Yes		Yes			Yes		3	0.38
Sierra Leone	Yes	Yes	Yes	Yes		Yes		5	0.63
Solomon Islands	Yes	Yes	Yes	Yes		Yes		5	0.63
Sri Lanka	Yes		Yes	Yes		Yes	Yes	5	0.63
Sudan	Yes	Yes	Yes	Yes		Yes		5	0.63

Country	(1)	(2)	(3)	(4)	(5)	(6)	(7)		
Suriname			Yes	Yes	Yes	Yes		5	0.63
Syria		Yes	Yes	Yes	Yes	Yes	Yes	4	0.50
Tajikistan	Yes	Yes	Yes	Yes		Yes		5	0.63
Tanzania	Yes	Yes	Yes	Yes		Yes		5	0.63
Timor-Leste	Yes	Yes	Yes	Yes	Yes	Yes		5	0.63
Tonga	Yes		Yes			Yes	Yes	3	0.38
Trinidad and Tobago	Yes		Yes	Yes		Yes		4	0.50
Tunisia	Yes	Yes	Yes	Yes	Yes	Yes	Yes	6	0.75
Turkmenistan	Yes	Yes	Yes	Yes	Yes	Yes		6	0.75
Uganda	Yes	Yes	Yes	Yes		Yes		5	0.63
Ukraine	Yes	Yes	Yes	Yes	Yes	Yes		6	0.75
United Arab Emirates	Yes		Yes	Yes		Yes		4	0.50
Uruguay	Yes	Yes	Yes	Yes		Yes		5	0.63
Uzbekistan	Yes	Yes	Yes	Yes	Yes	Yes		5	0.63
Vanuatu	Yes	Yes	Yes	Yes		Yes		5	0.63
Vietnam	Yes		Yes	Yes	Yes	Yes	Yes	4	0.50
Yemen	Yes		Yes	Yes		Yes		4	0.50
Zambia	Yes		Yes	Yes		Yes		4	0.50
Zimbabwe	Yes		Yes	Yes		Yes	Yes	5	0.63
Average									0.63
Satisfaction ratio (1 pt. in 7th crit.)	89%	56%	91%	90%	44%	94%	24%		
(2 pts. In 7th crit.)							7%		

Note: (1) no automatic procedure for government to obtain direct credit from central bank; (2) when available, credit extended to government at market interest rates; (3) credit is temporary; (4) for limited amount; (5) central bank does not participate in primary market for public debt; (6) central bank responsible for setting policy rate; and (7) central bank has no responsibility to oversee banking sector (two points) or shares responsibility with other institutions (one point).

[1] BCEAO includes Benin, Burkina Faso, Côte d'Ivoire, Guinea Bissau, Mali, Niger, Senegal and Togo.

[2] BEAC includes Cameroon, Central African Republic, Chad, Republic of Congo, Equatorial Guinea and Gabon.

[3] ECCB includes Anguilla, Antigua-Barbuda, Dominica, Grenada, Montserrat, St. Kitts-Nevis, St. Lucia, and St. Vincent-the-Grenadines.

Source: Authors' estimates.

Appendix VIII Independence: evolution for GMT sample (late 1980s–2003)

CBs	Political independence[1]										Economic independence[2]								
	Appointments				Relations with govt.		Constituting laws		Score	Stand. score	Monetary financing of public deficits					Monetary instruments		Score	Stand. score
	1	2	3	4	5	6	7	8			1	2	3	4	5	6	7		
Late 1980s																			
Australia		1					1	1	3	0.38	1	1	1	1	1	1		6	0.75
Japan							1		1	0.13	1		1	1	1	1	1	5	0.63
New Zealand									0	0.00			1			1	1	3	0.38
Austria					1	1	1		3	0.38		1	1	1	1	1		6	0.75
Belgium	1								1	0.13		1	1	1	1	1	1	6	0.75
Denmark		1		1		1			3	0.38		1	1	1		1	1	5	0.63
France		1		1					2	0.25	1		1	1	1	1		5	0.63
Germany		1		1	1	1	1	1	6	0.75	1	1	1	1	1	1	1	7	0.88
Greece			1					1	2	0.25		1		1				2	0.25
Ireland					1	1	1		3	0.38		1	1	1		1		4	0.50
Italy		1	1		1		1		4	0.50				1				1	0.13
Netherlands		1		1	1	1	1	1	6	0.75			1	1		1	1	4	0.50
Portugal					1				1	0.13				1		1		2	0.25
Spain				1	1				2	0.25			1	1		1		3	0.38
Switzerland		1		1	1	1	1		5	0.63		1	1	1	1	1	2	7	0.88
UK					1				1	0.13		1	1	1		1		5	0.63
Canada	1			1	1	1	1	1	4	0.50	1	1	1	1	1	1	2	7	0.88
USA		1			1	1	1	1	5	0.63	1	1	1	1	1	1	1	7	0.88
APD	0.00	0.33	0.00	0.00	0.00	0.00	0.67	0.33	1.33	0.17	0.33	0.33	1.00	0.67	0.67	1.00	0.33	4.33	0.54
EUR	0.08	0.54	0.15	0.38	0.54	0.46	0.46	0.38	3.00	0.38	0.15	0.46	0.54	0.92	0.54	0.85	0.54	4.00	0.50

	P1	P2	P3	P4	P5	P6	P7	P8	Total	Index[1]	E1	E2	E3	E4	E5	E6	E7	E8	Total	Index[2]
WHD	0.50	0.50	0.00	0.50	0.50	0.50	1.00	1.00	4.50	0.56	1.00	1.00	1.00	1.00	1.00	0.50	1.00	1.00	6.50	0.81
All	0.11	0.50	0.11	0.33	0.44	0.39	0.56	0.44	2.89	0.36	0.33	0.67	0.89	0.56	0.89	0.56	0.89	0.56	4.39	0.55

2003

	P1	P2	P3	P4	P5	P6	P7	P8	Total	Index[1]	E1	E2	E3	E4	E5	E6	E7	E8	Total	Index[2]
Australia	1						1		2	0.25	1	1	1	1	1	1	1	1	8	1.00
Japan							1		1	0.13		1	1	1	1	1		1	6	0.75
New Zealand			1				1		2	0.25		1	1	1	1	1			5	0.63
Austria	1	1	1	1	1	1	1	1	8	1.00	1	1	1	1	1	1		1	7	0.88
Belgium	1	1	1	1	1	1	1	1	8	1.00	1	1	1	1	1	1		1	7	0.88
Denmark	1	1	1	1	1	1	1	1	4	0.50	1	1	1	1	1	1	1	1	8	1.00
France	1	1	1	1	1	1	1	1	8	1.00	1	1	1	1	1	1		1	7	0.88
Germany	1	1	1	1	1	1	1	1	8	1.00		1	1	1	1	1		1	6	0.75
Greece	1	1	1	1	1	1	1	1	8	1.00		1	1	1	1	1			5	0.63
Ireland	1	1	1	1	1	1	1	1	8	1.00		1	1	1	1	1			5	0.63
Italy	1	1	1	1	1	1	1	1	8	1.00		1	1	1	1	1			5	0.63
Netherlands	1	1	1	1	1	1	1	1	8	1.00		1	1	1	1	1	1		6	0.75
Portugal	1	1	1	1	1	1	1	1	8	1.00		1	1	1	1	1			5	0.63
Spain	1	1	1	1	1	1	1	1	8	1.00		1	1	1	1	1	1		6	0.75
Switzerland	1	1	1	1	1	1	1		7	0.88	1	1	1	1	1	1	1	1	8	1.00
UK						1	1	1	3	0.38	1	1	1	1	1	1	1	1	8	1.00
Canada						1	1	1	3	0.38	1	1	1	1	1	1		1	7	0.88
USA	1			1	1	1	1		5	0.63	1	1	1	1	1	1		1	7	0.88
APD	0.00	0.33	0.00	0.33	0.00	0.00	1.00	0.00	1.67	0.21	0.33	1.00	1.00	1.00	1.00	0.67	1.00	0.67	5.33	0.67
EUR	0.77	0.92	0.85	0.92	0.92	1.00	1.00	1.00	7.23	0.90	1.00	1.00	1.00	1.00	1.00	0.23	0.69	5.92	0.74	
WHD	0.50	0.50	0.00	0.50	0.50	0.50	1.00	1.00	4.00	0.50	1.00	1.00	1.00	1.00	1.00	0.50	1.00	1.00	6.50	0.81
All	0.61	0.78	0.61	0.67	0.72	0.72	1.00	0.78	5.94	0.74	0.74	0.94	1.00	1.00	0.94	1.00	0.44	0.72	5.94	0.74

[1] Political independence: see Table 4.2 for the specification of the variables.
[2] Economic independence: see Table 4.2 for the specification of the variables.
Source: GMT (1991), and authors' estimates.

Appendix IX Independence: evolution for Cukierman sample (late 1980s–2003)

Central banks	Political independence[1]								Economic independence[2]						
	Appoint.		Relations with govt.		Constituting laws		Score	Stand. score	Monetary financing of public deficits					Score	Stand. score
	1	*2*	*5*	*6*	*7*	*8*			*1*	*2*	*3*	*4*	*5*		
Late 1980s															
Argentina			1.00		1.00		2.00	0.33	1.00		1.00	1.00		3.00	0.60
Bahamas					1.20		1.20	0.20	1.00		1.00	1.00		3.00	0.60
Barbados					1.00		1.00	0.17	1.00		1.00			2.00	0.40
Bolivia			1.00		1.00		2.00	0.33			1.00	1.00		2.00	0.40
Botswana							0.00	0.00	1.00		1.00	1.00		3.00	0.60
Brazil	1.00						1.00	0.17						0.00	0.00
Chile					1.00		1.00	0.17	1.00					1.00	0.20
China						1.50	1.50	0.25	1.00				1.00	2.00	0.40
Colombia	1.00						1.00	0.17	1.00		1.00			2.00	0.40
Costa Rica	2.00		2.00		2.00		6.00	1.00	1.00		1.00	1.00		3.00	0.60
Egypt	1.00		1.00		1.00		3.00	0.50	1.00		1.00	1.00		3.00	0.60
Ethiopia						1.20	1.20	0.20						0.00	0.00
Finland		1.20			1.20		2.40	0.40			1.00	1.00		2.00	0.40
Ghana		1.00					1.00	0.17	1.00		1.00	1.00		3.00	0.60
Honduras		1.00	1.00			1.00	3.00	0.50	1.00		1.00	1.00		3.00	0.60
Hungary	1.00						1.00	0.17		1.00	1.00	1.00		3.00	0.60
Iceland	1.00	1.00			1.00		3.00	0.50			1.00			1.00	0.20
India					1.00		1.00	0.17	1.00		1.00	1.00		3.00	0.60
Indonesia					1.00		1.00	0.17			1.00	1.00		2.00	0.40
Israel	1.00				1.00		2.00	0.33	1.00					1.00	0.20
Kenya					1.20		1.20	0.20	1.00		1.00	1.00		3.00	0.60

Country									
Korea					1.20	0.20	1.00	1.00	0.20
Lebanon			1.20	1.20	2.40	0.40	1.00	3.00	0.60
Luxembourg			1.20	1.20	2.40	0.40		1.00	0.20
Malaysia		1.00	1.00		1.00	0.17	1.00	3.00	0.60
Malta	1.00	1.00	1.00		3.00	0.50	1.00	2.00	0.40
Mexico	1.00	1.00	1.00		3.00	0.50		1.00	0.20
Morocco					0.00	0.00	1.00	2.00	0.40
Nepal					0.00	0.00		1.00	0.20
Nicaragua			1.20	1.20	2.40	0.40	1.00	3.00	0.60
Nigeria		1.00			1.00	0.17	1.00	3.00	0.60
Norway		1.00	1.00		2.00	0.33		1.00	0.20
Pakistan		1.00			1.00	0.17		1.00	0.20
Panama			1.20	1.20	2.40	0.40		0.00	0.00
Peru	1.00	1.00	1.00		3.00	0.50	1.00	3.00	0.60
Philippines		1.00	1.00		2.00	0.33	1.00	3.00	0.60
Poland		1.00			0.00	0.00	1.00	1.00	0.20
Qatar					1.00	0.17	1.00	0.00	0.00
Romania			1.00	1.00	2.00	0.33	1.00	1.00	0.20
Singapore			1.50	1.50	1.50	0.25	1.25	1.25	0.25
South Africa					0.00	0.00	1.00	1.00	0.20
Sweden	1.50				1.50	0.25		2.00	0.40
Tanzania		1.00	1.00		1.00	0.17	1.00	3.00	0.60
Thailand	1.00	1.00	1.00		2.00	0.33	1.00	2.00	0.40
Turkey	1.00	1.00	1.00		3.00	0.50	1.00	3.00	0.60
Uganda	1.00	1.00	1.00		2.00	0.33	1.00	3.00	0.60
Uruguay		1.00	1.00		1.00	0.17		0.00	0.00
Venezuela			1.00	1.00	2.00	0.33	1.00	1.00	0.20
Yugoslavia		1.00			1.00	0.17		0.00	0.00
Zambia	1.00				2.00	0.33		2.00	0.40
Zimbabwe		1.00			1.00	0.17	1.00	3.00	0.60

(Continued)

Appendix IX Continued

Central banks	Political independence[1]								Economic independence[2]						
	Appoint.		Relations with govt.		Constituting laws		Score	Stand. score	Monetary financing of public deficits					Score	Stand. score
	1	2	5	6	7	8			1	2	3	4	5		
AFR	0.10	0.10	0.10	0.00	0.62	0.12	1.04	0.17	0.80	0.00	0.90	0.90	0.00	2.60	0.52
APD	0.11	0.11	0.00	0.00	0.86	0.17	1.24	0.21	0.44	0.00	0.92	0.56	0.11	2.03	0.41
EUR	0.46	0.37	0.17	0.08	0.70	0.17	1.94	0.32	0.33	0.08	0.58	0.33	0.00	1.33	0.27
MCD	0.20	0.24	0.44	0.00	0.60	0.00	1.48	0.25	0.20	0.20	0.80	0.60	0.00	1.80	0.36
WHD	0.40	0.13	0.63	0.08	0.76	0.13	2.13	0.36	0.60	0.00	0.60	0.60	0.00	1.80	0.36
All	0.28	0.19	0.29	0.04	0.72	0.13	1.65	0.28	0.51	0.04	0.73	0.59	0.02	1.89	0.38
End 2003									*End 2003*						
Argentina		1.00	1.00	1.00	1.00	1.00	5.00	0.83	1.00	1.00	1.00	1.00	1.00	5.00	1.00
Bahamas		1.00	1.00		1.00		2.00	0.33	1.00		1.00	1.00		3.00	0.60
Barbados					1.00		1.00	0.17	1.00		1.00	1.00	1.00	4.00	0.80
Bolivia		1.00	1.00	1.00	1.00		4.00	0.67	1.00	1.00	1.00	1.00	1.00	5.00	1.00
Bosnia Herzegovina	1.00	1.00	1.00	1.00	1.00	1.00	6.00	1.00	1.00	1.00	1.00	1.00	1.00	5.00	1.00
Botswana					1.00		1.00	0.17	1.00		1.00	1.00	1.00	4.00	0.80
Brazil		1.00			1.00		2.00	0.33	1.00	1.00	1.00	1.00	1.00	5.00	1.00
Chile			1.00		1.00	1.00	3.00	0.50	1.00	1.00	1.00	1.00	1.00	5.00	1.00
China		1.00			1.00		2.00	0.33	1.00	1.00	1.00	1.00	1.00	5.00	1.00
Colombia			1.00		1.00		2.00	0.33	1.00	1.00	1.00	1.00	1.00	5.00	1.00
Costa Rica		1.00	1.00		1.00	1.00	4.00	0.67	1.00	1.00	1.00	1.00	1.00	5.00	1.00
Croatia	1.00	1.00	1.00	1.00	1.00	1.00	6.00	1.00	1.00	1.00	1.00	1.00	1.00	5.00	1.00
Egypt					1.00		1.00	0.17	1.00	1.00	1.00	1.00		4.00	0.80
Ethiopia		1.00			1.00		2.00	0.33	1.00		1.00	1.00	1.00	4.00	0.80
Finland	1.00	1.00	1.00	1.00	1.00	1.00	6.00	1.00	1.00	1.00	1.00	1.00	1.00	5.00	1.00
Ghana			1.00		1.00	1.00	3.00	0.50	1.00	1.00	1.00	1.00		4.00	0.80

Country						INT	FRAC					FIVE	NORM
Honduras				1.00		2.00	0.33	1.00	1.00	1.00	1.00	5.00	1.00
Hungary		1.00	1.00	1.00		4.00	0.67	1.00	1.00	1.00	1.00	5.00	1.00
Iceland		1.00	1.00	1.00		2.00	0.33	1.00	1.00	1.00	1.00	5.00	1.00
India			1.00		1.00	3.00	0.50	1.00	1.00	1.00	1.00	3.00	0.60
Indonesia		1.00	1.00	1.00		4.00	0.67	1.00	1.00	1.00	1.00	5.00	1.00
Israel			1.00			2.00	0.33	1.00	1.00	1.00	1.00	4.00	0.80
Kenya			1.00			2.00	0.33	1.00	1.00	1.00	1.00	4.00	0.80
Korea		1.00	1.00	1.00		3.00	0.50	1.00	1.00	1.00	1.00	4.00	0.80
Lebanon			1.00			3.00	0.50	1.00	1.00	1.00	1.00	4.00	0.80
Luxembourg	1.00	1.00	1.00	1.00		6.00	1.00	1.00	1.00	1.00	1.00	5.00	1.00
Macedonia	1.00	1.00	1.00	1.00		6.00	1.00	1.00	1.00	1.00	1.00	5.00	1.00
Malaysia	1.00		1.00	1.00		3.00	0.50	1.00	1.00	1.00	1.00	4.00	0.80
Malta			1.00		1.00	4.00	0.67	1.00	1.00	1.00	1.00	5.00	1.00
Mexico	1.00		1.00	1.00	1.00	4.00	0.67	1.00	1.00	1.00	1.00	5.00	1.00
Morocco		1.00	1.00	1.00		3.00	0.50	1.00	1.00	1.00	1.00	4.00	0.80
Nepal		1.00	1.00	1.00	1.00	4.00	0.67	1.00	1.00	1.00	1.00	4.00	0.80
Nicaragua			1.00	1.00		2.00	0.33	1.00	1.00	1.00	1.00	5.00	1.00
Nigeria			1.00	1.00		2.00	0.33	1.00	1.00	1.00	1.00	4.00	0.80
Norway	1.00		1.00	1.00		3.00	0.50	1.00	1.00	1.00	1.00	5.00	1.00
Pakistan	1.00		1.00	1.00	1.00	4.00	0.67	1.00	1.00	1.00	1.00	4.00	0.80
Panama			1.00	1.00		3.00	0.50	1.00	1.00	1.00	1.00	0.00	0.00
Peru			1.00	1.00		3.00	0.50	1.00	1.00	1.00	1.00	5.00	1.00
Philippines	1.00		1.00	1.00		5.00	0.83	1.00	1.00	1.00	1.00	4.00	0.80
Poland	1.00		1.00	1.00		6.00	1.00	1.00	1.00	1.00	1.00	5.00	1.00
Qatar	1.00		1.00			1.00	0.17	1.00	1.00	1.00	1.00	1.00	0.20
Romania	1.00		1.00	1.00		5.00	0.83	1.00	1.00	1.00	1.00	5.00	1.00
Serbia Montenegro	1.00		1.00	1.00		5.00	0.83	1.00	1.00	1.00	1.00	4.00	0.80
Singapore	1.00		1.00	1.00		3.00	0.50	1.00	1.00	1.00	1.00	2.00	0.40
Slovenia	1.00		1.00	1.00		6.00	1.00	1.00	1.00	1.00	1.00	5.00	1.00

(Continued)

Appendix IX *Continued*

Central banks	Political independence[1]								Economic independence[2]						
	Appoint.		Relations with govt.		Constituting laws		Score	Stand. score	Monetary financing of public deficits					Score	Stand. score
	1	2	5	6	7	8			1	2	3	4	5		
South Africa	1.00						1.00	0.17	1.00	1.00				2.00	0.40
Sweden		1.00	1.00	1.00	1.00	1.00	5.00	0.83	1.00	1.00	1.00	1.00	1.00	5.00	1.00
Tanzania			1.00		1.00		2.00	0.33	1.00	1.00	1.00	1.00		4.00	0.80
Thailand		1.00			1.00		2.00	0.33	1.00			1.00		2.00	0.40
Turkey	1.00		1.00		1.00	1.00	4.00	0.67	1.00	1.00	1.00	1.00	1.00	5.00	1.00
Uganda			1.00	1.00	1.00	1.00	4.00	0.67	1.00	1.00	1.00	1.00		4.00	0.80
Uruguay		1.00	1.00		1.00	1.00	4.00	0.67	1.00	1.00	1.00	1.00		4.00	0.80
Venezuela		1.00	1.00		1.00	1.00	4.00	0.67	1.00	1.00	1.00	1.00	1.00	5.00	1.00
Zambia			1.00	1.00	1.00	1.00	4.00	0.67	1.00		1.00	1.00		3.00	0.60
Zimbabwe					1.00		1.00	0.17	1.00		1.00	1.00		3.00	0.60
AFR	0.00	0.10	0.60	0.30	0.90	0.30	2.20	0.37	1.00	0.60	0.90	0.90	0.20	3.60	0.72
APD	0.11	0.33	0.67	0.56	1.00	0.56	3.22	0.54	0.89	0.67	0.89	0.89	0.33	3.67	0.73
EUR	0.75	0.63	0.88	0.75	0.94	0.81	4.75	0.79	1.00	0.88	1.00	1.00	1.00	4.88	0.98
MCD	0.20	0.20	0.60	0.40	1.00	0.00	2.40	0.40	0.80	0.40	0.80	0.80	0.60	3.40	0.68
WHD	0.00	0.47	0.80	0.40	0.93	0.40	3.00	0.50	0.93	0.80	0.93	0.93	0.80	4.40	0.88
All	0.25	0.40	0.75	0.51	0.95	0.49	3.35	0.56	0.95	0.73	0.93	0.93	0.65	4.18	0.84

[1] Political variables: see Table 4.2 for the specification of the variables.
[2] Economic variables: see Table 4.2 for the specification of the variables.

Note: The weight of Cukierman's (1992) missing variables ("NA"), which is always 1 as the index is unweighted, is divided by the number of the remaining variables and then added to the variables that have meaningful entries. The regional classification of central banks follows the organization of the IMF area departments.

Source: Cukierman (1992) and authors' estimates.

Central banks (number of CBs)	Late 1980s (narrow index for Cukierman) (full index for GMT)			End-2003 (narrow index)			(full index)		
	Political	Economic	Overall	Political	Economic	Overall	Political	Economic	Overall
All central banks									
Full sample (163)	**NA**	**NA**	**NA**	**NA**	**NA**	**NA**	**0.49**	**0.68**	**0.59**
GMT sample (18)	**0.36**	**0.59**	**0.48**	**NA**	**NA**	**NA**	**0.74**	**0.81**	**0.77**
Cukierman sample (50)	**0.28**	**0.39**	**0.33**	**0.52**	**0.82**	**0.66**	**0.42**	**0.73**	**0.57**
Advanced economies									
ECB							1.00	1.00	1.00
Australia	0.38	0.75	0.56				0.25	1.00	0.63
Austria	0.38	0.75	0.56				1.00	0.88	0.94
Belgium	0.13	0.75	0.44				1.00	0.88	0.94
Canada	0.50	0.88	0.69				0.38	0.88	0.63
Cyprus							0.38	0.75	0.56
Denmark	0.38	0.63	0.50				0.50	1.00	0.75
Finland	0.40	0.00	0.22	1.00	1.00	1.00	1.00	0.88	0.94
France	0.25	0.63	0.44				1.00	0.88	0.94
Germany	0.75	0.88	0.81				1.00	0.75	0.88
Greece	0.25	0.25	0.25				1.00	0.63	0.81
Hong Kong							0.38	0.38	0.38
Iceland	0.50	0.20	0.36	0.33	1.00	0.64	0.50	1.00	0.75
Ireland	0.38	0.50	0.44				1.00	0.63	0.81
Italy	0.50	0.13	0.31				1.00	0.63	0.81
Japan	0.13	0.63	0.38				0.13	0.75	0.44
Korea	0.20	0.20	0.20	0.50	0.80	0.64	0.25	0.88	0.56
Luxembourg	0.40	0.20	0.31	1.00	1.00	1.00	1.00	0.88	0.94
Netherlands	0.75	0.50	0.63				1.00	0.75	0.88
New Zealand	0.00	0.38	0.19				0.25	0.63	0.44
Norway	0.33	0.20	0.27	0.50	1.00	0.73	0.50	1.00	0.75

(Continued)

Appendix X Continued

Central banks (number of CBs)	Late 1980s (narrow index for Cukierman) (full index for GMT)			End-2003 (narrow index)			(full index)		
	Political	Economic	Overall	Political	Economic	Overall	Political	Economic	Overall
Portugal	0.13	0.25	0.19				1.00	0.63	0.81
Singapore	0.25	0.25	0.25	0.50	0.40	0.45	0.38	0.38	0.38
Spain	0.25	0.38	0.31				1.00	0.75	0.88
Sweden	0.25	0.40	0.32	0.83	1.00	0.91	0.88	1.00	0.94
Switzerland	0.63	0.88	0.75				0.88	1.00	0.94
United Kingdom	0.13	0.63	0.38				0.38	1.00	0.69
United States	0.63	0.88	0.75				0.63	0.88	0.75
Full sample (27)	NA	NA	NA	NA	NA	NA	**0.70**	**0.81**	**0.75**
GMT sample (18)	**0.36**	**0.59**	**0.48**	NA	NA	NA	**0.74**	**0.81**	**0.77**
Cukierman sample (7)	**0.33**	**0.21**	**0.28**	**0.67**	**0.89**	**0.77**	**0.64**	**0.86**	**0.75**
ESCB (13)	NA	NA	NA	NA	NA	NA	**1.00**	**0.78**	**0.89**
Emerging markets									
Argentina	0.33	0.60	0.45	0.83	1.00	0.91	0.75	0.75	0.75
Brazil	0.17	0.00	0.09	0.33	1.00	0.64	0.50	0.75	0.63
Bulgaria							1.00	0.75	0.88
Chile	0.17	0.20	0.18	0.50	1.00	0.73	0.50	0.88	0.69
China	0.25	0.40	0.32	0.33	1.00	0.64	0.38	0.75	0.56
Croatia	0.17	0.00	0.09	1.00	1.00	1.00	1.00	0.75	0.88
Czech Republic							0.88	0.88	0.88
Egypt	0.50	0.60	0.55	0.17	0.80	0.45	0.13	0.63	0.38
Estonia							0.63	1.00	0.81
Hungary	0.17	0.60	0.36	0.67	1.00	0.82	0.88	1.00	0.94
India	0.17	0.60	0.36	0.50	0.60	0.55	0.25	0.75	0.50
Indonesia	0.17	0.40	0.27	0.67	1.00	0.82	0.63	0.75	0.69

	1	2	3	4	5	6	7	8	9	10
Israel	0.55	0.20	0.27	0.53	0.80	0.55	0.63	0.13	0.75	0.38
Jordan							0.50	0.25	0.50	0.38
Latvia							1.00	1.00	1.00	1.00
Lithuania							0.75	0.88	0.75	0.81
Malaysia	0.17	0.60	0.36	0.50	0.80	0.64	0.75	0.25	0.75	0.50
Malta	0.50	0.40	0.45	0.67	1.00	0.82	0.88	0.50	0.88	0.69
Mexico	0.50	0.20	0.36	0.67	1.00	0.82	0.75	0.63	0.75	0.69
Morocco	0.00	0.40	0.18	0.50	0.80	0.64	0.75	0.25	0.75	0.50
Pakistan	0.17	0.20	0.18	0.67	0.80	0.73	0.63	0.38	0.63	0.50
Peru	0.50	0.60	0.55	0.50	1.00	0.73	1.00	0.38	1.00	0.69
Philippines	0.33	0.60	0.45	0.83	0.80	0.82	0.63	0.63	0.63	0.63
Poland	0.00	0.20	0.09	1.00	1.00	1.00	0.88	0.88	0.88	0.88
Romania	0.33	0.20	0.27	0.83	1.00	0.91	0.75	0.63	0.75	0.69
Russia							0.38	0.50	0.38	0.44
Slovakia							0.75	0.50	0.75	0.63
Slovenia	0.17	0.00	0.09	1.00	1.00	1.00	0.75	0.88	0.75	0.81
South Africa	0.00	0.20	0.09	0.17	0.40	0.27	0.38	0.13	0.38	0.25
Thailand	0.33	0.40	0.36	0.33	0.40	0.36	0.38	0.50	0.38	0.44
Turkey	0.50	0.60	0.55	0.67	1.00	0.82	1.00	0.63	1.00	0.81
Venezuela	0.33	0.20	0.27	0.67	1.00	0.82	0.88	0.50	0.88	0.69
Full sample (32)	**NA**	**NA**	**NA**	**NA**	**NA**	**NA**	**0.75**	**0.56**	**0.75**	**0.65**
Cukierman sample (22)	**0.27**	**0.38**	**0.32**	**0.56**	**0.87**	**0.70**	**0.75**	**0.47**	**0.75**	**0.61**
Developing countries										
Afghanistan							0.75	0.50	0.75	0.63
Albania							0.75	0.75	0.75	0.75
Algeria							0.63	1.00	0.63	0.81
Angola							0.38	0.25	0.38	0.31
Armenia							0.75	0.88	0.75	0.81
Aruba							0.38	0.75	0.38	0.56
Azerbaijan							0.50	0.75	0.50	0.63

(Continued)

Appendix X Continued

Central banks (number of CBs)	Late 1980s (narrow index for Cukierman) (full index for GMT)			End-2003 (narrow index)			(full index)		
	Political	Economic	Overall	Political	Economic	Overall	Political	Economic	Overall
Bahamas	0.20	0.60	0.38	0.33	0.60	0.45	0.13	0.50	0.31
Bahrain							0.25	0.63	0.44
Bangladesh							0.00	0.38	0.19
Barbados	0.17	0.40	0.27	0.17	0.80	0.45	0.13	0.63	0.38
BCEAO							0.50	0.88	0.69
BEAC							0.50	0.88	0.69
Belarus							0.50	0.38	0.44
Belize							0.13	0.63	0.38
Bermuda							0.13	0.75	0.44
Bhutan							0.13	0.50	0.31
Bolivia	0.33	0.40	0.36	0.67	1.00	0.82	0.50	1.00	0.75
Bosnia Herzegovina	0.17	0.00	0.09	1.00	1.00	1.00	1.00	0.75	0.88
Botswana	0.00	0.60	0.27	0.17	0.80	0.45	0.13	0.75	0.44
Burundi							0.38	0.38	0.38
Cambodia							0.38	0.75	0.56
Cape Verde							0.38	0.63	0.50
Cayman Islands							0.13	0.63	0.38
Colombia	0.17	0.40	0.27	0.33	1.00	0.64	0.13	0.88	0.50
Comoros							0.13	0.75	0.44
Costa Rica	1.00	0.60	0.82	0.67	1.00	0.82	0.50	0.88	0.69
Cuba							0.38	0.25	0.31
Dominican Republic							0.25	0.88	0.56
ECCB							0.63	0.63	0.63
Ecuador							0.88	1.00	0.94

Country									
El Salvador								1.00	0.81
Eritrea							0.63	0.63	0.50
Ethiopia	0.20	0.60	0.38	0.33	0.80	0.55	0.38	0.63	0.50
Fiji							0.38	0.63	0.50
Georgia							0.13	0.63	0.38
Ghana	0.17	0.40	0.27	0.50	0.80	0.64	0.88	0.63	0.75
Guatemala							0.38	0.63	0.50
Guinea Republic							0.63	0.88	0.63
Guyana							0.25	0.63	0.63
Haiti							0.50	0.75	0.50
Honduras	0.50	0.60	0.55	0.33	1.00	0.64	0.13	0.50	0.50
Iran							0.00	0.88	0.50
Iraq							0.50	0.75	0.38
Jamaica							0.13	0.75	0.63
Kazakhstan							0.63	0.63	0.38
Kenya	0.20	0.60	0.38	0.33	0.80	0.55	0.13	0.88	0.75
Kuwait							0.13	0.75	0.44
Kyrgyzstan							1.00	0.50	0.31
Laos							0.13	0.75	0.88
Lebanon	0.40	0.60	0.49	0.50	0.80	0.64	0.25	0.63	0.38
Lesotho							0.25	0.75	0.50
Liberia							0.25	0.63	0.44
Libya							0.38	0.63	0.50
Macau							0.25	0.63	0.44
Macedonia	0.17	0.00	0.09	1.00	1.00	1.00	0.50	0.38	0.44
Madagascar							1.00	0.75	0.88
Malawi							0.50	0.75	0.63
Maldives							0.13	0.63	0.38
Mauritius							0.38	0.38	0.38
							0.50	0.50	0.50

(Continued)

Appendix X Continued

Central banks (number of CBs)	Late 1980s (narrow index for Cukierman) (full index for GMT)			End-2003 (narrow index)			(full index)		
	Political	Economic	Overall	Political	Economic	Overall	Political	Economic	Overall
Moldova							0.75	0.75	0.75
Mongolia							1.00	0.50	0.75
Mozambique							0.38	0.50	0.44
Myanmar							0.25	0.50	0.38
Namibia							0.25	0.50	0.38
Nepal	0.00	0.20	0.09	0.67	0.80	0.73	0.38	0.63	0.50
Netherlands Antilles							0.38	0.50	0.44
Nicaragua	0.40	0.60	0.49	0.33	1.00	0.64	0.13	1.00	0.56
Nigeria	0.17	0.60	0.36	0.33	0.80	0.55	0.25	0.63	0.44
Oman							0.13	0.50	0.31
Palestine							0.38	0.63	0.50
Panama	0.40	0.00	0.22	0.50	0.00	0.27	0.50	0.25	0.38
Papua New Guinea							0.63	0.63	0.63
Paraguay							0.25	0.75	0.50
Qatar	0.17	0.00	0.09	0.17	0.20	0.18	0.13	0.25	0.19
Rwanda							0.50	0.63	0.56
São Tomé Príncipe							0.25	0.38	0.31
Saudi Arabia							0.25	0.75	0.50
Serbia Montenegro	0.17	0.00	0.09	0.83	0.80	0.82	0.63	0.63	0.63
Seychelles							0.13	0.38	0.25
Sierra Leone							0.50	0.63	0.56
Solomon Islands							0.13	0.63	0.38
Sri Lanka							0.50	0.63	0.56

Sudan							0.00	0.63	0.31
Suriname							0.13	0.63	0.38
Syria							0.38	0.50	0.44
Tajikistan							1.00	0.63	0.81
Tanzania	0.17	0.60	0.36	0.33	0.80	0.55	0.13	0.63	0.38
Timor-Leste							0.75	0.63	0.69
Tonga							0.25	0.38	0.31
Trinidad and Tobago							0.38	0.50	0.44
Tunisia							0.63	0.75	0.69
Turkmenistan							0.63	0.75	0.69
Uganda	0.33	0.60	0.45	0.67	0.80	0.73	0.50	0.63	0.56
Ukraine							0.88	0.75	0.81
United Arab Emirates	0.17	0.00	0.09	0.67	0.80	0.73	0.38	0.50	0.44
Uruguay							0.63	0.63	0.63
Uzbekistan							0.75	0.63	0.69
Vanuatu							0.13	0.63	0.38
Vietnam							0.38	0.50	0.44
Yemen							0.38	0.50	0.44
Zambia	0.33	0.40	0.36	0.67	0.60	0.64	0.38	0.50	0.44
Zimbabwe	0.17	0.60	0.36	0.17	0.60	0.36	0.25	0.63	0.44
Full sample (103)	NA	NA	NA	NA	NA	NA	**0.41**	**0.63**	**0.52**
Cukierman sample (21)	0.27	0.45	0.35	0.42	0.75	0.57	**0.29**	**0.67**	**0.48**
Monetary unions (3)	NA	NA	NA	NA	NA	NA	**0.54**	**0.79**	**0.67**

Source: Authors' estimates.

Appendix XI Accountability database (Q1-2006)

Sub-components[1,2]	Responsibility					Objectives								Ex post							Governance		
Central banks	1a	1b	1c	1d	2	3a	3b	3c	4	5a	5b	5c	5d	6a	6b	6c	7	8a	8b	8c	9a	9b	10
Albania	Y				N		Y		Y			Y		Y	Y	Y	Y	N	N	N	Y	Y	Y
Algeria	Y				N			Y	N				Y	Y	Y	Y		Y	Y		Y	Y	N
Argentina		Y			N	Y			Y	Y					Y		Y	N	N	N	Y	Y	Y
Armenia	Y				N	Y			Y	Y				Y			N	N	Y	Y	Y	Y	Y
Australia		Y			Y	Y		Y	Y	Y	Y			Y			Y	Y	Y	Y	Y	Y	Y
Austria	Y				N	Y		Y	Y			Y			Y		Y	Y	Y	Y	Y	Y	Y
Bahrain		Y			Y		Y		N					Y	Y		N	Y	Y	Y	Y	Y	N
Bangladesh	Y				Y			Y	Y	Y							Y	Y	Y	Y	Y	Y	Y
BCEAO	Y				Y			Y	Y		Y				Y	Y	N	N	Y	N	Y	Y	Y
BEAC	Y				N	Y			Y	Y				Y		Y	N	N	N	Y	Y	Y	Y
Belarus	Y	Y			Y			Y	Y	Y					Y	Y	N	N	N	N	Y	Y	N
Belgium	Y				N	Y		Y	Y			Y			Y	Y	N	Y	Y	Y	Y	Y	Y
Bolivia	Y				N	Y			N		Y			Y	Y		N	N	N	N	Y	Y	Y
Botswana	Y				Y		Y		Y	Y				Y	Y		Y	Y	Y	Y	Y	Y	Y
Brazil		Y			Y	Y		Y	Y	Y				Y	Y		Y	Y	Y	Y	Y	Y	N
Bulgaria			Y		N			Y	Y		Y				Y		N	N	Y	Y	Y	Y	Y
Canada		Y	Y		Y	Y		Y	Y	Y				Y	Y	Y	Y	Y	Y	Y	Y	Y	Y
Chile	Y				Y		Y		Y	Y				Y			N	N	N	N	Y	Y	N
China				Y	Y		Y		Y	Y					Y		N	N	N	N	Y	Y	N
Colombia	Y				Y	Y			Y					Y			Y	N	Y	Y	Y	Y	Y
Costa Rica	Y				Y		Y		Y		Y		Y	Y			Y	Y	N	Y	Y	Y	Y
Croatia	Y				N		Y		N					Y			N	N	Y	Y	Y	Y	Y
Czech Republic	Y				N	Y			Y			Y		Y	Y		Y	Y	Y	Y	Y	Y	Y
Denmark	Y				N			Y	Y		Y				Y		N	Y	N	Y	Y	Y	Y
ECB	Y				N	Y			Y			Y		Y	Y		Y	Y	N	N	Y	Y	Y
Ecuador	Y	Y			N	Y			Y				Y	Y	Y	Y	N	Y	N	N	Y	Y	Y

Country																				
Egypt		Y		Y		N						Y			Y	Z	Z	N	Y	N
El Salvador	Y			Z		Y	Y				Z	N	Y	Y	Y	Z	Z	N	Y	Y
Estonia	Y			Z		Y	Y			Y	Z	N	Y		Y	Z	Z	N	Y	Y
Finland	Y			Z		Y				Y	Z	Y	Y		Y	Z	Z	Y	Y	N
France	Y			Z		Y		Y		Y	Z	Y	Y		Y	Y	Y	Y	Y	Y
Georgia		Y		Z		Y				Y	Z	Y	Y		Y	Y	Y	Y	Y	Y
Germany	Y			Y		Y			Y	Y	Z	Y	Y		N	Z	Y	Y	Y	Y
Ghana	Y			Z		N			Y	Y	Z	Y			Y	Z	Y	Y	Y	Y
Greece	Y			Z		Y			Y	Y	Z	Y			Y	Z	Y	Y	Y	Y
Guatemala	Y			Y		Y			Y	Y	Z	Y	Y		Y	Y	Y	Y	Y	Y
Honduras	Y			Y		Y	Y		Y	Y	Y	Z	Y		Y	Y	Y	Y	Y	Y
Hungary	Y			Z		Y	Y		Y	Y	Y	Z	Y		Y	Z	Y	Y	Y	N
Iceland				Y		Y			Y	Y	Z	Y	Y		Y	Z	Z	Y	Y	N
India		Y		Y	Y	Y			Y	Y	Z	Y	Y		Y	Y	Y	Y	Y	Y
Indonesia	Y			Z	Y	Y		Y		Y	Y	Z	Y		Y	Z	Z	Y	Y	N
Iran		Y		Y		Y		Y		Y	Y	Z	Y		Y	Z	Z	Y	Y	N
Ireland	Y			Z		Y		Y		Y	Y	Z	Y		Y	Z	Z	Y	Y	Y
Israel			Y	Y		Y		Y		Y	Y		Y	Y	Y	Z	Y	Y	Y	N
Italy	Y			N		Y		Y		Y	Y	Y	Y		Y	Z	Y	Y	Y	N
Japan	Y			Y		Y			Y	Y	Y	Y	Y		Y	Z	Y	Y	Y	Y
Jordan	Y			Y		Y			Y	Y	Y	Y	Y		Y	Z	Y	Y	Y	Y
Kazakhstan	Y			Y		Y	Y		Y	Y	Y	Y	Y	Y		Z	Z	Y	Y	N
Kenya	Y			Y		Y	Y		Y	Y	Y	Y		Y	Y	Z	Y	Y	Y	Y
Korea		Y		Y	Y	Y		Y		Y	Y	Y	Y		Y	Z	Z	Y	Y	Y
Kyrgyzstan	Y			N	Y	Y		Y		Y	Y	Z	Y		Y	Z	Z	Y	Y	Y
Latvia	Y			Y		Y		Y		Y	Y	Z	Y		Y	Z	Z	Y	Y	Y
Lebanon	Y			Y	Y	N	Y	Y		N	Y	Y	Y		Y	Z	Z	Z	Y	Y
Lithuania	Y			N		Y		Y		Y	Y	Z	Y		Y	Z	Z	Z	Y	Y

(Continued)

Appendix XI Continued

Sub-components[1,2]	Responsibility				Objectives									Ex post							Governance		
Central banks	1a	1b	1c	1d	2	3a	3b	3c	4	5a	5b	5c	5d	6a	6b	6c	7	8a	8b	8c	9a	9b	10
Madagascar	Y				N	Y			Y	Y			Y	Y	Y	Y	N	N	N	N	Y		Y
Malaysia	Y				Y				N	Y				Y	Y		N	Y	Y	Y	Y		Y
Mexico	Y				Y		Y	Y	Y					Y	Y		Y	N	N	N	Y		Y
Moldova		Y			N		Y		Y			Y		Y	Y		Y	N	N	N	Y		Y
Mongolia	Y				N		Y		Y			Y		Y	Y		Y	Y	Y			Y	Y
Morocco		Y			Y			Y	Y			Y		Y			Y	N	N	N	N		N
Mozambique	Y				Y		Y		N				Y	Y		Y	N	N	N	N	Y		Y
Namibia	Y				Y			Y	Y	Y				Y	Y		N	Y	Y	Y	Y		Y
Netherlands	Y				N	Y			Y			Y			Y		Y	Y	Y	Y	Y		Y
New Zealand		Y			Y	Y			Y	Y			Y		Y		Y	Y	Y	Y	Y	Y	Y
Nicaragua	Y				Y	Y			N	Y				Y	Y		N	N	N	N	Y		Y
Nigeria	Y				Y			Y	Y	Y	Y			Y	Y	Y	N	N	N	N	Y		N
Norway				Y	Y			Y	Y					Y	Y	Y	Y	Y	Y	Y	Y		Y
Pakistan		Y			Y			Y	Y		Y			Y	Y		N	Y	N	Y	Y		Y
Paraguay		Y			Y	Y			Y				Y	Y	Y		Y	Y	Y	Y	Y		Y
Peru	Y				N	Y			Y	Y				Y	Y		N	N	N	N	Y		Y
Philippines		Y			N	Y			Y		Y			Y	Y	Y	N	Y	Y	Y	Y		Y
Poland	Y				N	Y	Y		Y			Y		Y	Y		N	N	Y	N	Y		Y
Portugal	Y				N	Y			Y			Y		Y	Y		Y	N	N	N	Y		Y
Romania	Y				N	Y			Y	Y				Y	Y	Y	N	N	N	N	Y		Y
Russia		Y			Y		Y	Y	Y	Y			Y	Y	Y		Y	Y	Y	N	Y		Y
Saudi Arabia	Y				Y			Y	N				Y	Y	Y		N	N	N	N	Y		N
Sierra Leone	Y				N		Y		Y				Y	Y	Y		N		Y		Y		Y
Singapore	Y				Y			Y	N	Y				Y	Y	Y	Y	N	N	N	Y		Y

Country	(1)	(2)	(3)	(4)	(5)	(6) outlook	(6) reporting	(7)	(8)	(9)	(10)
Slovakia	Y	N				Y	Y	N	N	Y	Y
Slovenia	Y	N				Y	Y	Y	Y	Y	Y
South Africa	Y	N		Y		Y	Y	N	Y	Y	Y
Spain	Y	N				Y	Y	Y	N	Y	Y
Sri Lanka	Y	Y			Y	Y	Y	N	Y	Y	Y
Sweden	Y	N	Y		Y	Y	Y	N	Y	Y	Y
Switzerland	Y	N			Y	Y	Y	Y	N	Y	Y
Syria		Y	Y	N			N	N	N	Y	N
Tanzania	Y	Y		Y		Y	Y	Y	N	Y	Y
Thailand	Y	Y			Y	Y	Y	Y	N	Y	N
Tunisia	Y	N		Y	Y		Y	N	N	Y	N
Turkey	Y	Y	Y		Y	Y	Y	Y	N	Y	Y
United Arab Emirates	Y	Y			Y	Y	Y	Y	N	Y	Y
Uganda	Y	Y		Y	N	Y	Y	Y	N	Y	Y
United Kingdom		Y		Y	Y	Y				Y	Y
Ukraine	Y	Y	Y		N	Y	Y	Y	Y	Y	Y
Uruguay	Y	N		Y	Y		Y	N	N	N	Y
United States	Y	N	Y	Y	Y		Y	Y	Y	N	Y
Venezuela	Y	Y	Y		Y	Y	Y	Y	Y	Y	Y
Zambia	Y	Y		Y	Y		Y	N	N	N	N

[1] (1) Who sets the objectives of monetary policy: a. CB; b. CB and government jointly; c. Set by statute; d. None/government. (2) Is the CB subject to possible interference in the conduct of monetary policy? (3) Clarity on final objective of monetary policy: a. Single and clearly defined objective; b. Multiple objectives without prioritization; c. Clear prioritization of multiple objectives. (4) Quantification of objective. (5) Publication of objective. (6) Reporting outlook: a. in the form of explicit forecasts; b. forecasts with assessment of risks; c. general statement only; d. no economic outlook. (6) Reporting mechanisms and procedures: a. to minister; b. to legislature; c. other (for example, board). (7) Regular appearances before parliament. (8) Conflict resolution procedures: a. definition of conflict; c. procedures to resolve conflict; c. clear outcomes in the case of failure to resolve conflict. (9) Decision-making structure: a. by committee; b. CEO only. (10) Clear and detailed explanation of appointment procedures.

[2] N: No; Y: Yes.

Source: Authors' estimates.

Appendix XII   Transparency database (Q1-2006)

Sub-components[1,2]	Operational										Economic					Procedural	
Central banks	1a	1b	1c	1d	1e	2	3a	3b	3c	3d	4	5	6a	6b	6c	7	8
Albania	Y	Y	Y	Y	Y	Y	Y				Y	N		Y		Y	N
Algeria	Y	Y	N	N	Y	N			Y		Y	N			Y	Y	N
Argentina	Y	Y	N	Y	Y	Y	Y				Y	Y			Y	N	N
Armenia	Y	Y	N	N	Y	N	Y				Y	Y			Y	N	N
Australia	Y	Y	Y	Y	Y	N	Y				Y	Y		Y		N	N
Austria	Y	Y	Y	Y	Y	Y	Y				Y	N		Y		N	N
Bahrain	N	Y	Y	N	N	N	Y				Y	Y		Y		Y	N
Bangladesh	Y	Y	Y	Y	Y	N	Y				Y	N			Y	N	N
BCEAO	Y	Y	Y	Y	Y	Y			Y		Y	Y		Y	Y	Y	N
BEAC	Y	N	N	Y	N	N			Y		Y	Y		Y		Y	N
Belarus	Y	N	N	N	Y	Y	Y				Y	N				N	N
Belgium	Y	Y	Y	Y	Y	Y	Y				Y	N		Y		N	N
Bolivia	Y	Y	N	Y	Y	Y			Y		Y	Y		Y		Y	N
Botswana	Y	N	Y	Y	Y	N	Y				Y	Y			Y	Y	N
Brazil	Y	Y	N	Y	Y	Y	Y				Y	Y		Y		Y	N
Bulgaria	N	Y	Y	Y	Y	N	Y				Y	N		Y		N	N
Canada	Y	Y	Y	Y	Y	Y	Y				Y	Y	Y			N	N
Chile	Y	Y	Y	Y	Y	Y	Y				Y	Y		Y		Y	N
China	Y	N	Y	N	N	N		Y			Y	N			Y	Y	N
Colombia	Y	N	Y	Y	Y	Y					Y	Y	Y			N	N
Costa Rica	Y	Y	N	Y	Y	N			Y		Y	Y	Y			Y	N
Croatia	Y	Y	Y	Y	Y	N	Y				Y	Y			Y	Y	N
Czech Republic	Y	Y	Y	Y	Y	Y	Y				Y	Y		Y		Y	Y
Denmark	Y	N	Y	Y	Y	Y	Y				Y	N		Y		N	N
ECB	Y	Y	Y	Y	Y	Y					Y	N		Y		N	N
Ecuador	N	Y	N	Y	N	Y	Y		Y		Y	N	Y			N	N

Country													
Egypt	N	N	N	Y	Y				Y	N	N	N	N
El Salvador	N	N	N	Y	N				N	N	Y	N	N
Estonia	Y	Y	Y	Y	N	Y		Y	Y	Y	Y	Y	N
Finland	Y	Y	Y	Y	Y	Y		Y	Y	Y	Y	Y	N
France	Y	Y	Y	Y	Y	Y		Y	Y	Y	Y	N	N
Georgia	Y	N	N	Y	N	Y		N	Y	Y	Y	N	N
Germany	Y	Y	Y	Y	Y	Y		Y	Y	Y	Y	Y	N
Ghana	Y	Y	Y	N	N	N		Y	Y	Y	Y	Y	N
Greece	Y	Y	Y	Y	Y	Y		N	Y	Y	Y	N	Y
Guatemala	Y	N	Y	Y	Y			N	N	Y	Y	N	N
Honduras	Y	Y	Y	Y	N		Y	Y	Y	Y	Y	N	Y
Hungary	Y	Y	Y	Y	N	Y		Y	Y	Y	Y	Y	Y
Iceland	Y	Y	Y	Y	Y	Y		Y	Y	Y	Y	Y	N
India	Y	Y	Y	Y	Y	Y		Y	Y	Y	Y	Y	N
Indonesia	Y	Y	Y	Y	N	Y		Y	N	Y	Y	Y	N
Iran	Y	Y	Y	Y	Y		Y	N	Y	N	Y	Y	N
Ireland	Y	Y	Y	Y	Y	Y		Y	Y	Y	Y	Y	N
Israel	Y	Y	Y	Y	Y	Y		Y	Y	Y	Y	Y	N
Italy	Y	Y	Y	Y	Y	Y		Y	Y	Y	Y	Y	N
Japan	Y	Y	Y	Y	Y	Y		Y	Y	Y	Y	Y	N
Jordan	N	N	N	Y	N	Y		Y	N	N	Y	Y	Y
Kazakhstan	Y	Y	N	Y	N	Y		Y	Y	Y	Y	Y	N
Kenya	Y	Y	Y	Y	Y	Y		Y	Y	Y	Y	Y	N
Korea	Y	N	Y	Y	Y	Y		Y	Y	Y	Y	Y	N
Kyrgyzstan	Y	Y	N	Y	N		Y	Y	Y	N	Y	Y	N
Latvia	Y	Y	Y	Y	Y		Y	Y	Y	Y	Y	Y	N
Lebanon	N	Y	N	N	N	Y	Y	N	N	Y	Y	Y	Y
Lithuania	Y	Y	N	Y	N		Y	Y	Y	Y	Y	Y	N
Madagascar	N	Y	N	Y	N		Y	N	N	Y	Y	Y	N
Malaysia	Y	Y	Y	Y	Y	Y		Y	Y	Y	Y	Y	N
Mexico	Y	Y	Y	Y	Y		Y	Y	Y	Y	Y	Y	N

Appendix XII Continued

Sub-components[1,2]	Operational										Economic					Procedural	
Central banks	1a	1b	1c	1d	1e	2	3a	3b	3c	3d	4	5	6a	6b	6c	7	8
Moldova	Y	Y	N	N	Y	N	Y				Y	N			Y	N	N
Mongolia	Y	N	N	Y	Y	N	Y				Y	N		Y		N	N
Morocco	Y	Y	Y	Y	Y	N		Y			Y	N			Y	N	N
Mozambique	N	Y	N	N	Y	Y	Y				N	N			Y	N	N
Namibia	Y	Y	N	Y	Y	N	Y				Y	N			Y	N	N
Netherlands	Y	Y	Y	Y	Y	Y	Y				Y	Y		Y		N	N
New Zealand	Y	Y	Y	Y	Y	Y	Y				Y	Y	Y			N	N
Nicaragua	Y	Y	Y	Y	Y	N			Y		Y	N	Y			Y	N
Nigeria	Y	Y	Y	Y	Y	Y			Y		Y	Y			Y	Y	N
Norway	Y	Y	Y	Y	Y	Y	Y				Y	Y		Y		Y	N
Pakistan	Y	Y	Y	Y	N	N	Y				Y	N		Y		Y	N
Paraguay	Y	Y	N	Y	Y	N			Y		Y	N		Y		N	N
Peru	Y	Y	N	Y	Y	Y	Y				Y	Y			Y	Y	N
Philippines	Y	Y	Y	Y	Y	N	Y				Y	Y		Y		Y	N
Poland	Y	Y	Y	Y	Y	Y	Y				Y	N		Y		Y	N
Portugal	Y	Y	Y	Y	Y	Y	Y				Y	N		Y		N	N
Romania	Y	Y	Y	N	Y	N	Y				Y	Y	Y			Y	N
Russia	Y	Y	N	Y	Y	Y	Y				Y	N			Y	N	N
Saudi Arabia	Y	N	Y	Y	N	N	Y				N	N			Y	N	N
Sierra Leone	N	Y	Y	Y	Y	N	Y				N	N			Y	N	N
Singapore	Y	Y	Y	Y	Y	Y	Y				Y	Y		Y		N	N

Country	1a	1b	1c	1d	1e	2	3a	3b	3c	3d	4a	4b	4c	5	6a	6b	6c	7	8
Slovakia	Y	Y	Y	Y	Y	Y	Y				Y			Y	Y			Y	N
Slovenia	Y	Y	Y	Y	Y	Y	Y				Y			Y	Y			Y	N
South Africa	Y	N	Y	Y	Y	Y	Y			Y	Y			Y	Y			Y	N
Spain	Y	Y	Y	Y	Y	Y	Y				Y	Y		N	N			N	N
Sri Lanka	Y	Y	Y	Y	Y	Y	N			Y	Y			N	N			N	N
Sweden	Y	Y	Y	Y	Y	Y	Y			Y	Y			Y	Y			Y	N
Switzerland	Y	Y	Y	Y	Y	Y	Y	Y			Y			N	N			N	N
Syria	N	N	N	N	N	Y	Y				N			N	N			N	N
Tanzania	Y	Y	Y	Y	Y	Y	Y		Y		Y			Y	N			Y	N
Thailand	Y	Y	Y	Y	Y	Y	Y	Y			Y			Y	Y			Y	N
Tunisia	N	Y	Y	Y	Y	Y	N		Y		Y			N	Y			Y	N
Turkey	Y	Y	Y	Y	Y	N	Y			Y	Y			Y	Y			Y	N
Uganda	N	Y	Y	Y	Y	Y	N		Y		Y			N	N			N	N
United Kingdom	Y	Y	Y	Y	Y	Y	Y			Y	Y			Y	Y			Y	Y
Ukraine	Y	N	N	Y	N	Y	N	Y			N			N	N			N	N
United Arab Emirates	N	N	N	Y	Y	N	N			Y	N			Y	N			N	N
Uruguay	Y	Y	Y	Y	Y	Y	Y			Y	Y			N	Y			Y	N
United States	Y	Y	Y	Y	Y	Y	Y			Y	Y			N	Y			Y	Y
Venezuela	Y	N	Y	Y	Y	N	N			Y	Y			N	Y			Y	Y
Zambia	Y	Y	N	N	Y	Y	N		Y		N			Y	N			N	N

[1] (1) Forms of communication: a. Statements or reports on inflation/monetary policy; b. Reports, bulletin on activities; c. Regular speeches; d. Economic research; e. Annual report/retrospective analysis. (2) Regular information published about how monetary policy decisions are made and their justification. (3) Official website: a. English website frequently updated; b. English website not frequently updated; c. No website available in English; d. No website. (4) Publication of a monetary policy strategy and/or limits of monetary policy. (5) Key assumptions in generating outlook. (6) Economic modeling procedures: a. Publicly available; b. Described or discussed but complete details not provided; c. No information provided. (7) Publication of minutes of CB meetings. (8) Publication of committee voting record.
[2] Y: Yes. N: No.

Sources: Authors' estimates.

Appendix XIII Detailed governance scores

	Region[1]	Income level[5]	Non-standardized scores										Standardized scores											
			Accountability					Transparency					Accountability				Transparency		Independence				Governance	
			Responsibility	Objectives	Ex post	Governance	Overall	Narrow[4]	Operational	Economic	Procedural	Overall	Overall	Ranking	Narrow[4]	Ranking	Overall	Ranking	Political	Economic	Overall	Ranking	Overall	Ranking
Australia	APD	A	0.66	1.66	2.32	2.00	6.64	5.98	3.50	2.50	0.00	6.00	0.66	48	0.75	10	0.63	32	0.25	1.00	0.63	53	0.64	48
Austria	WEU	A	2.00	2.33	1.33	2.00	7.66	5.66	4.50	1.50	0.00	6.00	0.77	13	0.71	24	0.63	32	1.00	0.88	0.94	3	0.78	8
Belgium	WEU	A	2.00	2.33	1.33	1.00	6.66	4.66	4.50	1.50	0.00	6.00	0.67	42	0.58	64	0.63	32	1.00	0.88	0.94	3	0.75	19
Canada	NAM	A	0.66	1.65	1.65	2.00	6.31	5.65	4.50	3.00	0.00	7.50	0.63	52	0.71	24	0.79	11	0.38	0.88	0.63	53	0.68	40
Denmark	WEU	A	2.00	1.66	0.33	2.00	5.99	3.99	4.00	1.50	0.00	5.50	0.60	66	0.50	81	0.58	56	0.50	1.00	0.75	31	0.64	48
ECB	WEU	A	2.00	2.33	1.33	2.00	7.66	5.66	4.50	1.50	0.00	6.00	0.77	13	0.71	24	0.63	32	1.00	1.00	1.00	1	0.80	7
Finland	WEU	A	2.00	2.33	1.33	1.00	6.66	4.66	4.50	1.50	0.00	6.00	0.67	42	0.58	64	0.63	32	1.00	0.88	0.94	3	0.75	19
France	WEU	A	2.00	2.33	1.33	2.00	7.66	5.66	4.50	1.50	0.00	6.00	0.77	13	0.71	24	0.63	32	1.00	0.88	0.94	3	0.78	8
Germany	WEU	A	2.00	2.33	1.33	2.00	7.66	5.66	4.50	1.50	0.00	6.00	0.77	13	0.71	24	0.63	32	1.00	0.75	0.88	11	0.76	13
Greece	WEU	A	2.00	1.83	1.66	2.00	7.49	5.49	4.50	1.50	0.00	6.00	0.75	27	0.69	42	0.63	32	1.00	0.63	0.81	19	0.73	23
Iceland	WEU	A	0.66	3.00	0.33	1.00	4.99	4.33	4.50	2.50	0.00	7.00	0.50	81	0.54	76	0.74	20	0.50	1.00	0.75	31	0.66	45
Ireland	WEU	A	2.00	2.33	1.33	1.00	6.66	4.66	4.50	1.50	0.00	6.00	0.67	42	0.58	64	0.63	32	1.00	0.63	0.81	19	0.70	33
Italy	WEU	A	2.00	2.33	1.33	2.00	6.66	4.66	4.50	1.50	0.00	6.00	0.67	42	0.58	64	0.63	32	1.00	0.63	0.81	19	0.70	33
Japan	APD	A	1.00	2.50	1.32	2.00	6.82	5.82	4.50	1.00	2.00	7.50	0.68	38	0.73	17	0.79	11	0.13	0.75	0.44	77	0.64	48
Korea	APD	A	0.66	1.33	2.65	2.00	6.64	5.98	4.50	1.00	1.00	6.50	0.66	48	0.75	10	0.68	29	0.25	0.88	0.56	61	0.64	48
Netherlands	WEU	A	2.00	2.33	1.33	2.00	7.66	5.66	4.50	1.50	0.00	6.00	0.77	13	0.71	24	0.63	32	1.00	0.75	0.88	11	0.76	13
New Zealand	APD	A	0.66	3.00	1.65	1.50	6.81	6.15	4.50	3.00	0.00	7.50	0.68	38	0.77	8	0.84	5	0.25	0.63	0.44	77	0.64	48
Norway	WEU	A	0.00	2.00	2.98	1.00	5.98	5.98	4.50	2.50	1.00	8.00	0.60	66	0.75	10	0.84	10	0.50	1.00	0.75	31	0.73	23
Portugal	WEU	A	2.00	2.00	2.33	2.00	7.66	5.66	4.50	1.50	0.00	6.00	0.77	13	0.71	24	0.63	32	1.00	0.63	0.81	19	0.74	22
Singapore	APD	A	1.00	1.00	1.99	2.00	5.99	4.99	4.50	2.50	0.00	7.00	0.60	66	0.62	57	0.74	20	0.38	0.38	0.38	90	0.57	65
Spain	WEU	A	2.00	2.33	1.33	2.00	7.66	5.66	4.50	1.50	0.00	6.00	0.77	13	0.71	24	0.63	32	1.00	0.75	0.88	11	0.76	13

Country																								
Sweden	WEU	A	2.00	2.50	1.32	2.00	7.82	5.82	4.50	2.50	1.00	8.00	0.78	10	0.73	17	0.84	5	0.88	1.00	0.94	3	0.85	4
Switzerland	WEU	A	2.00	2.66	0.99	2.00	7.65	5.65	4.50	3.00	0.00	7.50	0.77	13	0.71	24	0.79	11	0.88	1.00	0.94	3	0.83	5
United King.	WEU	A	0.00	2.16	1.65	2.00	5.81	5.81	4.50	3.00	2.00	9.50	0.58	69	0.73	17	1.00	1	0.38	1.00	0.69	42	0.76	13
United States	NAM	A	2.00	1.50	1.66	2.00	7.16	5.16	4.50	1.50	2.00	8.00	0.72	31	0.65	52	0.84	5	0.63	0.88	0.75	31	0.77	11
Argentina	LAM	E	1.66	3.00	1.33	2.00	7.99	6.33	4.00	0.00	0.00	6.00	0.80	5	0.79	4	0.63	32	0.75	0.75	0.75	31	0.73	23
Brazil	LAM	E	0.66	2.00	2.65	1.00	6.31	5.65	4.00	2.50	1.00	7.50	0.63	52	0.71	24	0.79	11	0.50	0.75	0.63	53	0.68	40
Bulgaria	TRS	E	1.33	2.66	1.66	2.00	7.65	6.32	3.00	1.50	0.00	4.50	0.77	13	0.79	4	0.47	68	1.00	0.75	0.88	11	0.70	33
Chile	LAM	E	1.00	2.50	1.65	2.00	7.15	6.15	4.00	2.50	1.00	7.50	0.72	31	0.77	8	0.79	11	0.50	0.88	0.69	42	0.73	23
China	APD	E	0.00	2.50	0.66	1.00	4.16	4.16	2.00	1.00	1.00	4.00	0.42	90	0.52	78	0.42	79	0.38	0.75	0.56	61	0.47	81
Croatia	TRS	E	2.00	0.50	0.66	2.00	5.16	3.16	3.00	1.00	1.00	5.00	0.52	77	0.40	89	0.53	59	1.00	0.75	0.88	11	0.64	48
Czech Rep.	TRS	E	2.00	2.33	1.66	2.00	7.99	5.99	4.50	2.50	2.00	9.00	0.80	5	0.75	10	0.95	2	0.88	0.88	0.88	11	0.87	2
Egypt	MCD	E	0.66	1.00	0.99	1.00	3.65	2.99	3.50	0.00	0.00	3.50	0.37	92	0.37	91	0.37	85	0.13	0.63	0.38	90	0.37	94
Estonia	TRS	E	2.00	2.50	1.33	2.00	7.83	5.83	3.50	2.50	1.00	7.00	0.78	10	0.73	17	0.74	20	0.63	1.00	0.81	19	0.78	8
Hungary	TRS	E	2.00	2.66	1.99	2.00	8.65	6.65	4.00	3.00	2.00	9.00	0.87	2	0.83	3	0.95	2	0.88	1.00	0.94	3	0.92	1
India	APD	E	0.66	1.33	1.65	1.00	4.64	3.98	4.50	0.50	0.00	5.00	0.46	86	0.50	81	0.53	59	0.25	0.75	0.50	67	0.50	77
Indonesia	APD	E	2.00	0.66	2.00	2.00	7.66	5.66	3.50	2.50	0.00	6.00	0.77	13	0.71	24	0.63	32	0.63	0.75	0.69	42	0.70	33
Israel	MCD	E	0.00	1.33	1.32	1.50	4.15	4.15	3.50	2.50	0.00	6.00	0.42	90	0.52	78	0.63	32	0.13	0.63	0.38	90	0.47	81
Jordan	MCD	E	1.00	0.50	1.33	2.00	4.82	3.83	3.00	1.00	1.00	5.00	0.48	82	0.48	83	0.53	59	0.25	0.50	0.38	90	0.46	84
Latvia	TRS	E	2.00	2.00	0.33	2.00	6.33	4.33	4.50	2.00	1.00	7.50	0.63	52	0.54	76	0.79	11	1.00	1.00	1.00	1	0.81	6
Lithuania	TRS	E	2.00	2.00	1.33	2.00	7.33	5.33	3.00	2.00	1.00	6.00	0.73	30	0.67	47	0.63	32	0.88	0.75	0.81	19	0.73	23
Malaysia	APD	E	1.00	1.00	1.65	2.00	5.65	4.65	3.50	1.00	0.00	4.50	0.57	71	0.58	64	0.47	68	0.25	0.75	0.50	67	0.51	75
Mexico	LAM	E	1.00	1.83	1.66	2.00	6.49	5.49	4.16	2.00	0.00	6.16	0.65	50	0.69	42	0.65	31	0.63	0.75	0.69	42	0.66	45
Morocco	MCD	E	0.66	1.33	0.66	1.00	3.65	2.99	3.16	1.00	0.00	4.16	0.37	92	0.37	91	0.44	78	0.25	0.75	0.50	67	0.43	91
Pakistan	APD	E	0.66	1.66	2.65	2.00	6.97	6.31	3.50	1.50	1.00	6.00	0.70	34	0.79	4	0.63	32	0.38	0.63	0.50	67	0.61	59
Peru	LAM	E	2.00	3.00	0.99	2.00	7.99	5.99	4.00	2.00	0.00	6.00	0.80	5	0.75	10	0.63	32	0.38	1.00	0.69	42	0.71	31
Philippines	APD	E	1.66	2.16	1.32	2.00	7.14	5.48	3.50	2.50	1.00	7.00	0.71	33	0.69	42	0.74	20	0.63	0.63	0.63	53	0.69	38
Poland	TRS	E	2.00	2.33	0.66	2.00	6.99	4.99	4.50	1.50	1.00	7.00	0.70	34	0.62	57	0.74	20	0.88	0.88	0.88	11	0.77	11
Romania	TRS	E	2.00	3.00	0.66	2.00	7.66	5.66	3.00	3.00	1.00	7.00	0.77	13	0.71	24	0.74	20	0.63	0.75	0.69	42	0.73	23
Russia	TRS	E	0.66	1.66	1.66	2.00	6.32	5.66	4.00	1.00	0.00	5.00	0.63	52	0.71	24	0.53	59	0.50	0.38	0.44	77	0.53	72

(Continued)

Appendix XIII (Continued)

		Non-standardized scores										Standardized scores											
		Accountability						Transparency				Accountability				Transparency		Independence				Governance	
	Region[1]	Income level[5]	Responsibility	Objectives	Ex post	Governance	Overall	Narrow[4]	Operational	Economic	Procedural	Overall	Overall	Ranking	Narrow[4]	Ranking	Overall	Ranking	Political	Economic	Overall	Ranking	Overall	Ranking
Slovakia	TRS	E	2.00	3.00	0.66	2.00	7.66	5.66	4.50	2.00	1.00	7.50	0.77	13	0.71	24	0.79	11	0.50	0.75	0.63	53	0.73	23
Slovenia	TRS	E	2.00	3.00	2.65	2.00	9.65	7.65	4.00	3.00	1.00	8.00	0.97	1	0.96	1	0.84	5	0.88	0.75	0.81	19	0.87	2
South Africa	AFR	E	2.00	2.66	1.65	2.00	8.31	6.31	4.50	2.50	1.00	8.00	0.83	3	0.79	4	0.84	5	0.13	0.38	0.25	97	0.64	48
Thailand	APD	E	1.00	2.00	0.33	1.00	4.33	3.33	4.50	3.00	1.00	8.50	0.43	88	0.42	87	0.89	4	0.50	0.38	0.44	77	0.59	63
Turkey	MCD	E	0.66	2.50	0.99	2.00	6.15	5.49	4.16	2.00	1.00	7.16	0.62	59	0.69	42	0.75	19	0.63	1.00	0.81	19	0.73	23
Venezuela	LAM	E	1.00	2.66	2.65	2.00	8.31	7.31	3.33	2.50	1.00	6.83	0.83	3	0.91	2	0.72	27	0.50	0.88	0.69	42	0.75	19
Albania	TRS	D	2.00	1.83	1.99	2.00	7.82	5.82	4.50	1.50	1.00	7.00	0.78	10	0.73	17	0.74	20	0.75	0.75	0.75	31	0.76	13
Algeria	MCD	D	2.00	0.00	1.65	1.00	4.65	2.65	1.83	1.00	1.00	3.83	0.47	84	0.33	93	0.40	84	1.00	0.63	0.81	19	0.56	66
Armenia	TRS	D	2.00	3.00	0.99	2.00	7.99	5.99	2.50	2.00	0.00	4.50	0.80	5	0.75	10	0.47	68	0.88	0.75	0.81	19	0.70	33
Bahrain	MCD	D	0.66	0.50	1.32	2.00	4.48	3.82	1.50	2.00	1.00	4.50	0.45	87	0.48	87	0.47	68	0.25	0.63	0.44	77	0.45	88
Bangladesh	APD	D	1.00	2.00	2.65	1.00	6.65	5.65	3.00	2.00	0.00	5.00	0.67	42	0.71	24	0.53	59	0.00	0.38	0.19	98	0.46	84
BCEAO[2]	AFR	D	1.00	1.66	0.99	2.00	5.65	4.65	3.83	1.00	1.00	5.83	0.57	71	0.58	64	0.61	53	0.50	0.88	0.69	42	0.62	56
BEAC[3]	AFR	D	1.66	2.00	1.32	2.00	6.98	5.32	1.33	2.50	1.00	4.83	0.70	34	0.67	47	0.51	67	0.50	0.88	0.69	42	0.63	55
Belarus	TRS	D	0.66	2.00	0.66	2.00	5.32	4.66	3.00	1.00	0.00	4.00	0.53	75	0.58	64	0.42	79	0.50	0.38	0.44	77	0.46	84
Bolivia	LAM	D	2.00	1.66	1.98	2.00	7.64	5.64	3.33	2.50	0.00	5.83	0.76	26	0.71	24	0.61	53	0.50	1.00	0.75	31	0.71	31
Botswana	AFR	D	1.00	2.50	1.32	2.00	6.82	5.82	3.00	2.00	0.00	5.00	0.68	38	0.73	17	0.53	59	0.13	0.75	0.44	77	0.55	69
Colombia	LAM	D	1.00	3.00	1.33	1.00	6.33	5.33	3.66	3.00	0.00	6.66	0.63	52	0.67	47	0.70	28	0.13	0.88	0.50	67	0.61	59
Costa Rica	LAM	D	1.00	2.16	1.00	2.00	6.16	5.16	2.33	3.00	0.00	5.33	0.62	59	0.65	52	0.56	57	0.50	0.88	0.69	42	0.62	56
Ecuador	LAM	D	1.33	1.50	1.32	2.00	6.15	4.82	2.33	2.00	0.00	4.33	0.62	59	0.60	61	0.46	76	0.88	1.00	0.94	3	0.67	44
El Salvador	LAM	D	2.00	1.83	0.99	2.00	6.82	4.82	2.16	2.00	1.00	5.16	0.68	38	0.60	61	0.54	58	0.63	1.00	0.81	19	0.68	40
Georgia	TRS	D	1.66	1.50	2.32	2.00	7.48	5.82	2.50	1.00	0.00	3.50	0.75	27	0.73	17	0.37	85	0.88	0.63	0.75	31	0.62	56
Ghana	AFR	D	1.00	0.83	0.99	2.00	4.82	3.82	3.00	1.50	0.00	4.50	0.48	82	0.48	83	0.47	68	0.38	0.63	0.50	67	0.49	78
Guatemala	LAM	D	2.00	2.33	1.66	2.00	7.99	5.99	4.00	3.00	1.00	8.00	0.80	5	0.75	10	0.84	5	0.38	0.88	0.63	53	0.76	13

Country	Region	Type																							
Honduras	LAM	D	1.00	2.16	0.99	2.00	6.15	5.15	2.33	1.00	0.00	3.33	0.62	59	0.64	54	0.35	88	0.13	0.88	0.50	67	0.49	78
Iran	MCD	D	0.66	1.00	0.00	1.00	2.66	2.00	2.16	0.00	0.00	2.16	0.27	96	0.25	95	0.23	95	0.00	0.75	0.38	90	0.29	98
Kazakhstan	TRS	D	1.00	2.50	0.66	1.00	5.16	4.16	3.00	2.00	0.00	5.00	0.52	77	0.52	78	0.53	59	0.63	0.88	0.75	31	0.60	62
Kenya	AFR	D	1.00	1.83	1.32	2.00	6.15	5.15	4.50	1.50	0.00	6.00	0.62	59	0.64	54	0.63	32	0.13	0.75	0.44	77	0.56	66
Kyrgyzstan	TRS	D	1.00	2.66	0.66	2.00	6.32	5.32	2.00	3.00	0.00	5.00	0.63	52	0.67	47	0.53	59	1.00	0.75	0.88	11	0.68	40
Lebanon	MCD	D	1.00	0.00	0.33	2.00	3.33	2.33	1.66	0.00	0.00	1.66	0.33	34	0.29	94	0.17	98	0.25	0.75	0.50	67	0.34	95
Madagascar	AFR	D	2.00	2.00	0.99	2.00	6.99	4.99	1.33	1.00	0.00	2.33	0.70	34	0.62	57	0.25	94	0.50	0.75	0.63	53	0.52	74
Moldova	TRS	D	1.66	1.83	0.66	2.00	6.15	4.49	2.50	1.00	0.00	3.50	0.62	59	0.56	73	0.37	85	0.75	0.75	0.75	31	0.58	64
Mongolia	APD	D	2.00	1.83	2.32	1.50	7.65	5.65	2.50	1.50	0.00	4.00	0.77	13	0.71	24	0.42	79	1.00	0.50	0.75	31	0.65	47
Mozambique	AFR	D	1.00	0.50	0.33	1.00	2.83	1.83	3.00	1.00	0.00	4.00	0.28	95	0.23	97	0.42	79	0.38	0.50	0.44	77	0.38	93
Namibia	AFR	D	1.00	1.00	1.65	2.00	6.65	5.65	3.00	0.00	0.00	3.00	0.67	42	0.71	24	0.32	90	0.25	0.50	0.38	90	0.45	88
Nicaragua	LAM	D	1.00	1.00	0.66	2.00	4.66	3.66	2.33	2.00	0.00	4.33	0.47	84	0.46	86	0.46	76	0.13	1.00	0.56	61	0.49	78
Nigeria	AFR	D	1.00	1.66	0.99	2.00	5.65	4.65	3.83	1.00	1.00	5.83	0.57	71	0.58	64	0.61	53	0.25	0.63	0.44	77	0.54	70
Paraguay	LAM	D	0.66	2.00	0.66	2.00	5.32	4.66	1.83	1.50	0.00	3.33	0.53	75	0.58	64	0.35	88	0.25	0.75	0.50	67	0.46	84
Saudi Arabia	MCD	D	1.00	0.00	0.33	1.00	2.33	1.33	2.50	0.00	0.00	2.50	0.23	98	0.17	98	0.26	93	0.25	0.75	0.50	67	0.33	96
Sierra Leone	AFR	D	2.00	1.50	0.99	2.00	6.49	4.49	3.00	0.00	0.00	3.00	0.65	50	0.56	73	0.32	90	0.50	0.63	0.56	61	0.51	75
Sri Lanka	APD	D	1.00	1.66	1.65	2.00	6.31	5.31	4.50	1.50	0.00	6.00	0.63	52	0.66	51	0.63	32	0.50	0.63	0.56	61	0.61	59
Syria	MCD	D	0.66	0.00	0.99	1.00	2.65	1.99	1.16	1.00	0.00	2.16	0.27	96	0.25	95	0.23	95	0.38	0.50	0.44	77	0.31	97
Tanzania	AFR	D	1.00	1.50	1.65	2.00	6.15	5.15	3.00	1.00	0.00	4.00	0.62	59	0.64	54	0.42	79	0.13	0.63	0.38	90	0.47	81
Tunisia	MCD	D	2.00	1.50	0.66	1.00	5.16	3.16	2.50	1.00	1.00	4.50	0.52	77	0.40	89	0.47	68	0.63	0.75	0.69	42	0.56	66
Uganda	AFR	D	1.00	1.16	1.65	2.00	5.81	4.81	3.00	1.50	0.00	4.50	0.58	69	0.60	61	0.47	68	0.50	0.63	0.56	61	0.54	70
Ukraine	TRS	D	0.66	1.00	1.99	2.00	5.65	4.99	2.16	0.00	0.00	2.16	0.57	71	0.62	57	0.23	95	0.88	0.75	0.81	19	0.53	72
United Arab E.	MCD	D	1.00	1.00	0.33	2.00	4.33	3.33	2.00	1.50	1.00	4.50	0.43	88	0.42	87	0.47	68	0.38	0.50	0.44	77	0.45	88
Uruguay	LAM	D	2.00	2.16	1.32	2.00	7.48	5.48	4.00	2.50	0.00	6.50	0.75	27	0.69	42	0.68	29	0.63	0.63	0.63	53	0.69	38
Zambia	AFR	D	0.66	1.50	1.99	1.00	5.15	4.49	3.00	0.00	0.00	3.00	0.52	77	0.56	73	0.32	90	0.38	0.50	0.44	77	0.42	92

1 APD: Asia & Pacific; AFR: Sub-Saharan Africa; LAM: Central & Latin America; MCD: Middle East & North Africa; NAM: North America; TRS: Transition Europe; WEU: Western Europe.

2 BCEAO includes Benin, Burkina Faso, Côte d'Ivoire, Guinea Bissau, Mali, Niger, Senegal and Togo.

3 BEAC includes Cameroon, Central African Republic, Chad, Republic of Congo, Equatorial Guinea and Gabon.

4 Narrow Accountability scores exclude the Responsibility component.

5 A: Advanced economies. D: Developing countries. E: Emerging market economies.

Source: Authors' estimates.

6
Independence and Inflation Performance: New Empirical Evidence

In this chapter[1] we return to the old debate about the benefits of CB independence for maintaining a low-inflation environment.[2] Inflation outcomes reflect actual monetary and fiscal policies, the external environment, and the general attitudes of policy-makers towards inflation, which may, or may not, be reflected in CB laws. Therefore, we examine to what extent strong legal frameworks for CB independence may have contributed to the reduction in average inflation levels, after controlling for other determinants of inflation.[3] Our analysis focuses on emerging markets and developing economies because these are the countries where the volatility in inflation outcomes has been most significant (see Figure 6.1). During the mid-1970s to the mid-1990s, recurring episodes of loose fiscal and monetary policies, combined with commodity price shocks, kept inflation high. By contrast, average inflation has fallen dramatically since the early 1990s – in many cases from double- and triple-digit levels[4] – to about 5 percent as of 2006.

A number of factors have contributed to the reduction of inflation in emerging markets. As discussed in Helbling, Jaumotte, and Sommer

---

[1] Martin Sommer contributed to this chapter.

[2] The early research on this issue includes Alesina and Summers (1993); Cukierman (1992); Cukierman, Webb, and Neyapti (1992); Grilli, Masciandaro, and Tabellini (1991); and Neyapti (1992). See Berger, Eijffinger, and de Haan (2000), Cukierman (2005), and Jácome and Vázquez (2005) for a recent treatment.

[3] De facto independence of CBs differs from de jure independence measured by our index. In any case, it is interesting to verify whether the de jure index has some predictive ability for inflation outcomes, even after controlling for a variety of other inflation determinants.

[4] In the Central and Eastern European countries, inflation spikes were associated with the initial stage of economic transformation.

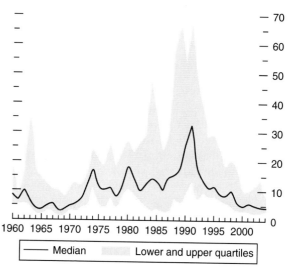

Figure 6.1 Inflation in emerging markets, 1960–2005 (annual percent change)
Source: Authors' estimates.

(2006), lower average inflation has generally reflected policy-makers' increasing preference for low and stable inflation. This policy shift in part resulted from the earlier experience with high and variable inflation in both emerging markets and advanced economies. In the early 1980s, the perceived costs of double-digit inflation increased, as high inflation coincided with low growth and rising unemployment. Governments in the advanced economies were the first to respond by strengthening institutional and policy frameworks to foster monetary stability – including by boosting CB independence and transparency and – in some countries – adopting an explicit inflation target. The combination of falling external inflation, learning from successful policies elsewhere, and public dissatisfaction with inflation explains much of the subsequent shift to low-inflation policies in emerging market and developing countries. Moreover, the gradual deepening of domestic financial markets and greater CB independence have made inflationary financing of fiscal deficits less common.[5] Aside from these factors, globalization may also have strengthened policy-makers' incentives to conduct prudent

---

[5] See Arnone, Laurens, Segalotto, and Sommer (2008).

monetary policy (Rogoff 2003). For instance, international capital markets may have had a disciplining effect on monetary policy, including through the risk of a reduction in foreign investment (Tytell and Wei 2004).[6]

In sum, the low inflation environment in emerging markets and developing countries has resulted from a variety of factors. But has greater CB independence contributed to better inflation outcomes after controlling for all the other important explanations of low inflation? To provide a tentative answer to this question, we have estimated an econometric model that links the likelihood of good inflation performance – defined as annual inflation below 10 percent – to the various determinants of inflation discussed above.[7] Specifically, the model specification includes trade openness, inflation in advanced economies, the fiscal balance scaled by the depth of the domestic financial sector, the exchange rate regime, and two alternative measures of CB independence.[8] The estimation results (Table 6.1) suggest that CB independence has indeed helped to keep inflation low. On average, a move from no independence to full independence increases the likelihood of maintaining low inflation by about 50 percent. In our sample, the average independence of CBs in emerging markets increased from 0.3 to about 0.7 over the past couple of decades, which implies an average increase in the likelihood of low inflation by about 20 percentage points. We also examine how the measure of independence calculated in Chapters 4 and 5 performs compared with an alternative measure of independence, TOR (turnover of CB governors – Cukierman, Webb, and Neyapti 1992), which has been traditionally used in panel regressions. Both independence measures are correlated so the horserace regression in

---

[6] For a detailed analysis, see Helbling, Jaumotte, and Sommer (2006).

[7] The probit model is estimated for 24 emerging market economies (Argentina, Brazil, Chile, China, Colombia, Czech Republic, Dominican Republic, Ecuador, Egypt, Hungary, India, Indonesia, Korea, Malaysia, Mexico, Peru, Philippines, Poland, Romania, Russia, South Africa, Thailand, Turkey, and Venezuela) over 1960–2004. The data are five-year averages.

[8] See Catão and Terrones (2005) and the IMF's May 2001 *World Economic Outlook* for an analysis of the relationship between fiscal deficits and inflation. Boschen and Weise (2003) find that US inflation is a useful predictor of inflation spurts in the OECD countries. Ghosh et al. (1997) provide evidence that the fixed exchange rate regime can help reduce inflation, although in the long term, the currency peg may incur large output and inflation costs if it is not supported by appropriate policies and breaks down (Mishkin 1999).

Table 6.1 Inflation in emerging markets (probit estimates, five-year averages)[1]

Dependent variable	Probability of achieving low inflation[2]			
	(1)	(2)	(3)	(4)
Central bank independence	0.57*	0.73**	–	0.37
Turnover rate of governor[3]	–	–	−5.9	−2.2
Openness[4]	0.88***	0.61**	0.86***	0.95***
Fiscal balance/ financial depth[5]	0.21	0.53*[1]	0.07	0.16
Inflation in advanced economies[6]	−7.29***	−6.1***	−9.44***	−9.27***
Pegged exchange rate regime[7]	57.4***	51.1***	53.8***	49.0**
Sample	1960–2004	1960–2004	1960–2004	1960–2004
Number of observations	107	111	85	78

[1] All explanatory variables in the probit model are lagged by one (five-year) period – except in specification (2) where the fiscal balance/financial depth ratio is contemporaneous – to reduce problems associated with endogeneity that has not been treated in some earlier cross-country studies. The estimation results are qualitatively similar when low inflation is defined as annual average inflation below 5 or 15 percent, respectively; they are also similar when countries from Central and Eastern Europe are excluded (price controls typically reduced inflation prior to 1990, while liberalization increased inflation in the early nineties).

[2] Low inflation is defined as annual inflation below 10 percent. The probability is scaled between 0 and 100. All data are five-year averages. Explanatory variables are lagged by one period (i.e., by one five-year average), except in specification (2) where the fiscal balance/financial depth ratio is contemporaneous. *** denotes statistical significance at the 1 percent level, ** denotes significance at the 5 percent level, and * denotes statistical significance at the 10 percent level.

[3] Higher turnover may be associated with lower independence.

[4] Trade in percent of GDP.

[5] Central government balance relative to the depth of financial sector (measured by narrow money).

[6] Expressed as a percentage. The group of advanced economies consists of Australia, Canada, France, Germany, Italy, United Kingdom, and the United States.

[7] The dummy takes value of 1 (peg) or 0 (otherwise) and is calculated from the Reinhart-Rogoff (2002) dataset.

Sources: IMF, International Financial Statistics; Reinhart and Rogoff (2002); World Bank, World Development Indicators; World Economic Outlook; and authors' calculations.

specification (4) does not produce statistically conclusive results. However, it is worth noting that the coefficient on CB independence is reduced only by one-third when TOR is included (see specifications (1) and (3)), but the coefficient on TOR falls by about two-thirds in the specification that also includes CB independence (specifications (3) and (4)).[9]

The model confirms the important role of the inflation determinants other than CB independence. Since average openness in the sample increased from approximately 30 to 60 percent over the past four decades, globalization has increased the probability of low inflation by about 20 percentage points for emerging markets. The model also attributes a significant weight to the inflation performance in advanced economies. The disinflation that took place there in the early 1980s is estimated to have increased the likelihood of low inflation in emerging markets by 30 percentage points or more. Fiscal policy – a traditional source of inflation pressure – is also identified as an important determinant of inflation.[10] Finally, a fixed exchange rate regime can on average improve inflation performance, although sustaining currency pegs has proven difficult in the long term.

---

[9] The time series data on independence were constructed as follows. First, we identified years in which there was a significant change in the independence-related legislation in each country. Subsequently, we took the simplifying assumption that independence before the break-year was the same as independence as of the end of the 1980s; and independence after the break-year equals actual independence as of 2003. This assumption introduces measurement error into our independence variable, but its size is limited by the fact that most changes in independence occurred over the past couple of decades (Cukierman 2005) and our regressions use five-year data averages.

[10] In some countries, fiscal deficits may have fallen after greater CB independence constrained the ability of governments to monetize. However, we assume that any changes to the fiscal deficit are exogenous. This assumption *reduces* the likelihood that we will indeed find a relationship between independence and inflation.

7
Policy Lessons from Global Trends

Overview

Our assessment of CBs' governance framework shows that CBs have changed dramatically in the past three decades in ways that would have been inconceivable back in the late 1970s or early 1980s. Building on the literature that highlights their benefits, CBs, irrespective of the country's income level, have been granted higher independence; have become more accountable to those which have granted them independence; and have significantly boosted the transparency of their operations. Such a framework for CB governance which developed over time is based on the consensus that CBs should be entrusted with the primary mandate to preserve the public good of stability. This broad-based consensus stems from the view, backed by empirical analysis, that price stability is the best contribution that monetary policy can make to help the economy achieve its maximum potential output, and that any attempts to sacrifice the medium-term goal of price stability for efforts to meet other short-term objectives will adversely affect the credibility and effectiveness of the CB and ultimately weaken long-term economic growth. To allow the CB to achieve its delegated responsibility of protecting price stability, it must be made independent from the government so that its decisions are not influenced by short-term political and electoral objectives.[1] However, independence does not mean isolation, and the CB must be accountable to those from whom it receives its mandate and independence. Finally, transparency makes possible actual and effective accountability

---

[1] Arnone, Laurens, and Segalotto (2006a); Arnone, Laurens, Segalotto, and Sommer (2008).

by facilitating a proper understanding of the CB's objectives and actions by the public at large and the institutions representing it.

While CB governance features have converged, there are still noticeable differences among CBs, including among those which operate under comparable market environments. In particular, while CB objectives have converged and communication has increased significantly worldwide, there are significant differences in the way CBs talk to the general public or financial markets, most noticeably with regard to how much of the internal debate is made public. Some CBs only disclose the consensus view among the members of the decision-making bodies, while others provide also information about how individual policy-makers perceive developments. Such differences are clearly evidenced by the wide dispersion of scores for our procedural component of transparency, with average scores for CBs in advanced countries lower than the average for emerging market economies, as well as a wide dispersion among CBs. This result points to the lack of consensus about the benefits to be expected from full transparency about the internal debate and the range of views among the members of the CB's decision-making body, including among CBs in advanced economies.

Relationships between the pillars of central bank governance

Figure 7.1 summarizes the relationships between the three pillars of CB governance and stakeholders (i.e., the public at large, parliament, the government, and financial markets) as well as the ways in which these pillars relate to each other. Independence, accountability, and transparency, rather than being independent pillars are intertwined and positively, although at times negatively, correlated. Independent CBs in modern democracies take their legitimacy from their accountability vis-à-vis those (i.e., the public at large and parliament) who have delegated to them the tasks of preserving the public good of price stability. The need for transparency vis-à-vis the public at large and parliament, which arises from accountability, has also become a necessity vis-à-vis the financial markets as a consequence of their rapid expansion and the related shift to market-based instruments of monetary policy. At the same time, accountability enhances independence as it promotes its legitimacy, while transparency enhances accountability as it facilitates its actual exercise.

The most fundamental policy implication of our findings is that CB reforms must encompass all three pillars of CB governance if they are to

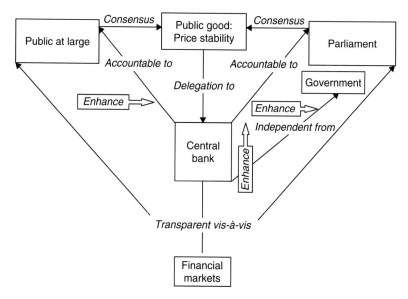

Figure 7.1 Pillars of central bank governance
Source: Authors' elaborations.

produce their expected benefits, in particular increased monetary policy credibility. At the same time, the concomitant development of the three pillars can help dispel the fear that may generate a narrowly conceived concept of CB independence as it will highlight that it does not signify the solitude of the CB or the lack of dialogue: independence implies accountability, which is not only the fact of being responsible, but also the transparency of decisions and the ability to account for one's actions. More broadly, the broad-based consensus among practitioners as well as academics about the key pillars of CB governance can help bridge divergences of views among stakeholders; it also provides a long-term perspective for CB reforms.

The global trends that we have identified can help policy-makers and the public at large appreciate what can and what cannot be expected from the CB when it operates in the context of financial globalization. CBs are expected to protect a fundamental public good: price stability and confidence in the currency. To be able to achieve this primary objective, they need to be granted instrument and political independence, in recognition of the fact that elected politicians face monetary temptations in the short term which conflict with price stability and that monetary policy is a technical matter which should be delegated to this special-ized institution. In return for the independence granted by the public authorities, the CB has a duty to communicate in a transparent manner on the results and achievement (or not) of the assigned mandate. This implies establishing a dialogue between the CB and the public at large, including but not only through a specific exercise of accountability to political institutions. CBs must also be able to explain their policies to the markets. These evolutions lead to the three pillars of modern CB gov-ernance: independence, accountability, and transparency. We are indeed very far from the conception of the CB as a tool of the government's eco-nomic and financial policy. We have also resolutely moved away from a view that was common in a not so distant past, that at least some of the tasks of the CB could be best achieved outside the limelight.

Potential points of conflict between the pillars of CB governance have to do with CB independence and accountability. A case of negative cor-relation between these two pillars has to do with an *override mechanism*, a component of the accountability pillar, whereby the government or parliament can influence CB behavior, which may undermine CB inde-pendence. Therefore, when an override mechanism exists, it is critical that the conditions under which it can be applied are clearly specified and made public so as to ensure that it is not misused and it does not lead to undesirable political influence on the CB. Otherwise, an over-ride clause would undermine both CB accountability and independence. A similar comment can be made regarding the *dismissal power* of the gov-ernment of CB officials on the grounds of poor performance, which can be a mechanism of ex post accountability. Such areas of potential conflict between independence and accountability call for a careful balancing exercise in the specification of the override mechanisms and dismissal powers, that needs to take into account countries' circumstances and in particular the specificities of the political system.[2]

While accountability is directly linked to independence, it is interest-ing to note that a consensus on transparency has emerged not only in countries with strong traditions of democratic accountability or CB inde-pendence. Greater transparency has become important to policy-makers as an urgent necessity in countries which have shifted from a command to a market economy, as clearly evidenced by the experience of tran-sition economies or in countries with a fast pace of financial market development. One underlying factor is undoubtedly the link between

---

[2] See the discussion in Eijffinger and Hoeberichts (2000).

transparency, credibility, and policy effectiveness when monetary policy relies on market-based operating instruments and procedures.

In some countries, de facto CB independence, as well as accountability and transparency of action may have preceded their statutory or de jure characterization. Often, this is a reflection of the personality of CB governors or the fact that a consensus has emerged in that country on the benefits that CB independence, accountability, and transparency bring to society in general and economic performance in particular. The relatively low scores for some CBs in our sample certainly reflect such a reality. One may argue that what matters most after all is actual practice, and it is true that, at least in times of limited economic stress and uncertainties, practice may suffice to bring all the expected benefits that can be achieved from sound CB governance. However, in troubled times legally well-defined pillars of CB governance can have stabilizing effects on markets as they bring about greater predictability and certainty about the behavior of the CB. Therefore, policy-makers in those countries should strive to make sure that actual good practice is firmly enshrined into legislation. It is expected that the findings and considerations in this book will provide an incentive for those countries whose legal frameworks have lagged behind actual good practice to fill the gap by bringing their CB legislation in line with actual practice.

Consensus views

Our analysis reveals that CBs share six principles which represent the "consensus view" among policy-makers with regard to governance frameworks, irrespective of the level of economic development of the countries in which they operate. All six principles are consistent with the views developed in the literature on how policy-makers should achieve separation between monetary and fiscal policies, and more broadly, limit the impact of political cycle on the conduct of monetary policy (see also Lybek 1998; Arnone, Laurens, and Segalotto 2006a). With such strong conceptual backing, the development of CB governance has been the fruit of a very pragmatic historical evolution. Often, the practice has preceded the literature, as clearly reflected in those countries where the practice of central banking has been ahead of what is laid down in legislation (i.e., de facto CB independence, accountability, or transparency is higher than their de jure characterization). The fact that some CBs in transition economies have scores of independence, accountability, and transparency which are higher than some of the CBs in advanced economies is also an illustration of that reality. Benefiting from the advances in CB practice and in the literature that developed subsequently, transition economies were able to move to state-of-the-art CB legislation, without a need for a gradual transition.

Principle 1: set price stability as one of the primary objectives of monetary policy

This principle has been the starting point for the evolution of CB governance frameworks. Currently, almost all CBs are legally obliged to pursue price stability as one of their primary objectives. CBs in some countries have been assigned more than one objective, but price stability has often been given priority status. Typically, the CB law formulates the objectives of the CB in a manner that identifies price stability as the most effective way in which the CB can contribute to economic growth.[3] This approach is in sharp contrast with policies of the 1970s in a number of countries, whereby CBs were expected to channel financial resources to priority sectors, thereby making them akin to development banks. The current approach to CB independence acknowledges that governments may have several competing economic objectives, particularly in the short term. Accordingly, they may tend to ignore the medium-term inflationary effects of an expansionary monetary policy. This time-inconsistency causes a credibility problem. Therefore, entrusting price stability to an autonomous agency (i.e., the CB) helps strengthen credibility (see Lybek 1998).

Principle 2: curtail direct lending to governments

Most CBs have provisions in place limiting their ability to provide unrestricted credit to the government. Today, almost all CB laws stipulate that lending to the government, if allowed at all, cannot be automatic, must be temporary, and subject to quantitative limits. In addition, a ban on CB participation in the primary market for public debt – which was not widespread in the late 1980s – is a distinctive characteristic of the most recent legislation. In addition, the provision that, when available, CB credit to the government should be at market rates, has also become a widespread practice.

---

[3] China is of particular interest as a country where the objective of monetary policy is to maintain the stability of the currency and thereby promote economic growth (see Laurens and Maino 2007). The United States is another example of a country that does not have clearly ranked macroeconomic objectives at the statutory level, although it is well understood that price stability is a precondition for achieving this mix of objectives.

Therefore, a consensus view has emerged that strong monetary policy requires direct CB lending to the government to be limited in nature, i.e., generally short term (or temporary) with restrictions on the amount. Setting the interest rate on such borrowing with reference to market interest rates strengthens the independence of the CB. That said, direct CB credit aims at facilitating cash management by the Treasury in countries with shallow money markets or a weak public debt management framework (see Laurens 2005).

Principle 3: ensure full independence for setting the policy rate

Most CBs have been granted full independence for setting their policy rate. At the most basic level, this condition is necessary for the CB to pursue its goals. But from another angle, such a practice also suggests that most policy-makers have accepted the view that a policy rate (typically a short-term inter-bank interest rate) is the appropriate operational target of monetary policy.[4] Therefore, the CB should be granted full independence to set its policy rate. A corollary to that consensus view is the desire to ensure that the CB has full independence for the design of its monetary policy instruments.

Principle 4: ensure no government involvement in policy formulation

That no government approval should be required for the formulation of monetary policy is a fourth principle that has been adopted by the majority of CBs around the world. A corollary to that principle is the existence of procedures to resolve conflicts between the CB and the government, as is apparent from the high degree of correlation between the scores on these two criteria among countries. Furthermore, when such procedures for conflict resolution are in place, government representation in a policy-making board (i.e., the CB board) is not necessary. This observation is also supported by the high correlation of scores for this criterion with the two preceding ones (i.e., no government approval for policy formulation and existence of conflict resolution procedures).

---

[4] The operational target can be defined as the variable which the CB aims at controlling and indeed can control to a very large extent on a day-by-day basis through the use of its monetary policy instruments.

Principle 5: ensure that accountability corresponds to the level of independence

As we have discussed, CB independence has wide-ranging implications, not only for the CB itself, but also for the whole macroeconomic management process, in particular regarding the coordination of monetary and fiscal policy. Therefore, it is almost inevitable that such a process will be a gradual one. During that process, it is critically important to ensure that independence and accountability move in tandem. Obviously, accountability should not be lagging behind, and care is needed to ensure that as a result of higher independence, the CB is made more politically accountable to public opinion and parliament. Accountability becomes a condition for the CB to build its credibility and to be accepted by public opinion. Also, care is needed to ensure that accountability is not ahead of independence, so as to ensure that the CB is not unduly made responsible for actions which are not of its making. This could potentially undermine its credibility, making it difficult later on to benefit from the expected benefits of CB independence.

Principle 6: ensure that transparency corresponds to the level of accountability and financial market deepening

Equally important is the need to ensure that CB transparency moves in tandem with the level of accountability and financial market deepening. Increasing transparency involves costs for the CB which, as we have noted, can be high for countries in the developing world or for small countries. Therefore, while one could argue that "the more the better" irrespective of any other considerations, it would be quite acceptable for a CB to apply judgement so as to avoid unnecessary expenses or tasks.[5] The CB's objective should be to provide the necessary information so that financial markets and stakeholders can anticipate short-term and medium-term monetary policy moves. It is, however, important to recognize that not all CBs need the same level of transparency and communication. This is certainly the pillar of CB governance where one size does not fit all.[6] The differences that remain among CBs with regard to transparency and the related communication policy reflect to a large degree their audience and specific economic challenges. In particular, in countries where financial markets are shallow and financial intermediation mostly relies on commercial banks, the transmission of monetary

---

[5] For a comprehensive discussion on CBs and the markets see Banque de France (2000).

[6] See Bank for International Settlements (2004: 73–80).

policy is mainly through the credit channel and there is less need for financial markets to have easy access to the range of information that is needed in countries where the interest rate channel dominates monetary policy transmission. Also, the level of transparency vis-à-vis the financial markets is not the same for a CB which operates mainly through rule-based monetary instruments and one which relies predominantly on market-based monetary instruments.

Role of central banks in financial supervision

Theoretical considerations

The debate over the role of CBs in financial supervision has received new impetus with the 2007–8 financial market crisis that began in the US sub-prime mortgage market, and its implications for the global financial system. The unfolding of the crisis confirmed that market developments within the financial services sector had blurred the traditional lines of demarcation between banking, securities, and insurance,[7] leading to the emergence of diversified financial conglomerates involved in banking, insurance, and securities business, which pose regulatory and supervisory challenges. In a number of countries, the regulatory architecture did not evolve accordingly, leading to regulatory gaps. Arnone and Gambini (2007) look at these issues and they ask two questions: Should prudential supervision be integrated, covering banking, securities, and insurance, or decentralized in multiple specialized authorities, one for each sub-sector? And should banking supervision be conducted inside or outside CBs?

The pros and cons of consolidated versus decentralized supervision have been discussed at length. The proponents of consolidated supervision argue that it provides a more efficient and effective supervision of financial conglomerates on a consolidated basis; therefore helping avoid problems of regulatory arbitrage, competitive inequality, duplication, overlapping responsibilities, and gaps which can arise in a system of multiple agencies. It also helps in resolving conflicts emerging between different regulatory goals; it promotes better understanding of overall financial markets, risk transfer techniques, and better equipment to monitor these risk transfer motivations; it allows a better response to market developments and to changes in the financial landscape; and it improves the accountability of regulation. From an operational point of view, consolidated supervision allows *economies of scale and scope* from

---

[7] See Briault (1999).

the point of view of both the government and market participants and it facilitates attracting and maintaining professional staff and expertise. Finally, consolidated supervision provides for greater transparency in the exercise of financial supervision. On the other hand, several potential shortcomings of consolidated supervision are cited in the literature, including the fact that such a supervisory agency would be extremely powerful and could possibly turn into an inefficient bureaucracy in which there may be a danger of not having a clear focus on the objectives of regulation. In addition, a single supervisor might not be able to recognize the unique characteristics of the banking, securities, and insurance industries, which still persist, though made less evident by the introduction of financial conglomerates. Also, moral hazard may be increased in so far as the public could assume that creditors of all institutions supervised by the integrated agency will receive equivalent protection; therefore, investors might decide to implement high risk financial operations believing that all financial institutions supervised by the same regulatory agency would be treated equally. From an efficiency point of view, the critics of consolidated supervision also argue that it could imply the adoption of a single supervisory approach; hence, that valuable information arising from the experience of different approaches to supervision could be lost and diseconomies of scale might emerge from an excessive bureaucracy of the integrated authority, while synergies between different functions have not yet been assessed. While the debate has been intense, limited empirical evidence has been advanced so far due to the fact that most of the combined regulators have been created in the second half of the 1990s.

The desirability of the involvement of CBs in financial supervision has also been frequently debated in the literature, and reasonable arguments have been made both in favor and against maintaining a role for the CB, but limited empirical analysis is available.[8] The most cited argument for combining monetary policy and financial supervision is an informational one, based on the synergies between the flows of information required for the conduct of monetary policy and financial supervision. Availability of information is particularly important in times of crisis, when only direct supervision can deliver information allowing timely responses by the CB. The CB's mandate for financial stability and the prevention of financial crises is another argument in favor of involvement of the CB in financial supervision. The point has been

---

[8] Goodhart and Shoenmaker (1992, 1995); Haubrich (1996); Briault (1999); Abrams and Taylor (2000); Padoa-Schioppa (2003).

made that, particularly in the case of small countries, CBs' involvement allows economies of scale. Some authors have suggested that entrusting financial supervision to the CB allows advantage to be taken of progress achieved with regard to CB governance, therefore implicitly granting the financial supervisor a higher level of independence, accountability, and transparency than may be the case if it were granted to a newly created agency.[9]

On the other hand, the literature has also pointed to the potential disadvantages of combining monetary and regulatory responsibilities in a single institution. In particular, a conflict of interests may arise for the CB, leading to a loosening of monetary policy out of concerns for financial institutions' health. A related moral hazard argument is often raised, since supervised institutions may take high risks in the belief that, in case of difficulties, access to the lender of last resort facilities may be easier. The critics of CB involvement in financial supervision have also argued that in the event of a bank failure, the credibility of the CB could suffer, hence undermining its capacity to fulfill its primary mandate of preserving price stability. Finally, merging financial stability and price stability in one single institution could lead to an excessive concentration of power which may either hinder the system of checks and balances on which CB accountability relies, or increase the risk for potential political or financial industry pressure on the CB. So far, empirical evidence on the disadvantages of CBs' involvement in financial supervision has been inconclusive.

Survey of practices

Responsibility for banking supervision varies widely from country to country (Table 7.1).[10] In three-quarters of cases reported in the table (157 out of 209 countries in the sample) CBs are responsible for banking supervision.[11] Furthermore, in the majority of countries (121 out of 209),

---

[9] This argument is highly relevant in countries where human capital with advanced skills is limited.

[10] The profiles of the prudential supervisory frameworks were elaborated using the information contained in Courtis (2005) and from the website of the Heuerman Fund for the Study of Investment, Law, and Regulation at University of Toledo: http://law.utoledo.edu/financialregulators/pages.htm

[11] In this category we consider those cases in which banking supervision is entrusted to CBs that, thus, have a total and exclusive responsibility, but also where CBs are not the primary supervisors, but retain at least a partial, but substantial power of supervision.

Table 7.1 Central banks' involvement in financial supervision (2005)

	Central bank	*Non-central bank*	*Total*
Banks alone	111	10	121
Banks and securities	6	8	14
Banks and insurance	29	8	37
Banks, securities, and insurance	11	26	37
Total	157	52	209

Source: Arnone and Gambini (2007), based on Courtis (2005).

the bank supervisor is responsible only for banks and not for other financial institutions. The CB as the sole banking supervisor is the most common model, making up around 53 percent of supervisory structures.[12] Two other models account for nearly 13 percent of the cases: the CB supervising banks and insurance companies and a single prudential regulator for all financial institutions outside the CB. The residual 20 percent is allocated between the five remaining supervisory frameworks.

With regard to the organization of regulatory institutions, and based on a sub-sample of 114 countries where the three main financial sub-sectors (i.e., banking, insurance, and securities) are supervised out of the 209 countries sample considered above, in 41 countries banks, securities companies, and insurance firms are supervised by dedicated agencies responsible for each single sub-sector (Table 7.2); only in 10 countries is the CB responsible for all supervised entities; there are 27 countries where a unified prudential regulator, responsible for the full range of financial institutions and markets, has been established outside the CB. Many cases of integration also arise, in which the powers to supervise two of the main financial intermediaries have been centralized in one agency. In 21 countries banking and insurance supervision are combined within the same agency, while securities are supervised by a separate agency; in 10 cases securities and insurance supervisions are combined; only in 5 jurisdictions is insurance regulated by a specialist agency and securities and banks are supervised by the same authority.

---

[12] In considering such a large sample of countries, we have to take into account that the choice of the institutional organization is not always available; for developing countries supervisory architecture may follow from the limited development of the financial system. In such circumstances the CB may be the only institution with sufficient autonomy and expertise to function as banks' and financial supervisor.

Table 7.2 Structure of financial sector supervisory frameworks

Supervisory frameworks	Number of countries
Single agency	
– Central bank	10
– Other	27
Separated agencies for each sub-sector	41
Banks alone, securities and insurance combined	10
Securities alone, banks and insurance combined	21
Insurance alone, banks and securities combined	5
Total	114

Source: Arnone and Gambini (2007), based on Courtis (2005).

In the last two decades a number of countries, especially European and OECD members, have been reconsidering the organizational structure of their financial supervision and, following the leading example of Scandinavian countries and Canada at the end of the 1980s, many of them have adopted an integrated or unified supervision by merging prudential banking supervision with the supervisor of one or two sectors; in no country with banking supervision outside the CB were the regulatory and supervisory powers moved under the control of the monetary authority. Despite the diversity of practices around the world, one can identify a trend towards less CB responsibility for banking supervision, and the creation of new supervisors responsible for a wider range of financial institutions on an integrated or unified basis. Considering the possible combinations deriving from the two basic issue we have discussed (i.e., consolidated supervision and scope of involvement of the CB), two models of financial supervision seem to prevail: on one side, a high level of unification of supervisory powers and weak CB involvement, and on the other side a low level of unification and strong CB involvement.

The way forward

Our analysis revealed that CBs in many emerging market and developing countries have retained their key role in the area of banking supervision. Although less pervasive, such practice is also observed in a few large advanced economies. This practice goes against the argument often made in the literature that implementation of monetary policy and banking supervision are two separate functions and that underlying structural problems in the financial sector should be addressed directly by a specialized agency (see Arnone and Gambini 2007 for a review of the literature). This argument is based on some country experiences showing that relaxing monetary policy to mitigate financial sector problems, which the CB may be more tempted to do if it is in charge of banking supervision, may exacerbate financial sector problems and undermine monetary policy.

However, practical considerations have led to a departure from these conceptual arguments.[13] In emerging markets and developing countries, the greater availability of skilled staff and resources at the CB has often played a role in deciding whether supervisory functions should be retained at the CB. There is also the view that, given the increased CB independence, in particular in emerging markets and developing countries, locating financial supervisory functions in the CB allows supervisors to "piggyback" and enjoy the same degree of independence. The considerations which have led a number of CBs to increase their focus on financial stability, as evidenced by an increasing number which publish a financial stability report (Čihák 2006), also support a departure from the conceptual arguments presented in the literature.

Empirical evidence presented in Arnone and Gambini (2007) shows that a higher degree of compliance with the Basel Core Principles is achieved by those countries implementing an integrated supervision of banks together with securities and/or insurance companies; they also find statistically significant results in favor of placing both banking supervision and an integrated supervision inside the CB.

Finally, price stability and financial sector soundness may be compatible, at least in the longer term.[14] Hence, entrusting monetary policy implementation and financial supervision to the CB could be desirable, particularly if the CB has a clear objective and enjoys a high degree of independence and accountability and, therefore, will not be tempted to use second-best instruments (in this case monetary policy) to achieve financial stability objectives. Therefore, the argument presented in part of the literature that CBs should not be involved in supervisory functions is open to question. In particular, as the 2007–8 financial crisis unfolded, voices in favor of a formal involvement of CBs in financial supervision have gained strength. In particular,

---

[13] See Arnone and Gambini (2007) for a review of the literature, and Quintyn and Taylor (2002) for an earlier discussion on the location of supervisory functions.

[14] While inadequate monetary policies could lead to inflation and contribute to financial sector weaknesses, a weak financial system can lead to a systemic financial crisis and impinge on monetary policy and price stability.

policy-makers are increasingly accepting the argument often made by the US Federal Reserve, that its ability to deal with threats to financial stability depends critically on the information, expertise, and powers that it holds by virtue of being both a bank supervisor and a CB.[15] In addition, some policy-makers have noted that episodes of financial crises have shown that conflicts of interest can

> hamper the necessary transmission of information on critical institutions from the supervisory authority to the central bank, even within the same country, in the hope that weak institutions would be bailed out by liquidity injections rather than by addressing the solvency problem . . . The lesson to be learned is that if supervisory functions are entrusted to a separate authority, outside the central bank, voluntary cooperation between the two is not sufficient. There must be an obligation for the former to provide the central bank with a whole series of detailed information.[16]

All of this does not mean that the CB should necessarily become *the* supervisor of individual financial institutions. Such a course of action may be desirable in the case of small countries for the sake of economies of scale. However, in large countries, or countries with diversified financial systems, it may not be optimal to combine monetary and regulatory responsibilities in a single institution for a number of reasons which are discussed in this book. However, the case can be made that in those countries the CB cannot ignore financial stability issues, hence it needs to be involved, in ways which may differ based on countries' specific circumstances and history, in financial supervision so that the CB is in a position to identify systemic risks in the financial sector.

Sequencing of reforms

Our analysis in the previous chapters and sections of this book has shown that CB governance frameworks have evolved over time and that those changes have been driven to a large extent by changes in the instruments

---

[15] See Bernanke (2007).

[16] Comments by Lorenzo Bini Smaghi, Member of the Executive Board of the ECB at the Roundtable discussion "How to strengthen Europe's financial stability framework?" at the conference "A Financial Stability Framework for Europe: Managing Financial Soundness in an Integrated Market," held in Frankfurt am Main on September 26, 2008 (http://www.ecb.int/press/key/date/2008/html/sp080926.en.html).

CB have relied upon to conduct their business. In turn, CBs' operating procedures have followed the general trend towards enhancing the role of price signals in the general economy. The process of improvement in CB governance generally starts with establishing the political foundations of an independent CB as well as setting price stability as its primary objective, followed by steps to strengthen its economic and political independence as well as its accountability and transparency as its operating frameworks become more and more market oriented.

This final section is an attempt to link the various dimensions of CB business with the process of financial market deepening, so as to offer a possible sequencing of reforms to enhance CB governance frameworks, which associates its three components – independence, accountability, and transparency – with structural changes in the economic and financial system. Our analysis relies on the four-stage process presented in Laurens (2005) and is summarized in Figure 7.2. While there is no single way to proceed, following such a sequence can help country authorities plan and execute the reform process and periodically assess progress before making a new policy move. Stage zero describes the situation of post-conflict countries. At this stage monetary policy is largely confined to currency management. Stage 1 involves developing the role of banks in financial intermediation. Stage 2 involves fostering the development of inter-bank operations. Stage 3 is focused on developing financial markets so that the money market is well integrated with the other segments of the financial markets, including the secondary market for government securities and the foreign exchange market.

Stage 1: clarify objectives and establish basic instrument independence

In post-conflict cases where there is no functioning monetary authority, financial reforms involve a gradual approach to re-establishing key functions in areas where a CB typically has responsibilities. Establishing clear objectives early on in the process of CB modernization is critical for setting a legal framework for the CB which ensures a proper allocation of responsibilities between government agencies. Conceptual considerations as well as practice point to price stability as the most desirable primary objective for the CB, although in a context of very limited financial intermediation monetary policy is unlikely to have a significant role to play (it will be confined to currency management) except for ensuring that direct CB credit to the government is under control. Price stability will be predominantly the outcome of sound fiscal management. Such a situation is likely to remain until the end of Stage 1, during which

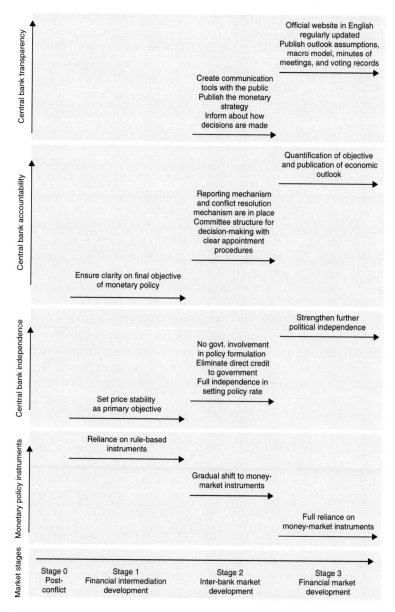

Figure 7.2 Pillars of central bank governance at different stages of market development

Source: Authors' elaborations, based on Laurens (2005).

financial reforms aim at enhancing the role of banks in financial inter-mediation, so that a credit function can grow. At this stage, the CB is still likely to provide a broad range of banking services to the government, including direct credit. Therefore, monetary stability will be contingent upon the establishment of clear limits and charging market rates for such financing, so as to pave the way for establishing a separation between money creation and government funding as soon as market conditions allow (i.e., the government issues debt in the market). Concomitantly, a minimum level of economic independence is required. In this process, instrument independence (i.e., the ability for the CB to conduct liquid-ity management independently of budget financing considerations) is an important first step towards establishing an autonomous CB. In par-ticular, early on in the process, limits must be placed on the ability of the government to obtain CB credit, or on the ability of commercial banks to have discretionary access to CB credit, so that the CB can control its balance sheet. Such measures are critical for enhancing the control of the CB over the money supply.[17]

Stage 2: establish the building block of accountability

As countries move from Stage 1 to Stage 2, the basic frameworks should be in place for allowing the CB to design and implement monetary policy. In particular the CB should be in a position to develop a monetary strategy, including indicators or intermediate targets for monetary policy. Mar-ket developments should also allow a clearer separation between money creation and government funding, making it possible to strengthen CB independence and accountability, which may not have been feasible in the early stages of financial market development. As a minimum, direct CB credit to the government should be at market rates, and intended to facilitate short-term cash management by the Treasury. There are several conditions for moving towards full independence for monetary policy and public debt management, which will allow separation of monetary and fiscal policy responsibilities. Especially important is the develop-ment of a government securities market, where market forces determine the conditions under which a budget deficit may be financed, and a public debt management capacity at the Treasury. This makes it possible to phase out direct CB credit to the government. At the end of Stage 2 the government should no longer be involved in the formulation of

---

[17] See Laurens (2005) for a review of country experiences in this area and Fry (1998) for the relationship between the CB's instrument independence and its ability to promote fiscal discipline.

monetary policy; the CB should be fully responsible for setting its policy rates; reporting mechanisms to parliament should be in place; conflict resolution mechanisms should exist; a committee structure should be in place for the decision-making process at the CB; and communication tools should be in place to allow the CB to communicate with the public about its operating procedures and decision-making process.

Stage 3: strengthen further political independence, accountability, and transparency

When financial markets become diversified (Stage 3: Financial market diversification), there is additional scope for strengthening further the political independence of the CB by ensuring that CB governing bodies are appointed without much political interference and for longer terms. Such provisions help to establish a total separation between monetary and fiscal policies. In such an environment, financial markets are expected to react to monetary policy signals, and the credibility of monetary policy is critical for maintaining orderly market conditions. Concomitantly, accountability must also be strengthened further through the definition and publication of a quantitative objective and the publication of an economic outlook, including the key assumptions for the outlook as well as the key specifications of the macroeconomic model used by the CB. At this stage, the existence of a regularly updated official CB website becomes highly desirable, as would the publication of the minutes of the meetings of the decision-making body at the CB as well as voting records at the meetings.

References

Abrams, R. K. and M. Taylor (2000) "Issues in the Unification of Financial Sector Supervision," *IMF Working Paper* No. 00/213.

Acemoglu, D., S. Johnson, P. Querubin, and J. A. Robinson (2008) "When Does Policy Reform Work? The Case of Central Bank Independence," paper presented at the conference Brookings Papers on Economic Activity, Spring (Washington, DC: The Brookings Institution). Available at http://www.brookings.edu/economics/bpea/bpea_conferencepapers_spring 2008.aspx, accessed October 12, 2008.

Akhand, H. A. (1998) "Central Bank Independence and Growth: a Sensitivity Analysis," *Canadian Journal of Economics*, Vol. 31, No. 2, 303–17.

Alesina, A. (1988) "Macroeconomics and Politics," *NBER Macroeconomics Annual 1988*, 13–52.

Alesina, A. (1989) "Politics and Business Cycles in Industrial Democracies," *Economic Policy*, Vol. 8, 55–98.

Alesina, A. and R. Gatti (1995) "Independent Central Banks: Low Inflation at No Cost," *American Economic Review*, Vol. 85, 196–200.

Alesina, A. and L. H. Summers (1993) "Central Bank Independence and Macroeconomic Performance: Some Comparative Evidence," *Journal of Money, Credit and Banking*, Vol. 25, No. 2, 151–62.

Arnone, M. and A. Gambini (2007) "Architectures of Supervisory Authorities and Banking Supervision," in D. Masciandaro and M. Quintyn (eds), *Designing Institutions for Financial Stability: Independence, Accountability and Governance* (Cheltenham, UK and Northampton, MA, USA: Edward Elgar).

Arnone, M., B. J. Laurens, and J. F. Segalotto (2006a) "The Measurement of Central Bank Autonomy: Survey of Models, Indicators, and Empirical Evidence," *IMF Working Paper* 06/227 (Washington: International Monetary Fund).

Arnone, M., B. J. Laurens, and J. F. Segalotto (2006b) "Measures of Central Bank Autonomy: Empirical Evidence for OECD and Developing Countries, and Emerging Market Economies," *IMF Working Paper* 06/228 (Washington: International Monetary Fund).

Arnone, M., B. J. Laurens, J. F. Segalotto, and M. Sommer (2008) "Central Bank Autonomy: Lessons from Global Trends," *IMF Staff Papers*, advance online publication, 23 September 2008; doi:10.1057/imfsp.2008.25. An earlier version is available as *IMF Working Paper* 07/88, 2007 (Washington: International Monetary Fund).

Bade, R. and M. Parkin (1977) "Central Bank Laws and Monetary Policies: A Preliminary Investigation" (London, Ontario, Canada: University of Western Ontario). Also available in M. G. Porter (ed.), *The Australian Monetary System in the 1970s* (Monash University, 1978), 24–39.

Bade, R. and M. Parkin (1985) "Central Bank Laws and Monetary Policies" (unpublished; London, Ontario, Canada: University of Western Ontario). Also available in a 1988 version.

Ball, L. (1994) "What Determines the Sacrifice Ratio?" in N. G. Mankiw (ed.), *Monetary Policy* (NBER and University of Chicago Press), 155–82.

Ball, L., N. G. Mankiw and D. Romer (1988) "The New Keynesian Economics and the Output-Inflation Tradeoff," *Brookings Papers on Economic Activity*, 1, 1–65.

Banaian, K., R. C. K. Burdekin, and T. D. Willett (1995) "On the Political Economy of Central Bank Independence," in K. D. Hoover and S. M. Sheffrin (eds), *Monetarism and the Methodology of Economics: Essays in Honor of Thomas Mayer* (Brookfield, VT).

Banaian, K., R. C. K. Burdekin, and T. D. Willett (1998) "Reconsidering the Principal Components of Central Bank Independence: The More the Merrier?" *Public Choice*, Vol. 97, 1–12.

Banque de France (2000) "Independence and Accountability: Developments in Central Banking," Bicentennial Symposium (Paris: Banque de France).

Bank for International Settlements (2004) *Annual Report*, June (Basel: Bank for International Settlements).

Barro, R. J. and D. Gordon (1983) "Rules, Discretion, and Reputation in a Model of Monetary Policy," *Journal of Monetary Economics*, Vol. 12, 101–21.

Berger, H., J. de Haan, and S. C. W. Eijffinger (2000) "Central Bank Independence: An Update of Theory and Evidence," *CEPR Discussion Papers* No. 2353 (London: Centre for Economic Policy Research). Published in 2001 in *Journal of Economic Surveys*, Vol. 15, No. 1, 3–40.

Bernanke, B. (2007) "Central Banking and Bank Supervision in the United States," remarks at the Allied Social Science Association Annual Meeting, Chicago, January 5.

Bindseil, U., A. Manzanares, and B. Weller (2004) "The Role of Central Bank Capital Revisited," *European Central Bank Working Paper* No. 392 (Frankfurt am Main: ECB).

Bini-Smaghi, L. and D. Gros (2000) *Open Issues in European Central Banking* (Basingstoke: Macmillan).

Bini-Smaghi, L. and D. Gros (2001) "Is the ECB Accountable and Transparent?" European Institute of Public Administration (EIPA), Maastricht; based on Bini-Smaghi and Gros (2000).

Blinder, A. S. (1999) "Central Bank Credibility: Why Do We Care? How Do We Build It?" *NBER Working Papers* No. 7161 (Cambridge, MA: National Bureau of Economic Research).

Boschen, J. F. and C. L. Weise (2003) "What Starts Inflation: Evidence From the OECD Countries," *Journal of Money, Credit and Banking*, Vol. 35, No. 3, 323–49.

Bouwman, K., R. M. Jong-a-Pin, and J. de Haan (2005) "On the Relationship Between Central Bank Independence and Inflation: Some More Bad News," *Applied Financial Economics Letters*, 1, 381–85.

Briault, C. B. (1999) "The Rationale for a Single National Financial Services Regulator," *FSA Occasional Paper* No. 2.

Briault, C. B., A. G. Haldane, and M. A. King (1996) "Independence and Accountability," *Bank of England Working Paper* No. 49 (London: Bank of England).

Brumm, H. J. (2000) "Inflation and Central Bank Independence: Conventional Wisdom Redux," *Journal of Money, Credit and Banking*, Vol. 32, No. 4, 807–19.

Brumm, H. J. (2002) "Inflation and Central Bank Independence Revisited," *Economic Letters*, Vol. 77, 205–209.

Bruno, M. and J. Sachs (1985) *The Economics of Worldwide Stagflation* (Cambridge, MA: Harvard University Press).

Calmfors, L. and J. Driffill (1988) "Centralization of Wage Bargaining and Macroeconomic Performance," *Economic Policy*, Vol. 6, 13–61.

Cameron, D. (1984) "Social Democracy, Corporatism, Labor Quiescence and the Representation of Labor Interest in Advanced Capitalist Society," in J. Goldethorpe (ed.), *Order and Conflict in Contemporary Capitalism* (New York: Oxford University Press).

Campillo, M. and J. A. Miron (1997) "Why Does Inflation Differ across Countries?" in C. D. Romer and D. H. Romer (eds), *Reducing Inflation: Motivation and Strategy* (Chicago: University of Chicago Press), 335–57.

Cargill, T. F. (1995) "The Statistical Association Between Central Bank Independence and Inflation," *Banca Nazionale del Lavoro Quarterly Review*, Vol. 193, 159–72.

Castellani, F. (2002) "A Model of Central Bank Accountability," *HEI Working Paper* 04/2002 (Geneva: Graduate Institute of International Studies).

Catão, L. A. V. and M. E. Terrones (2005) "Fiscal Deficits and Inflation," *Journal of Monetary Economics*, Vol. 52, No. 3, 529–54.

Čihák, M. (2006) "How Do Central Banks Write on Financial Stability?" *IMF Working Paper* No. 06/163 (Washington: International Monetary Fund).

Čihák, M. and Podpiera, R. (2006) "Is One Watchdog Better Than Three? International Experience with Integrated Financial Sector Supervision," *IMF Working Paper* No. 06/57 (Washington: International Monetary Fund).

Courtis, N. (ed.) (2005) *How Countries Supervise Their Banks, Insurers, and Securities Markets* (London: Central Banking Publications).

Crosby, M. (1998) "Central Bank Independence and Output Variability," *Economic Letters*, Vol. 60, 67–75.

Cukierman, A. (1992) *Central Bank Strategy, Credibility, and Independence* (Cambridge, MA: MIT Press).

Cukierman, A. (1994) "Central Bank Independence and Monetary Control," *The Economic Journal*, Vol. 104, 1437–48.

Cukierman, A. (2002) "Does a Higher Sacrifice Ratio Mean that Central Bank Independence is Excessive?" *Annals of Economics and Finance*, Vol. 3, 1–25.

Cukierman, A. (2005) "Central Bank Independence and Monetary Policy-Making Institutions – Past, Present and Future," Lecture at the Annual Meeting of the Chilean Economic Society, September.

Cukierman, A., P. Kalaitzidakis, L. H. Summers, and S. B. Webb (1993) "Central Bank Independence, Growth, Investment, and Real Rates," *Carnegie-Rochester Conference Series on Public Policy*, Vol. 39, 95–140.

Cukierman, A. and F. Lippi (1999) "Central Bank Independence, Centralization of Wage Bargaining, Inflation and Unemployment: Theory and Some Evidence," *European Economic Review*, Vol. 43, 1395–1434.

Cukierman, A. and S. B. Webb (1995) "Political Influence on the Central Bank: International Evidence," *The World Bank Economic Review*, Vol. 9, No. 3, 397–423.

Cukierman, A., S. Webb, and B. Neyapti (1991) "The Measurement of Central Bank Independence and its Effects on Policy Outcomes," paper presented at the NBER Conference on Political Economics, Cambridge, MA, November 15–16.

Cukierman, A., S. B. Webb, and B. Neyapti (1992) "Measuring the Independence of Central Banks and its Effects on Policy Outcomes," *World Bank Economic Review*, Vol. 6, 353–98.

Debelle, G. (1996) "The End of Three Small Inflations: Australia, New Zealand and Canada," *Canadian Public Policy*, Vol. 22, 56–78.

Debelle, G. and S. Fischer (1994) "How Independent Should a Central Bank Be?" in J. Fuhrer (ed.), *Goals, Guidelines, and Constraints Facing Monetary Policymakers*, proceedings of a conference sponsored by the Federal Reserve Bank of Boston, Conference Series No. 38, 195–221.

de Haan, J. (1999) "The Case for an Independent European Central Bank: a Comment," *European Journal of Political Economy*, Vol. 15, 759–62.

de Haan, J. and F. Amtenbrink (2003) "A Non-Transparent European Central Bank? Who is to Blame?" Univeristy of Groningen, mimeo. Available at *SSRN Working Paper Series*: http://ssrn.com/abstract=1138224

de Haan, J., F. Amtenbrink, and S. Eijffinger (1998) "Accountability of Central Banks: Aspects and Quantification," *Discussion Paper* 54, Tilburg University Center for Economic Research. Published in 1999 in *Banca Nazionale del Lavoro Quarterly Review*, Vol. 209, 169–93.

de Haan, J., F. Amtenbrink, and S. Waller (2004) "The Transparency and Credibility of the European Central Bank," *Journal of Common Market Studies*, Vol. 42, No. 4, 775–94.

de Haan, J. and W. J. Kooi (1997) "What Really Matters: Conservativeness or Independence?," *Banca Nazionale del Lavoro Quarterly Review*, Vol. 200, 23–38.

de Haan, J. and W. J. Kooi (2000) "Does Central Bank Independence Really Matter? New Evidence for Developing Countries Using a New Indicator," *Journal of Banking and Finance*, Vol. 24, 643–64.

de Haan, J. and J. E. Sturm (1992) "The Case for Central Bank Independence," *Banca Nazionale del Lavoro Quarterly Review*, Vol. 182, 305–27.

de Haan, J. and G. J. Van't Hag (1995) "Variation in Central Bank Independence Across Countries: Some Provisional Empirical Evidence," *Public Choice*, Vol. 85, 335–51.

Demertzis, M., A. Hughes Hallett, and N. Viegi (1998) "Independently Blue? Accountability and Independence in the New European Central Bank," *CEPR Discussion Paper* No. 1842.

Eijffinger, S. C. W. and P. Geraats (2002) "How Transparent are Central Banks?" *CEPR Discussion Paper* No. 3188. Also available as *Cambridge Working Paper in Economics* No. 0411/2004. Published in 2006 in *European Journal of Political Economy*, Vol. 22, No. 1, 1–21.

Eijffinger, S. C. W. and M. Hoeberichts (2000) "Central Bank Accountability and Transparency: Theory and Some Evidence," *Discussion Paper* 6/00, Economic Research Center of the Deutsche Bundesbank.

Eijffinger, S. C. W. and E. Schaling (1993) "Central Bank Independence in Twelve Industrial Countries," *Banca Nazionale del Lavoro Quarterly Review*, Vol. 184, 49–89.

Eijffinger, S. C. W., M. Van Rooij, and E. Schaling (1996) "Central Bank Independence: a Panel Data Approach," *Public Choice*, Vol. 89, No. 1–2, 163–82.

Eusepi, S. (2003) "Does Central Bank Transparency Matter for Economic Stability?" University of Warwick and New York University, mimeo. Available in 2004 in *Computing in Economics and Finance* Working Paper No. 176.

Eusepi, S. (2005) "Central Bank Transparency under Model Uncertainty," *Federal Reserve Bank of New York Staff Report* No. 199.

Fair, D. (1980) "Relationships Between Central Banks and Governments in the Determination of Monetary Policy," *SUERF Series*, 31A (Vienna: Société Universitaire Européenne de Recherches Financières).

Fischer, A. M. (1996) "Central Bank Independence and Sacrifice Ratios," *Open Economies Review*, Vol. 7, 5–18.

Fischer, S. (1996) "Why are Central Banks Pursuing Long-Run Price Stability?" paper presented at the Federal Reserve Bank of Kansas City Symposium, Achieving Price Stability, Jackson Hole, Wyoming, August 29–31.

Flood, R. and P. Isard (1989) "Monetary Policy Strategies," *IMF Staff Papers*, Vol. 36 (March), 612–32.

Forder, J. (1998a) "The Case for a European Central Bank: a Reassessment of Evidence and Sources," *European Journal of Political Economy*, Vol. 14, 53–71.

Forder, J. (1998b) "Central Bank Independence: Conceptual Clarifications and Interim Assessment," *Oxford Economic Papers*, Vol. 50, 307–34.

Forder, J. (1999) "Central Bank Independence: Reassessing the Measures," *Journal of Economic Issues*, Vol. 33, No. 1, 23–40.

Franzese, R. J., Jr. (1999) "Partially Independent Central Banks, Politically Responsive Governments, and Inflation," *American Journal of Political Science*, Vol. 43, No. 3, 681–706.

Fry, M. J. (1998) "Assessing Central Bank Independence in Developing Countries: Do Actions Speak Louder Than Words?" *Oxford Economic Papers*, Vol. 50, 512–29.

Fuhrer, J. C. (1997) "Central Bank Independence and Inflation Targeting: Monetary Policy Paradigms for the Next Millennium?" *New England Economic Review*, Vol. 1–2, 19–36.

Gartner, M. (1995) "Central Bank Independence and the Sacrifice Ratio: the Dark Side of the Force," *Discussion Paper* No. 9506, University of St. Gallen, Switzerland.

Geraats, P. (2000) "Why Adopt Transparency? The Publication of Central Bank Forecasts," *CEPR Discussion Paper* No. 2582.

Geraats, P. (2002) "Central Bank Transparency," *Economic Journal*, Vol. 112, No. 483, 532–65.

Ghosh, A. R., A. M. Gulde, J. D. Ostry, and H. C. Wolf (1997) "Does the Nominal Exchange Rate Regime Matter?" *NBER Working Paper* No. 5874 (Massachusetts: National Bureau of Economic Research).

Glastra, R. M. (1997) "European Monetary Union and Central Bank Independence," in M. Andenas, L. Gormley, C. Hadjiemmanuil, and I. Harden (eds), *European Economic & Monetary Union: the Institutional Framework* (London: Kluwer Law International).

Goodhart, C. and D. Schoenmaker (1992) "Institutional Separation between Supervisory and Monetary Agencies," *Giornale degli Economisti e Annali di Economia*, No. 51, 353–439.

Goodhart, C. and D. Schoenmaker (1995) "Should the Functions of Monetary Policy and Banking Supervision be Separated?" *Oxford Economic Papers*, No. 47, 539–60.

Greenspan, A. (1993) *Statement before the Committee on Banking, Finance, and Urban Affairs*, US House of Representatives, October 13.

Grilli, V., D. Masciandaro, and G. Tabellini (1991) "Political and Monetary Institutions and Public Financial Policies in the Industrial Countries," *Economic Policy*, Vol. 13, 341–92.

Grubb, S., R. Jackman, and D. Layard (1983) "Wage Rigidity in OECD Countries," *European Economic Review*, Vol. 21, 11–39.

Haubrich, J. G. (1996) "Combining Bank Supervision and Monetary Policy," *Economic Commentary*, No. 11, Federal Reserve Bank of Cleveland.

Havrilesky, T. (1993) *The Pressures on American Monetary Policy* (Dordrecht: Kluwer Academic Publishers).

Healey, J. (2001) "Financial Stability and the Central Bank: International Evidence," in *Financial Stability and Central Banks*, Bank of England editors, Central Bank Governors' Symposium Series (London: Routledge).

Helbling, T., F. Jaumotte, and M. Sommer (2006) "How has Globalization Influenced Inflation?" *World Economic Outlook*, April (Washington: International Monetary Fund).

International Monetary Fund, *Central Bank Legislation Database* (Washington: International Monetary Fund).

Ize, A. (2005) "Capitalizing Central Banks: a Net Worth Approach," *IMF Working Paper* No. 05/15 (Washington: International Monetary Fund).

Jácome, L. (2001) "Legal Central Bank Independence and Inflation in Latin America During the 1990s," *IMF Working Paper* No. 01/212 (Washington: International Monetary Fund).

Jácome, L. and F. Vázquez (2005) "Any Link between Central Bank Independence and Inflation? Evidence from Latin America and the Caribbean," *IMF Working Paper* No. 05/75 (Washington: International Monetary Fund).

Jenkins, M. A. (1996) "Central Bank Independence and Inflation Performance: Panacea or Placebo?" *Banca Nazionale del Lavoro Quarterly Review*, Vol. 197, 241–70.

Kilponen, J. (1999) "Central Bank Independence and Wage Bargaining Structure: Empirical Evidence," *Bank of Finland Discussion Paper* 9/99.

Laurens, B. (2005) "Monetary Policy at Different Stages of Market Development," *IMF Occasional Paper* No. 244 (Washington: International Monetary Fund).

Laurens, B. and R. Maino (2007) "China: Strengthening Monetary Policy Implementation," *IMF Working Paper* No. 07/14 (Washington: International Monetary Fund).

Laurens, B. and H. de la Piedra (1998) "Coordination of Monetary and Fiscal Policies," *IMF Working Paper* No. 98/25 (Washington: International Monetary Fund).

Levine, R. and D. Renelt (1992) "A Sensitivity Analysis of Cross-Country Regressions," *American Economic Review*, Vol. 82, 942–63.

Lohman, S. (1992) "The Optimal Degree of Commitment: Credibility versus Flexibility," *American Economic Review*, Vol. 82, 273–86.

Lybek, T. (1998) "Elements of Central Bank Autonomy and Accountability," *MAE/IMF Operational Paper* No. 98/1 (Washington: International Monetary Fund).

Lybek, T. (1999) "Central Bank Autonomy, and Inflation and Output Performance in the Baltic States, Russia, and Other Countries of the Former Soviet Union, 1995–97," *IMF Working Paper* No. 4/99 (Washington: International Monetary Fund).

Lybek, T. (2004) "Central Bank Governance: a Survey of Boards and Management," *IMF Working Paper* No. 04/226 (Washington: International Monetary Fund).

Mangano, G. (1998) "Measuring Central Bank Independence: a Tale of Subjectivity and of its Consequences," *Oxford Economic Papers*, Vol. 50, 468–92.

Masciandaro, D. and M. Quintyn (eds) (2007) *Designing Financial Supervision Institutions: Independence, Accountability and Governance* (Cheltenham, UK and Northampton, MA, USA: Edward Elgar).

Masciandaro, D. and G. Tabellini (1988) "Fiscal Deficits and Monetary Institutions: a Comparative Analysis," in H. Cheng (ed.), *Challenges to Monetary Policy in the Pacific Basin Countries* (Dordrecht: Kluwer Academic Publishers).

McCallum, B. (1995) "Two Fallacies Concerning Central Bank Independence," *American Economic Review*, Papers and Proceedings, Vol. 85, 207–11.

Mishkin, F. S. (1999) "International Experiences with Different Monetary Policy Regimes," *Journal of Monetary Economics*, Vol. 43, No. 3, 576–606.

Oatley, T. (1999) "Central Bank Independence and Inflation: Corporatism, Partisanship, and Alternative Indices of Central Bank Independence," *Public Choice*, Vol. 98, 399–413.

Organization for Economic Cooperation and Development (OECD) (1997) "Economic Performance and the Structure of Collective Bargaining," *Employment Outlook* (Paris: Organization for Economic Cooperation and Development), 63–92.

Padoa-Schioppa, T. (2003) "Financial Supervision: Inside or Outside Central Banks?" in J. Kremers, D. Schoenmaker, and P. Wierts (eds), *Financial Supervision in Europe* (Cheltenham, UK and Northampton, MA, USA: Edward Elgar).

Padoa-Schioppa, T. and C. Randzio-Plath (2000) "The ECB: Independence and Accountability," *Policy Paper* B00-16, ZEI/Center for European Integration Studies.

Persson, T. and G. Tabellini (1993) "Designing Institutions for Monetary Stability," *Carnegie-Rochester Conference Series on Public Policy*, Vol. 39, 53–84.

Posen, A. S. (1993) "Why Central Bank Independence does not Cause Low Inflation: There is no Institutional Fix for Politics," in R. O'Brien (ed.), *Finance and the International Economy* (Oxford: Oxford University Press), 40–65.

Posen, A. S. (1995) "Declarations are not Enough: Financial Sector Sources of Central Bank Independence," *NBER Macroeconomics Annual Report 1995*, 253–74.

Posen, A. S. (1998) "Central Bank Independence and Disinflationary Credibility: a Missing Link?" *Oxford Economic Papers*, Vol. 50, 493–511.

Quintyn, M. and M. Taylor (2002) "Regulatory and Supervisory Independent and Financial Stability," *MAE/IMF Operational Paper* No. 02/6 (Washington: International Monetary Fund).

Reinhart, C. M. and K. S. Rogoff (2002) "The Modern History of Exchange Rate Arrangements: a Reinterpretation," *NBER Working Paper* No. 8963.

Roger, S. (2006) "An Overview of Inflation Targeting in Emerging Market Economies," paper presented at the Symposium, Challenges to Inflation Targeting in Emerging Countries, held at the Bank of Thailand, November 13–14 (Washington: International Monetary Fund).

Rogoff, K. (1985) "The Optimal Degree of Commitment to an Intermediate Monetary Target," *Quarterly Journal of Economics*, Vol. 100, 1169–90.

Rogoff, K. (2003) "Globalization and Global Disinflation," paper presented at the Federal Reserve Bank of Kansas City conference, Monetary Policy and Uncertainty: Adapting to a Changing Economy, Jackson Hole, Wyoming.

Sargent, T. J. and N. Wallace (1981) "Some Unpleasant Monetarist Arithmetic," *Federal Reserve Bank of Minneapolis Quarterly Review*, Vol. 5, No. 3, 1–17.

Sikken, B. J. and J. de Haan (1998) "Budget Deficits, Monetization, and Central Bank Independence in Developing Countries," *Oxford Economic Papers*, Vol. 50, 493–511.

Siklos, P. (2002) *The Changing Face of Central Banking: Evolutionary Trends since World War II* (Cambridge: Cambridge University Press).

Stasavage, D. (2003) "Transparency, Democratic Accountability and the Economic Consequences of Monetary Institutions," *American Journal of Political Science*, Vol. 47, No. 3, 389–402.

Stella, P. (1997) "Do Central Banks Need Capital?" *IMF Working Paper* 83/97 (Washington: International Monetary Fund).

Stella, P. (2003) "Why Central Banks Need Financial Strength," *Central Banking Journal*, Vol. 14, No. 2, 23–9.

Stella, P. (2006) "Central Bank Financial Strength, Transparency, and Policy Credibility," *IMF Staff Papers*, Vol. 52, No. 2, 335–65.

Sturm, J. E. and J. de Haan (2001) "Inflation in Developing Countries: Does Central Bank Independence Matter? New Evidence Based on a New Data Set," *CCSO Working Papers* No. 200101 (Groningen, The Netherlands: University of Groningen, CCSO Centre for Economic Research). Published in 2001 in *Ifo Studien*, Vol. 47, No. 4, 389–403.

Svensson, L. E. O. (1997) "Optimal Inflation Targets, 'Conservative' Central Banks, and Linear Inflation Contracts," *American Economic Review*, Vol. 87, 98–114.

Temple, J. (1998) "Central Bank Independence and Inflation: Good News and Bad News," *Economic Letters*, Vol. 61, 215–19.

Tytell, I. and S. Wei (2004) "Does Financial Globalization Induce Better Macroeconomic Policies?" *IMF Working Paper* 04/84 (Washington: International Monetary Fund).

Visser, J. (1991) "Trends in Trade Union Membership," *OECD Economic Outlook* (Paris: OECD).

Wagner, H. (1999) "Central Bank Independence and the Lessons from Developed and Developing Countries," *Comparative Economic Studies*, Vol. 41, No. 4, 1–22.

Waller, S. and J. de Haan (2004) "Credibility and Transparency of Central Banks: New Results Based on IFO's World Economic Survey," *CESIFO Working Paper* No. 1199.

Walsh, C. (1994) "Central Bank Independence and the Cost of Disinflation in the EC," University of California–Santa Cruz, unpublished, June.

Walsh, C. (1995) "Optimal Contracts for Central Bankers," *American Economic Review*, Vol. 85, 150–67.

Winkler, B. (2000) "Which Kind of Transparency? On the Need for Clarity in Monetary Policy-Making," *ECB Working Paper* No. 26.

Index